# Information Technology Law in Japan

# Information Technology Law in Japan

**Masao Yanaga**

This book was originally published as a monograph in the International Encyclopaedia of Laws/Privacy and Technology Law.

Founding Editor: Roger Blanpain
General Editor: Frank Hendrickx
Volume Editor: Jos Dumortier, Pieter Gryffroy, Ruben Roex & Yung Shin Van Der Sype

Wolters Kluwer

*Published by:*
Kluwer Law International B.V.
PO Box 316
2400 AH Alphen aan den Rijn
The Netherlands
E-mail: lrs-sales@wolterskluwer.com
Website: www.wolterskluwer.com/en/solutions/kluwerlawinternational

*Sold and distributed by:*
Wolters Kluwer Legal & Regulatory U.S.
7201 McKinney Circle
Frederick, MD 21704
United States of America
E-mail: customer.service@wolterskluwer.com



ISBN 978-94-035-4965-1

e-Book: ISBN 978-94-035-4625-4
web-PDF: ISBN 978-94-035-4635-3

# The Author

Masao Yanaga (born in 1961) is a professor of Law and Accounting at Graduate School of Professional Accountancy, Meiji University. He studied at Meiji University (BA in Economics) and at the University of Tokyo (LLB). After having passed the bar examination, he became a research associate in the Faculty of Law at the University of Tokyo. He is qualified as a chief telecommunications engineer (in data interchange), a first-class technical radio operator for on-the-ground services (Ministry of Posts and Telecommunications) and a systems auditor (Ministry of Trade and Industry). Professor Yanaga was a member of the Study Group for Electronic Commerce Legislation at the Ministry of Justice and a non-voting member of the Company Law Modernization Committee under the Council of the Judicial System at the Ministry of Justice.

Several prizes were awarded to him, including the Japan Bankers Association Research Foundation Prize (2014), the *Osumi Ken-ichiro* Prize (2000), the *Ota-Kurosawa* Prize (1999) and the Japanese Institute of Certified Public Accountants Academic Publication Prize (1998). The author wrote many articles on company law, electronic commerce and banking regulation, *Legal Aspect of Fair Value Accounting* (Nihon Hyoron sha, 1996), *Accounting for Income Tax* (Chuo Keizai sha, 1997) (with Hiroshi Ashida), *Financial Accounting and Company Law* (Chuo Keizai sha, 1998), *Limiting Auditors' Liability* (Yuhikaku, 2000), *Auditors' Independence in Appearance* (Shoji Homu, 2002), *Accounting for Shareholders' Equity* (Chuo Keizai sha, 2003), *Accounting Standards and Law* (Chuo Keizai sha, 2013), *Challenges for Statutory Auditors* (Doubunkan, 2015) and *AI/Robots and the Law* (Yuhikaku, 2018) (co-editor) (in Japanese) being his best-known academic works. He also wrote textbooks on: *Company Law* (fifteenth edition, Yuhikaku, 2021), *Law on Bills and Cheques* (third edition, Yuhikaku, 2018) and *Law on Commercial Transactions* (third edition, Yuhikaku, 2019) (in Japanese). He is also the principal contributor to *Commentary on the Implementing Regulation for the Companies Act and the Regulation on Electronic Public Notice* (third edition, Shoji Homu, 2021) and *Commentary on the Regulation on Company Accounting and the Implementing Regulation for the Commercial Code* (fourth edition, Shoji Homu, 2022) (in Japanese).

## The Author

# Table of Contents

# List of Abbreviations

| | |
|---|---|
| ANS | American National Standards |
| ANSI | American National Standards Institute |
| API | Application Interfaces |
| ATM | Automated/Automatic Teller Machine |
| BOJ | Bank of Japan |
| BOJ-NET | Bank of Japan Financial Network System |
| BS | British Standards |
| BSI | British Standards Institution |
| CIO | Chief Information Officer |
| CPS | Certification Practice Standards |
| ECOM | Electronic Commerce Promotion Council of Japan |
| FEYCS | Foreign Exchange Yen Clearing System |
| FY | Fiscal Year |
| ICT | Information and Communications Technology |
| ISP | Internet Service Provider |
| IT | Information Technology |
| JASC | Japan Accreditation System for Product Certification Bodies of JIS Mark |
| JGS | Japanese Government Securities |
| JIS | Japanese Industrial Standards |
| JISC | Japanese Industrial Standards Committee |
| JNLA | Japanese National Laboratory Accreditation |
| JPNIC | Japan Network Information Centre |
| *Kaminshu* | Lower Courts Civil Cases Reporter (*Kakyu saibansho minji saibanreishu*) |
| METI | Ministry of Economics, Trade and Industry |
| *Minroku* | Supreme Tribunal Civil Cases Reporter (*Daishin'in minji hanketsuroku*) |
| *Minshu* | Supreme Court Civil Cases Reporter (*Saiko saibansho minji hanreishu*) |

## List of Abbreviations

| | |
|---|---|
| *Daishin'in Minshu* | Supreme Tribunal Civil Cases Reporter (*Daishin'in minji hanreishu*) |
| MIC | Ministry of Internal Affairs and Communications/Minister of Internal Affairs and Communications |
| MITI | Ministry of International Trade and Industry |
| NTT | Nippon Telephone & Telegram Co. Ltd |
| PIN | Personal Identification Number |
| PHS | Personal Handyphone System |
| RR | Radio Regulations |
| RTGS | Real-Time Gross Settlement System |
| SRE | Specified Radio Equipment |
| TSP | Telecommunication Service Provider |

# Preface

The author is very grateful for the opportunity to present an outline of cyber law in Japan. To cope with the rapid evolution in Information and Communications Technology and with internationalization, new bills have been introduced and statutes are constantly being amended with regard to cyber law. It is far from easy to catch up with such developments and the author hopes readers will comprehend the essence of Japanese cyber law and understand Japanese efforts in this terrain.

The author is indebted to the *Max Planck Institut für ausländisches und internationales Privatrecht* (Hamburg) and Interdisciplinary Centre for Law and IT (KU. Leuven) for the opportunity to undertake research on electronic commerce, and cordially thanks Ms Yumi Oba (attorney-at-law, *Asuka kyowa*) for her advice and material regarding the practices in this field.

# General Introduction

## Chapter 1. General Background of the Country

### §1. Geography and Population

*1.* Japan is a 3,000 km-long archipelago with a total surface area of 377,972 $km^2$, stretching in a north-to-southwardly direction in the Pacific Ocean. About 73% of the total land area is mountainous. In Tokyo, the capital city, the average daily maximum and minimum temperatures are 30°C and 22°C in August and 8°C and -2°C in January. The population of Japan numbers 127 million, which ranks eleventh in the world.

### §2. State Organs

*2.* The 1946 Constitution explicitly stipulates that sovereignty lies with the people. It envisages a parliamentary cabinet system based on the separation of powers, stating that the Emperor is but the symbolic head of state, without any governmental powers.

Legislative power is vested in the Diet, composed of the House of Representatives, elected for four years unless dissolved by the Prime Minister, and the House of Councillors, elected for six years with half of the seats being up for election every three years. The former's decisions prevail over the latter's decisions regarding the appointment of the Prime Minister, the budget and the ratification of treaties. The former's decisions may override the latter's regarding other matters, if there is a two-thirds majority, except for constitutional amendments, which require a two-thirds vote in both houses.

Administrative power belongs to the Cabinet, which is elected by the Diet and consists of the Prime Minister and the other Ministers of State. The Cabinet owes accountability to the Diet and has to resign en masse or dissolve the House of Representatives were the House to adopt a vote of no confidence.

The Judiciary, with the Supreme Court at its apex, is independent of both the Diet and the Cabinet and is granted the power to review the acts of the Diet and the Cabinet by the Constitution.

§3. Court System

## I. The Organization of the Courts (Court Act (Law No. 59 of 16 April 1947), Articles 6 Through 32)

### A. *The Supreme Court* (Saiko Saibansho)

*3.* The Supreme Court consists of fifteen judges (Court Act, Article 5). They are divided into three petty benches (*sho-hotei*), each of which consists of five judges. All the judges sit together as the grand bench (*dai-hotei*) for cases involving a constitutional issue for which there exists no Supreme Court precedent, for cases involving non-constitutional issues in which a petty bench has considered it appropriate to overrule a precedent set by the Supreme Court (Court Act, Article 10), for cases in which a petty bench has felt it appropriate to decide in the grand bench and for cases where the verdict of the judges in a petty bench ended in a tie.

### B. *The High Court* (Koto Saibansho)

*4.* A High Court is usually the first appellate (*koso*) court. But there are some exceptions. It acts as second appellate (*jokoku*) court for minor civil cases (Civil Procedure Code, Article 311, paragraph 1), in which case the losing party may only bring the case before the Supreme Court if the decision of the High Court is inconsistent with the Constitution (special appeal (*tokubetsu jokoku*)) (Civil Procedure Code, Article 327). However, a High Court has original jurisdiction on insurrection cases (Court Act, Article 16, paragraph 4) as well as certain types of administrative cases, reviewing the decisions by the Fair Trade Commission according to the Anti-Monopoly Act (Anti-Monopoly Act, Articles 85 and 86) or reviewing the decisions by the Patent Agency regarding some intellectual property rights (Patent Act, Article 178, paragraph 1, etc.). In principle, cases are heard by three judges (Court Act, Article 18, paragraph 2), while in certain serious criminal cases (Penal Code, Articles 77 through 79) and in certain cases provided for in the Anti-Monopoly Act (Anti-Monopoly Act, Article 87, paragraph 2) the bench consists of five judges.

### C. *The District Court* (Chiho Saibansho)

*5.* District Courts have original jurisdiction unless a law provides in particular that other courts have original jurisdiction. They are the first appellate courts for the decisions made by a summary court in civil matters. In principle, cases are heard by one judge (Court Act, Article 26, paragraph 1), while three judges sit in cases provided for in paragraphs 2 through 4 of Article 26.

*D. The Summary Court* (Kan'i Saibansho)

*6.* Summary Courts handle minor civil (if the amount in controversy does not exceed JPY 1,400,000) and criminal cases. In cases where the amount in controversy does not exceed JPY 300,000, the plaintiff may request a simplified procedure for small amounts of claims (Civil Procedure Code, Article 386). The party dissatisfied with the decision in the small amount claim procedure may not lodge an appeal with a higher court but may lodge an objection with the court that made the decision (Civil Procedure Code, Articles 377 and 378). Cases are heard by a single judge (Court Act, Article 35).

*E. The Family Court* (Katei Saibansho)

*7.* Family Courts have original jurisdiction over juvenile delinquency cases and civil cases involving matters regarding domestic relations.

## II. Appeals in Civil Cases

*A. First Appeal* (Koso)

*8. Koso* may be lodged whenever the party is dissatisfied with the judgment (*hanketsu*) of the Court of First Instance, except for judgments in small claim procedures. The appellate court deals with the facts in the same manner as the trial in the first instance.

*B. Second Appeal* (Jokoku)

*9.* Second appeal (reappeal) may be lodged only on the grounds that the judgment of the original court contained a constitutional issue, the composition of the original court was illegal, the original court did not have jurisdiction because of exclusive jurisdiction, an attorney did not have the authority to represent the party, the original court failed to make the oral proceedings public or the decision of the original court was given without any reason or with inconsistent reasons (Civil Procedure Code, Article 312, paragraphs 1 and 2).

Second appeal to a High Court may also be lodged on the grounds that the judgment of the original court is in contravention of laws or orders which would probably affect the conclusion of the judgment (Civil Procedure Code, Article 312, paragraph 3). In addition, upon the application by a party, the Supreme Court may, at its discretion, accept a *Jokoku* when it deems that the original judgment was in contravention of a precedent of the Supreme Court (where there is no precedent, precedents of the *Daishin-in* (the antecedent of the Supreme Court) or the High Courts) or when it considers it to be of great importance in interpreting laws or orders (Civil Procedure Code, Article 318).

The second appellate court makes decisions on questions of law and is, in principle, bound by the facts as established by the original courts. In other words, they do not review the propriety of the facts as established by the original court as this is outside of their jurisdiction (Civil Procedure Code, Article 321, paragraph 1).

## §4. Characteristics of Japanese Law

*10.* In the nineteenth century, Japan implemented a legal system imported mainly from Germany and France. French law had much influence on the Civil Code, German law on the Constitution, the Commercial Code and the Civil Procedure Code. After World War II, American law influenced Japanese law, especially the Constitution, the Criminal Procedure Act and joint-stock company law.

*11.* The low number of lawsuits is well known. It should be noted that the role of judges has been important in shaping the law in Japan because it often took much time to introduce new statutes. Especially, the courts have made good use of general clauses (*ippan joko*) to find an appropriate and equitable conclusion. General clauses are written in the Codes in abstract or vague terms. In fact, the courts have used general clauses to create 'law'. The examples of the general clauses are set out below.

### I. Public Policy (*Kojo*) and Public Morals (*Ryozoku*)

*12.* Article 90 of the Civil Code provides that a juridical act is null and void if its object deals with matters that are contrary to public policy or good morals.

### II. Abuse of Rights (*Kenri Ran'yo*)

*13.* Article 1, paragraph 3 of the Civil Code provides that abuse of rights is not permitted. Courts have often referred to this doctrine to reach desirable results, but it is not necessarily clear whether to rely on this doctrine or on the doctrine of fidelity and good faith. This clause has been employed in relation to commercial law, especially in relation to laws on promissory notes and on other payment instruments.

### III. Fidelity (*Shingi*) and Good Faith (*Seijitsu*)

*14.* Article 1, paragraph 2 of the Civil Code provides that rights shall be exercised and duties performed with fidelity and in good faith. Though these provisions (Article 1 of the Civil Code) were only added in 1947, the courts had steadily adopted the doctrine of fidelity and good faith even before the amendments. The principle of fidelity and good faith has often been referenced in the context of contract law.

*15.* Though these general clauses might make the decisions of the courts less transparent, they have been accepted as reasoning in order to reach a fair conclusion or as substantial law-making in case of a lack of appropriate statutes. Thus, judicial precedents are very important to foresee the decisions the courts will make, even though Japan has adopted a continental code law system. The Supreme Court must sit as an entire bench when it overrules its own precedents (Court Act, Article 10, No. 3).

## §5. Sources of Law

### I. The Constitution (*Kempo*)

*16.* The Constitution (3 November 1946) is the supreme source of law in Japan. No statutes, ordinances, decrees or other acts regarding affairs of state are legally valid when they are contradictory to the provisions of the Constitution (Constitution, Article 98, paragraph 1). The Supreme Court is the competent authority ruling on the final judgment on the Constitutionality of all the statutes, ordinances, regulations or measures taken by organs of the state (Constitution, Article 81).

### II. Statutes (*Horitsu*)

*17.* Statutes are only enacted by the Diet (Constitution, Article 41). Among the many statutes, it is said that the Civil Code (Law No. 89 of 1898), the Commercial Code (Law No. 48 of 1899), the Penal Code (Law No. 45 of 1907), the Civil Procedure Code (Law No. 109 of 1996) and the Criminal Procedure Code (Law No. 131 of 1948) are the most important. These five statutes and the Constitution are often called *roppo* (literary, six laws).

### III. Ordinances

*18.* There are two types of ordinances: Cabinet ordinances and ministerial ordinances. The Cabinet may enact Cabinet ordinances (*seirei*) in order to enforce the provisions in the Constitution or statutes (Constitution, Article 73, No. 6). The Prime Minister may promulgate Prime Minister's Office ordinances in order to enforce the provisions in statutes or Cabinet ordinances or in accordance with the specific delegation by statutes or Cabinet ordinances (Act Concerning the Establishment of the Prime Minister's Office (Law No. 89 of 1999), Article 7, paragraph 3) while Ministers of state may promulgate ministerial ordinances in order to enforce the provisions in statutes or Cabinet ordinances or in accordance with the specific delegation by statutes or Cabinet ordinances (National Administrative Organization Act (Law No. 120 of 1948), Article 12, paragraph 1). Though there are no decrees under the present Constitution, some imperial decrees (*chokurei*), established under the former Constitution, still have a legal effect (Cabinet ordinance No. 14 of 1947).

## IV. Custom

*19.* Article 3 of Act on the General Rules of Application of Laws stipulates that customs (*kanshu*) not contrary to public policy shall have the same effect as law to the extent that they are authorized by a statute or a statutory instrument, or that they concern matters not otherwise prescribed by a statute or a statutory instrument.

*20.* Article 92 of the Civil Code also provides that a custom that is different from statutory provisions but not contrary to the mandatory provisions (provisions providing public order) shall be applied where the parties have an intention to follow the custom. In other words, customs may have greater value than non-mandatory statutory provisions. Moreover, Article 1 of the Commercial Code stipulates that commercial customs shall apply in commercial cases in the absence of provisions in the Commercial Code. In addition, the Decree of *Dajokan* No. 103 of 1875[1] stated that the judge should decide according to custom in the absence of written law in civil cases (Article 3).

## V. Case Law

*21.* The court is not legally bound by precedents in other cases,[2] but the judgments by the Supreme Court have strong influence on the lower courts' decisions. As mentioned in section IV 'Custom', above, the court has made new 'law'.

## VI. *Jori* (Recta Ratio)

*22.* Article 3 of the Decree of *Dajokan* No. 103 of 1875 provided that the judge should give a decision in civil cases, taking *jori* into account where there are neither written laws nor customs. Though there are no precedents decided solely on *jori*, courts have given decisions making use of general provisions, when no appropriate written law or custom exists.

---

1. It is unclear whether the Decree of *Dajokan* No. 103 of 1875 still has a legal effect now.
2. The court is legally bound to a judgment of a superior court with respect to the case with which it concerned (Court Act, Art. 4).

## Chapter 2. Telecommunications Infrastructure

*23.* The number of telecommunications carriers in Japan reached 22,397 by August 2021. Among them, there were 330 registered telecommunications carriers and 22,067 notified telecommunications carriers. While the number of mobile phone contracts is growing steadily, reaching 195.1 million by the end of 2020, the number of fixed-line telephone contracts (excluding 0ABJ Type IP telephone contracts) by the end of 2020 numbered 17.16 million compared to 62.85 million in December 1997.

*24.* Mobile Internet services – Internet connection services via cell phones – enable the subscriber to access information services, buy tickets, do online banking and other financial transactions and so on. For such purposes, moving image services and navigation services for cell phone users have become quite popular in Japan.

## Chapter 3. The Information and Communications Technology (ICT) Market

*25.* The real gross domestic product (base year: 2015) of the information and communications industry has been growing and amounted to JPY 108.4 trillion in 2019, though a 0.5% decrease from 2018.

*26.* The number of Internet users has been rapidly increasing and reached about 100.8 million by the end of 2019. The penetration rate within the population was 83.4%, whereas the rate for large enterprises was nearly 100% in 2020.

## Chapter 4. e-Commerce: Facts and Figures

*27.* The B-to-B market grew to JPY 353 trillion in 2019, while 2020's figure shows a 5.1% decrease due to COVID-19.

*28.* The B-to-C market grew to JPY 19.4 trillion in 2019, while 2020's figure shows a 0.43% decrease. The C-to-C market has been, however, expanding dramatically until 2019, a 73.4% increase compared to that in 2013.

# Chapter 5. e-Government Initiatives

## §1. The New IT Reform Strategy

*29.* Article 10 of the Framework Act on the Formation of an Advanced Information and Telecommunications Network Society (Law No. 144 of 2000) provides that the national government has the responsibility for formulating and implementing measures meant to establish an advanced information and telecommunications network society in accordance with the basic ideas provided in Articles 3 through 9. The basic ideas are as follows:

(1) realizing a society in which the people can enjoy the benefits of information and telecommunications technology (Article 3);
(2) promoting the economic structural reform and enhancing the international competitiveness of industry (Article 4);
(3) realizing citizen life that evokes feelings of comfort and affluence (Article 5);
(4) realizing vital local communities and improvement of the welfare of residents (Article 6);
(5) role sharing between the national/local governments and the private sector (Article 7);
(6) filling gaps in the opportunities for access to information and telecommunications technology (Article 8); and
(7) dealing with new problems that emerge in line with changes in the socioeconomic structure (Article 9).

*30.* Local governments have the responsibility of formulating and implementing measures of their own, which reflect the distinctive features of the territories of the relevant local governments with regard to the formation of an advanced information and telecommunications network society, while appropriately sharing the roles with the national government (Article 11). The national and local governments mutually cooperate so that measures for an advanced information and telecommunications network society will be implemented expeditiously and intensively (Article 12). The national government will take legal, fiscal and other actions necessary for implementing measures to establish an advanced information and telecommunications network society (Article 13).

*31.* According to Article 25 of this Act, the Strategic Headquarters for Promoting an Advanced Information and Telecommunications Network Society (hereinafter referred to as the 'Headquarters') is established in the Cabinet. The Headquarters is responsible for making a priority policy program for the formation of advanced information and telecommunications network society (hereinafter referred to as the 'priority policy program'). At the same time, it is the mission of the Headquarters to plan important measures to establish an advanced information and telecommunications network society, and also to implement such measures (Article 26). The priority policy program should have provisions with respect to:

(1) the basic policy concerning measures which the government should implement expeditiously and intensively in order to establish an advanced information and telecommunications network society;
(2) the measures that the government should implement expeditiously and intensively in order to drive the Japanese society forward to the most advanced information and telecommunications society in the world;
(3) the measures that the government should implement expeditiously and intensively in order to promote education/learning as well as to develop human resources with respect to information and telecommunication technology;
(4) the measures that the government should implement expeditiously and intensively to facilitate e-commerce, etc.;
(5) the measures that the government should implement expeditiously and intensively to make administrative procedures digitized, applying information and telecommunications technology to the public sector;
(6) the measures that the government should implement expeditiously and intensively to ensure the security and reliability of advanced information and telecommunications networks; and
(7) other measures that are required which the government must drive forward expeditiously and intensively in order to realize an advanced information and telecommunications network society (Article 35, paragraph 2).

*32.* The Headquarters consists of all the State Ministers and of those who have superior insight into the formulation of an advanced information and telecommunications network society and have been appointed by the Prime Minister (Article 30).

*33.* The Information Technology (IT) Strategy Council published *The IT Fundamental Strategy* in November 2000 and the e-Japan Strategy was implemented. Based on five years of experience, it published *New IT Reform Strategy* in January 2006.

*34.* The IT Strategy Council published *Priority Policy Program 2007* in July 2007. In order to realize the goals set forth by the *New IT Reform Strategy* and its Policy Package, the *Priority Program 2007* has organized, in accordance with the prioritized tasks and strategy fields cited in the *New IT Reform Strategy* and the Policy Package, the basic principles to which the policy implementation should comply. The government intends to develop a standardized model for an e-administration platform that allows various administrative processes to be carried out in a 'one-stop' process by Fiscal Year (FY) 2010, together with preparing the groundwork for the drafting of a user-friendly software manual for the use of the comprehensive e-administration service, accessible to small business owners among others.

§2. A NEW STRATEGY IN ICT

*35.* The IT Strategy Council published *A New Strategy in Information and Communications Technology* in May 2010. According to the document, the government will enforce an IT revolution within the government to achieve a citizen-oriented electronic administration for promoting citizens' sovereignty, recreate bonding in local communities by taking utmost advantage of what IT applications might offer and aim at innovatively creating new markets and internationally expanding them.

*36.* In order to attain the goals, the government was planning to take several measures:

(1) to identify among the administrative services only those services which are most frequently used, hence the most beneficial to the citizens if offered twenty-four hours, seven days a week (e.g., issuance of the Certificates of Residence, Certificates of Registered Seal, and Certified Copies of Family Register); and provide such services online, or offline (e.g., at public administration terminal booths) possibly upon collaboration from the private sector;
(2) to develop a citizen identification (ID) system to serve as the common infrastructure for electronic administration, usable by the governmental and private sectors alike, which would enhance the citizen's confidence in the social security system and will be implemented integrally with the taxation system as well as systems that will allow individuals to monitor and control the way the government utilizes their own personal information;
(3) to instal government Chief Information Officer (CIO) that will be the commanding post specifically mandated to advance electronic administration to streamline the administration in conjunction with administrative reforms, reviewing the cost-effectiveness of previous IT-related governmental investments and compiling the lessons learned from them;
(4) to provide rigorously administration-held information in formats that are convenient for secondary use, and as a rule, offer all such information over the Internet for easy access;
(5) to create national-level information service so as to allow the citizens to electronically manage and utilize their own medical and health-related information in order to create an environment where the citizens may receive medical care based on their medical records anywhere in the country and undertake their own health management;
(6) to apply IT to promote senior citizen employment and social participation; to enable families and others to check on the conditions of lone seniors; and to make care-related information available to those providing medical, care and other services at the recipients' homes;
(7) to develop an environment conducive to creating an appropriate school system for the twenty-first century. In such a school system, information and communications technologies will be used to: (i) develop easy-to-understand classroom environment where children teach and learn from one

another; (ii) reduce the burden on the teachers and staff; and (iii) expand children's capability to utilize information.

(8) to promote various measures in order to make community sovereignty a reality through IT applications, such as: utilizing white space (in broadcasting) and such to expanding the citizens' media nationally; producing and transmitting hometown content on the community culture, tourism, and products; revitalizing rural areas through IT applications; sharing of disaster information among the disaster-prevention agencies throughout the country for fast and appropriate response to a disaster; and distributing information to the residents;

(9) to promote Smart Grid in Japan and abroad by integrating energy networks and IT to achieve a low-carbon society where environmental technology and ICT are integrated, as well as energy-saving houses and offices taking advantage of IT applications, and green transport of people and goods through an intelligent transport system (ITS), and facilitate the development, standardization and propagation of new technologies using IT or in the IT field that achieves a reduced environmental burden;

(10) to focus resources on research and development in the particular IT-related fields in which our country excels, and aim at putting the resultant products on the market;

(11) to develop an environment that is conducive to taking advantage of the capabilities of the younger 'digital native' generations, and to promote the creation and development of new content- and IT-related enterprises;

(12) to set our sights on developing a suitable environment – such as creation of new industries that take advantage of available data, promotion of data centres in Japan and standardization of relevant technologies – to ensure the competitiveness of cloud computing services, which would contribute to improving public convenience and expanding the scope of the user industry;

(13) to facilitate strategic acquisition and deployment of intellectual property rights and international standards, and export and investment on major foreign markets in strategic fields that hold high promise for growth by developing an all-Japan structure across the government agencies, private and industrial sectors, and intensifying research and development efforts; and

(14) to study the possibility to digitize the political activities such as election campaigns on the Internet, electronic voting to facilitate the exercise of voting rights by the voters and dissemination of the information on the activities of the Diet.

## §3. Declaration to Be the World's Most Advanced IT Nation

*37.* The Strategic Headquarters for the Promotion of an Advanced Information and Telecommunications Network Society published the *Declaration to be the World's Most Advanced IT Nation* in 2013 and revised it in 2014, 2015 and 2016.

*38.* In this document, one of the goals of the Japanese government is to provide one-stop public services that anyone can access and use at any time. It is pointed out that existing measures for electronic government services have produced certain results in terms of digitalizing services and developing one-stop services, but in many cases they follow rules and procedures from the analogue period and service desks and paper forms remain fundamental, with the online provision of services serving in a supplementary role. In addition, the vertical organization of ministries and agencies or the vertical organization of bodies within ministries and agencies is often the cause of the failure to provide services that are convenient from users' perspectives.

*39.* In light of this analysis of the present state, it is noted, it is the government's responsibility that the citizen may access government services electronically, and comprehensive utilization of cloud computing and MYNUMBER System will make possible the creation of convenient lifestyles where anyone can obtain one-stop electronic government services from anywhere, at any time, using any type of terminal.

*40.* According to this document, in order to cut costs extensively and conduct administrative operations efficiently, a new model for an electronic government capable of sustainable development should be created. To this end, it is necessary to improve the environment indispensable for collaboration with private services and implementing these measures centred on a cooperative relationship between the public and private sectors. The function of the government to provide services will be opened to the private sector and highly convenient services will be created through collaboration between by the public and private sectors. Open user environments that utilize cloud computing are being developed through the standardization and sharing of data format, terminologies, codes, and characters and the public release of application interfaces (API) to facilitate active participation by members of the public as stakeholders. Efforts will be made based on the *Policy for Improving Convenience of Online Procedures* (adopted at Liaison committee of ministries CIOs on 1 April 2014)[3] and the *Action Plan for Development of Disclosed IT Utilization Environment in the field of Administration* (adopted at Liaison committee of ministries CIOs on 25 April 2014). Websites will be reviewed to create sites that are more convenient from users' perspectives by progressively publicly disclosing API for government websites and taking other measures. The government information systems will be reviewed to build the Certification Platform which enables collective identity verification using individual number cards, etc. for realizing seamless access between systems.

*41.* Reform of government information systems at the national and local levels will be put in place. For this purpose, portfolio management in regard to government investment in IT will be implemented. Based on the roadmap for government information system reforms, redundant information systems and networks will be consolidated, and systems with low demand will be reviewed under the direction of the government CIO and its transition to a common government platform will be

---

3. Available in Japanese at http://www.kantei.go.jp/jp/singi/it2/cio/dai55/siryou1_2a.pdf.

accelerated. At the same time, environment and functions of the government common platform as government private clouds including development environment and remote desktop functions will be improved and enriched. As for the review of the government information system, the government common platform will be utilized and use of package software will be promoted. Furthermore, standards related to the use of private cloud services will be organized.

*42.* To reinforce IT governance in government, an investment plan for government information systems will be adopted and implemented under the leadership of the government CIO.[4] Common rules relating to information system procurement and project management will be adopted, a pool system for government CIO aides, databases for managing government information system assets created and put into operation, and review systems introduced. A new assessment system will be created under the IT Strategic Headquarters, and monitoring functions will be reinforced for large-scale and high-risk projects. Moreover, training programs will be reviewed and across-the-board measures taken to improve those programs in order to foster IT human resources within government.

## §4. Framework Act on Utilization of Public and Private Sector Data

*43.* The Framework Act to Promote Utilization of Public and Private Sector Data (Act No. 103 of 2016) provides essential matters for utilization of public and private sector data.

*44.* First, Article 8 provides that the government shall establish a Basic Plan for Promoting Utilization of Public and Private Sector Data to ensure the comprehensive and effective promotion of measures to promote the utilization of public and private sector data.

*45.* Second, the national government shall implement necessary measures to ensure that an application, notification, notice of a disposition or any other procedure pertaining to an administrative organ, etc. is, in principle, proceeded by means of an electronic data-processing system or any other information and telecommunications technology; to promote an offer of a contract or any other procedure by a private company, etc. to be proceeded by means of an electronic data-processing system or any other information and telecommunications technology; and to implement legislative and other necessary measures to ensure that a person who was delegated with mandate by a representative of a corporation is able to implement an offer of a contract or any other procedure by exclusively using an electronic data-processing system (Article 10). Moreover, Both the national government and local public entities implement necessary measures in regard to the public and private sector data held by themselves, to enable citizens to easily use such data via the

4. 'IT dashboard' (a structure that enables members of the public to confirm at a glance via the Internet the status of IT investment by individual government ministries and agencies) has been in operation since FY 2014. http://www.itdashboard.go.jp/.

Internet or any other advanced information and telecommunications network while ensuring that the rights and interests of individuals and corporations, national security, etc. are not damaged. Companies are requested to do in a similar way. The national government shall review systems for the smooth circulation of public and private sector data (including the system for the smooth circulation of content) and implement other necessary measures (Article 11). Furthermore, the national government and local public entities shall, in coordination with each other, develop standards for their own information systems, secure compatibility among those systems, review their own business, and implement other necessary measures to contribute to the utilization of public and private sector data (Article 15, paragraph 1). The national government ensures consistency among measures taken by itself and local public entities and implements other measures necessary to utilize public and private sector data (Article 19).

*46.* Third, the national government shall promote the development and provision of services as well as the development and dissemination of technology through utilizing public and private sector data and implement other measures necessary to rectify the disparity among citizens in their opportunitics or ability to make use of information and telecommunications technology regardless of geographical constraints, age, physical circumstances and other factors (Article 14). Moreover, it shall also implement measures necessary to promote research, development and substantiation of the technology-related top artificial intelligence, Internet of Things, cloud computing service, and any other state-of-the-art technology, and shall disseminate the outcomes thereof (Article 16) while it shall implement measures necessary to develop and secure human resources who have technical knowledge or skills pertaining to utilizing public and private sector data at the same time (Article 17).

## §5. Basic Plan for Promoting Public and Private Sector Data Utilization

*47.* Declaration to be the World's Most Advanced IT Nation as well as the Basic Plan for Promoting Public and Private Sector Data Utilization, formulated in accordance with Article 8, paragraph 6 of the Framework Act to Promote Utilization of Public and Private Sector Data and approved by the Cabinet in May 2017, was revised and renamed as Declaration to be the World's Most Advanced Digital Nation as well as the Basic Plan for Promoting Public and Private Sector Data Utilization in June 2018.

*48.* In the Basic Plan, eight fields have been defined as priority (digital government; healthcare/medical/nursing care; tourism; finance; agriculture/forestry/fisheries; manufacturing; infrastructure/disaster prevention and mitigation; and mobility) in light of a number of issues (e.g., economic recovery and fiscal soundness, local revitalization, and the securing of safety and security) to be addressed intensively since Japan becomes a society in which the birth rate is decreasing and the population is aging at exceptional rates. Japan will implement measures to be taken as priority in each field by 2020 while maintaining a focus on cross-sectoral data linkages.

*49.* The Basic Plan expects that, for example, utilizing data linkages and AI will enable effective, efficient, high-quality healthcare, medical, and nursing care services to be realized and a society in which citizens can remain active their entire lives to be created; productivity will be increased and profitable agricultural sector will be established by utilizing data; and automated driving will be achieved through linkages of public and private sector data for dynamic maps and other such applications and the development of systems in order to bring about the world's safest, smoothest traffic society.

## §6. On the Direction of New IT Policy in the Digital Era

*50.* Advanced Information and Communication Network Society Promotion Strategy Headquarters, Public-Private Data Utilization Promotion Strategy Council formulated a policy document, *On the Direction of New IT Policy in the Digital Era* (19 December 2018).

*51.* According to the document, based on free and fair rules on the domestic and international transfer of data, the government will take necessary measures to establish an international data circulation environment for personal data and operational data of important industries, etc. with highly transparent rules securing personal information protection and security mutually so that the rights and interests of individuals and corporations and the safety of Japan will not be impaired.

*52.* Moreover, the government will promote not only the digitization of the administration but also teleworking, which is a flexible way of working that enables workers to effectively utilize their time and place, and the digitization of private businesses, especially those that belong to critical industries. It will also implement measures necessary to effectively utilize Japan's strengths in real data as well as leading-edge technologies such as AI and to realize Japan's competitiveness.

*53.* Furthermore, the government will develop infrastructure, rules and standards to support the Digital Era, such as nationwide deployment of 5G as the next-generation communication infrastructure, formulating rules for new business forms such as platformers enhancing the functions to develop standards and architectures that form the foundation of the Digital Era.

# Part I. Digital Market Regulation

## Chapter 1. Legal Status of Standardization and Technical Specifications

### §1. Industrial Standardization Act

*54.* The purpose of Industrial Standardization Act (Law No. 185 of 1949) is to promote industrial standardization in Japan in order to improve the quality of industrial products, to rationalize production, to promote fair business practices and to rationalize use and consumption through enactment and diffusion of Japanese Industrial Standards (JIS) and operation of the JIS Mark system and the laboratory accreditation system (Article 1).

### §2. Japanese Industrial Standards

*55.* Japanese Industrial Standards (JIS), which are set by the competent Ministers (i.e., the Minister of Economy, Trade and Industry, the Minister of Education, Culture, Sports, Science and Technology, the Minister of Environment, the Minister of Public Management, Internal Affairs, Post and Communication, the Minister of Agriculture, Forestry and Fisheries, the Minister of Land, Infrastructure and Transport and the Minister of Health, Labour and Welfare), are national standards (Article 11), just as the American National Standards (ANS) of the American National Standards Institute (ANSI) in the United States (US) or the British Standards of the British Standards Institution (BSI) in the United Kingdom (UK). JIS are established or revised on the basis of a consensus among producers, consumers, regulators and related parties. The JIS cover industrial and mineral products. The JIS have been influenced by the standards established by various industrial associations for their specific needs, or the standards established by many companies called for by the company standards (operation manuals, products specifications, etc.). In other words, the need for common practices in companies belonging to the same industrial sector leads to the establishment of industrial association standards, and the same need in terms of wider applications has promoted the establishment of JIS.

*56.* A number of statutes contain technical regulations providing binding legislative rules for the protection of human life, health, and the environment, for example, and for electronic appliances under the Electrical Appliance and Material Safety Law (Law No. 234 of 1961). These technical regulations should respect JIS where appropriate, under the Industrial Standardization Law. In fact, several thousands of JIS items are quoted by the technical regulations in Japan.

## §3. JIS Marking System

*57.* In order to promote the use of industrial standardization, the Industrial Standardization Law provides for the JIS Marking System. The JIS Marking System is a voluntary certification scheme (Article 19, paragraph 1 and Article 25, paragraph 1). Factories manufacturing products that satisfy JIS are certified to affix the JIS Mark on their products if their company standards and practices of quality control are judged by the competent Ministers or the JIS Mark Certification Body to guarantee continuous production of products satisfying JIS. The aims of JIS and the JIS Marking System are, among others, to improve the quality of products, rationalize production, and to ensure fair and simplified trade through the establishment and dissemination of appropriate and rational standards.

## §4. Japanese Industrial Standards Committee

*58.* The Japanese Industrial Standards Committee (JISC) is a consultative body for the competent Ministers. The JISC consists of many national committees and plays a central role in standardization activities in Japan.

*59.* The task of JISC can be summarized as follows:

(1) establishment and maintenance of JIS;
(2) administration of accreditation and certification;
(3) participation in and contribution to international standardization activities; and
(4) development of measurement standards and technical infrastructure for standardization.

## §5. Amendments to the Industrial Standardization Act in 1997

### I. Speeding-Up of JIS Development Process

*60.* In order to reflect the current rapid advance in technology and industrial activities, the JIS development process has been improved and simplified in cases when a draft JIS is proposed by the private sector according to the eleventh item of the Industrial Standardization Act. The new procedure has eliminated the Ministers' preliminary assessment process of a proposed draft JIS, so that a JIS can be established in a timely manner.

## II. Japan Accreditation System for Product Certification Bodies of JIS Mark

*61.* The 1997 Amendment of the Industrial Standardization Act introduced two accreditation systems (Japan Accreditation System for Product Certification Bodies of JIS Mark (JASC) and Japanese National Laboratory Accreditation (JNLA)).

*62.* JASC is an accreditation system of the certification bodies, in the private sector under a JIS Marking System and operated based on ISO/IEC Guides 65 and 61. An accredited certification body (JIS Mark Certification Body) is able to issue a JIS Mark certificate. Taking into account perspectives such as the improvements in the certification capability in the private sector, the requirements of the World Trade Organization/Technical Barriers to Trade Agreement, and the promotion of deregulation, it was considered appropriate to allow accredited certification bodies to certify the use of the JIS Mark. Under JASC, any organization, including companies established by private laws, is qualified to apply for the designation as a JIS Mark Certification Body. These certification bodies are expected to compete with each other to serve the market needs for JIS Marking.

*63.* The accreditation criteria for JIS Mark Certification Bodies are those included in ISO/IEC Guide 65. In addition, in order to improve market access of foreign manufacturers to the Japanese market and facilitate 'mutual recognition', the accreditation scheme is open to the foreign certification bodies.

## III. JNLA System

*64.* The testing laboratory accreditation system constitutes the basis for legal certification systems and certification systems in the private sector. The JNLA System, based on ISO/IEC Guide 58 and ISO/IEC 17025, was introduced in order to promote the suppliers' declaration of conformity with more confidence and to help the establishment of infrastructure to accelerate deregulation of such systems. An accredited testing laboratory may issue test reports with a logo of the JNLA within the scope of the accredited testing fields (scopes).

*65.* It is expected that the JNLA System will enhance the reliability of tests conducted by accredited testing laboratories in Japan on the international level. As test results obtained by testing laboratories are essential to various certification systems, the JNLA System, which is in accordance with international rules, represents a significant step toward an international one-stop test (results tested once are valid worldwide).

# Chapter 2. Legal Status of Standard Terms and Conditions

## §1. General

*66.* Standard contracts and the incorporation by reference of general conditions are common in ICT contract practice. This common practice has a lot of advantages for contract parties, especially for ICT service providers, because it enables businesses to save money and time. However, it is closely linked to the issue of unfair contract terms. It may enable one party (the ICT service provider), to dictate its terms to the other (the user, consumer) because the terms in standard contracts cannot be negotiated and it is likely that careless or lazy users will not read these terms, which makes it easy for the drafter to draft the terms to his advantage. As a result, standard contracts are sometimes subject to administrative control.

*67.* Moreover, some rules have been developed by the courts to prevent one party, who has drafted a standard contract, from abusing his dominant bargaining power.

*68.* Furthermore, the Consumer Contracts Act declares some types of clauses in consumer contracts void and null.

*69.* In addition, the Act amending the Civil Code, etc. (Law No. 44 of 2017) introduced the provisions (effective from 1 April 2020) governing *teikei yakkan* (pre-formulated clauses/ adhesive terms and conditions), mainly regarding the requirements for the incorporation of such clauses into contracts and the invalidity of unfair standard clauses (Articles 548*bis* through 548*quater*).

## §2. Ministry of Economics, Trade and Industry Guidelines

*70.* The Ministry of Economics, Trade and Industry (METI) formulated in 2002 and recently revised in 2020 the Interpretative Guidelines on Electronic Commerce Promotion Council of Japan (ECOM) and Information Property Trading, based on the results of deliberation by the Working Group on Rule Establishment for the Business Utilizing IT under the Information Economy Subcommittee of the Commerce, Distribution and Information Committee, Industrial Structure Council. The interpretative guidelines are intended to explain how the relevant laws and regulations, including the Civil Code, are applied and interpreted with respect to various types of legal problems in the field of ECOM and to promote facilitation of transactions by enhancing predictability for the parties involved.

## §3. Consumer Contracts Act

*71.* First, Article 8, paragraph 1 of the Consumer Contracts Act provides that some types of clauses exempting businesses from their liability are null and void:

(1) clauses that totally exclude a business from liability to compensate damages to a consumer arising from that business's non-performance;
(2) clauses which partially exclude a business from liability to compensate damages to a consumer arising from that business's non-performance (such non-performance is limited to instances where the same arises by wilful misconduct or gross negligence on the part of the business, the business's representative or an employee);
(3) clauses that totally exclude a business from liability to compensate damages to a consumer arising from a tort provided in the Civil Code, committed on occasion of the business's performance of a consumer contract;
(4) clauses which partially exclude a business from liability to compensate damages to a consumer arising from a tort (such torts are limited to instances where the same arises from gross negligence or wilful misconduct on the part of the business, the business's representative or an employee) provided in the Civil Code committed on occasion of the business's performance of a consumer contract;
(5) clauses which totally exclude a business from liability to compensate for damages to a consumer caused by a defect if a consumer contract is a contract for value and if there exists a latent defect in the material subject to that consumer contract (in case a consumer contract is a contract for work, a defect should exist in the object of the work). However, this clause will not be null and void (Article 8, paragraph 2) to the extent that the consumer contract provides that the business is responsible to deliver substitute goods without defects or to repair the subject if any defects exist in the material subject to the consumer contract, or another contract between the consumer and another business entrusted by the business or a contract between the business and another business for the benefit of the consumer, which is concluded before or simultaneously with the consumer contract, provided that the other business is responsible to compensate the whole or a part of the damage caused by the defect, deliver substitute goods without defects or repair the subject if any defect exists in the material, subject to the consumer contract.

Article 8*bis* of the Consumer Contracts Act stipulates other types of clauses deemed as null and void: clauses that a consumer gives up the right to rescind the contract due to non-performance or incomplete performance by the business; clauses that a consumer gives up the right to rescind the contract due to hidden defects in case of a contract for value.

*72.* Second, clauses to deem that a consumer has indicated his/her intention to offer or accept a new consumer contract by the consumer's non-feasance and other clauses which restrict the rights of consumers or expand the duties of consumers beyond the restrictions and expansions that would otherwise apply by application of the provisions of the Civil Code, the Commercial Code, and other such statutes not concerned with the public order and which, at the same time, unilaterally impair the interests of consumers against the fundamental principle provided in the second paragraph of Article 1 of the Civil Code, are null and void (Consumer Contracts Act, Article 10).

*73.* Third, Article 9 of the Consumer Contracts Act stipulates that some types of clauses in a consumer contract are null and void to a limited extent. With respect to clauses stipulating the amount of damages in case of a rescission or to clauses fixing the penalty, part of the clauses are null and void to the extent that the total amount of liquidated damages, in addition to the penalty, exceeds the average amount of damages by the rescission of a contract of the same kind to the business in accordance with the reason, the time of the rescission or other factors. As to clauses stipulating the amount of damages or fixing the penalty in case of total or partial default (in case payments should be made twice or more, every failure of payment is deemed as a default) of a consumer who is overdue, the clauses are null and void to the extent that the total amount of liquidated damages in addition to the penalty exceeds the amount calculated by deducting the amount of money actually paid by the appointed deadline from the amount of money which should have been paid and multiplying it by 14.6% a year in accordance with the number of days from the appointed deadline to the day on which the money is actually paid.

# Chapter 3. International Private Law Applied to the Online Environment

## §1. Adjudicative Jurisdiction

### I. Arbitration Agreement

*74.* If an action is filed for a civil dispute which is subject to an arbitration agreement, the Japanese court dismisses the action without prejudice (Arbitration Act, Article 14, paragraph 1).

### II. Rules for International Jurisdiction

*75.* The Code of Civil Procedure provides the rules on international jurisdiction, which applies to cases where there is no arbitration agreement.

#### *A. General Rules*

*76.* As a general rule, the courts have jurisdiction over an action that is brought against a person domiciled in Japan; against a person without a domicile or of domicile unknown, whose residence is in Japan; and against a person without a residence or of residence unknown, who was domiciled in Japan before the action was filed (unless the person has been domiciled in a foreign country after last being domiciled in Japan) (Article 3*bis*, paragraph 1). The courts have jurisdiction over an action that is brought against a corporation or any other association or foundation whose principal office or business office is located in Japan, and against a corporation, association, or foundation without a business office or other office, or with a business office or other office of unknown location, whose representative or other person principally in charge of its business is domiciled in Japan (Article 3*bis*, paragraph 3).

*77.* In addition, Japanese courts have the jurisdiction, for example, over: (a) an action on a claim for performance of a contractual obligation; on a claim involving benevolent intervention in another's affairs that has been done, or unjust enrichment that has arisen, in connection with a contractual obligation; on a claim for damages due to non-performance of a contractual obligation; or on any other claim involving a contractual obligation in cases where the contractually specified place for performance of the obligation is within Japan, or in cases where the law of the place adopted under the contract gives a place within Japan as the place for performance of the obligation; (b) an action on a property right in cases where the subject matter of the claim is located within Japan, or if in cases where an action is a claim for the payment of monies, and seizable property of the defendant is located within Japan (except for cases where the value of such property is extremely low); (c) an action against a person with an office or a business office, which is filed in connection with the business conducted at that person's office or business office, in case where the office or business office is located within Japan; (d) an action against a person that conducts business in Japan (including a foreign company (Article 2, Item 2 of the Companies Act) that regularly carries out transactions in Japan) in cases where the action involves the business that the person conducts in Japan; (e) an action for a tort in cases where the place where the tort occurred is within Japan (excluding the cases where the consequences of a wrongful act committed in a foreign country have brought about within Japan but it would not ordinarily have been possible to foresee the such consequences would be brought about within Japan) (Article 3*ter*, items 1, 3, 4, 5 and 8).

### B. *Rules Applicable to Consumer Contracts*

*78.* An action involving a contract concluded between a consumer (a natural person who does not enter the contract as a part of a business undertaking or for business purposes) and an entrepreneur (a corporation or any other association or foundation or a natural person who enters the contract as a part of a business undertaking or for business purposes) (excluding a labour contract; hereinafter referred to as a 'Consumer contract'), which is brought by the consumer against the entrepreneur, may be filed with the Japanese courts if the consumer is domiciled in Japan at the time the action is filed or at the time the Consumer contract is concluded (Article 3*quater*, paragraph 1).

*79.* Parties may, however, choose, by agreement, the country in which they are permitted to file an action with the courts. The agreement is not valid unless it is made regarding actions that are based on a specific legal relationship, and executed by means of a paper document or an electromagnetic record (a record in computer data processing which are created in electronic form, magnetic form, or any other form that is otherwise unperceivable through the human senses alone)(Article 3*septies*, paragraphs 1, 2 and 3). As an exception, an agreement on jurisdiction which covers Consumer contract disputes that may arise in the future is valid only in cases where: (a) the agreement provides that an action may be filed with the courts of the country where the consumer was domiciled at the time the Consumer contract was concluded (except for (b), any agreement that an action may be filed only with a court of such a country is deemed not to preclude the filing of an action with a court of any other country); or the consumer, in accordance with said agreement, has filed an action with the courts of the agreed-upon country, or if an entrepreneur has filed an action with the Japanese courts or with the courts of a foreign country and the consumer has invoked the agreement (Article 3*septies*, paragraph 5).

*C. Other Rules*

*80.* Where the defendant presents an oral argument on the merits of the case or submits a statement in preparatory proceedings without presenting the affirmative defence that the Japanese courts lack jurisdiction, the courts have jurisdiction (Article 3*octies*).

*81.* Even in cases where any Japanese court has jurisdiction over an action (except for cases where an action is filed under an agreement that only permits parties to file an action with the Japanese courts), the court may dismiss the whole or part of an action without prejudice if it finds that there are special circumstances that would cause inequity to either party or prevent a fair and speedy trial, in consideration of the nature of the case, the degree of burden that the defendant would have to bear in responding to the action, the location of evidence, and other circumstances if the Japanese courts were to conduct a trial and reach a judicial decision in the action (Article 3*nonies*).

## §2. Applicable Law

### I. CISG

*82.* As Japan is a Contracting State of the United Nations Convention on Contracts for the International Sale of Goods (CISG), the CISG applies to contracts of sale of goods between parties whose places of business are in different States: when the States are Contracting States; or when the rules of private international law (i.e., Act on General Rules for Application of Laws in Japan) lead to the application of the law of a Contracting State (CISG, Article 1, paragraph 1).

*83.* This CISG does not, however, apply to sales:

(a) of goods bought for personal, family or household use, unless the seller, at any time before or at the conclusion of the contract, neither knew nor ought to have known that the goods were bought for any such use;
(b) by auction;
(c) on execution or otherwise by authority of law;
(d) of stocks, shares, investment securities, negotiable instruments or money;
(e) of ships, vessels, hovercraft or aircraft;
(f) of electricity (CISG, Article 2).

*84.* In addition, the parties may exclude the application of the CISG or, subject to Article 12 of the CISG, derogate from or vary the effect of any of its provisions (CISG, Article 6).

## II. The Act on General Rules for Application of Laws

*85.* The Act on General Rules for Application of Laws governs determination of the applicable law.

*86.* The legal capacity of a person to act is governed by his/her national law. Unless a juridical act is to be governed by the provisions of family law or inheritance law, or a juridical act relating to real property situated in a place governed by a different law from the law of the place where the act was done, a person who has performed a juridical act is subject to the limitation of his/her capacity to act under his/her national law but has full capacity to act under the law of the place where the act is done (*lex loci actus*) is deemed, however, to have full capacity to act, only in cases where all the parties were present in a place governed by the same law at the time of the juridical act (Article 4).

*87.* The formation and effect of a juridical act is governed by the law of the place chosen by the parties at the time of the act (Article 7). In the absence of a choice of law by the parties, the formation and effect of a juridical act is governed by the law of the place with which the act is most closely connected at the time of the act. In cases where only one of the parties is to effect the characteristic performance involved in a juridical act, the law of the habitual residence of the party effecting the performance (in cases where the party has a place of business connected with the juridical act, the law of the place of business; in cases where the party has two or more places of business that are connected with the juridical act and governed by different laws, the law of the principal place of business) is presumed to be the law of the place with which the act is most closely connected (Article 8).

*88.* In this context, the 'characteristic performance' means any performance which distinguishes a certain type of contract from others. In a sale of goods, whether tangible or intangible, the seller of goods is the party who is to effect the 'characteristic performance'. Where a Japanese entrepreneur sells goods to a person abroad via its website, for example, the Japanese law is presumed to be the law that governs the place most closely related with the transaction.

*89.* In case of supplying software, the copyright licence contract is concluded with the licenser of the software in question in many cases in addition to the contract with the entity supplying the software. In such cases, the seller is the party effecting characteristic performance related to the supply contract while the licenser is the party effecting characteristic performance related to the copyright licence contract.

*90.* The parties may change the law otherwise applicable to the formation and effect of a juridical act; provided, however, that if such change prejudices the rights of a third party, it may not be asserted against the third party (Article 9).

*91.* The formalities for a juridical act are governed by a law applicable to the formation of the act (the initial applicable law prior to the change shall govern if the applicable law was changed after the juridical act had been done) while the formalities that comply with the law of the place where the act was done is applicable unless the juridical act to establish or dispose of a right in rem with regard to movable or immovable, or any other right requiring registration. In this context, with regard to a declaration of intention to a person in a place governed by a different law, the place from where the notice of the declaration was dispatched is deemed to be the place where the act was done.

*92.* These rules do not, however, apply to the formalities for a contract concluded between persons in places governed by different laws. In such a case, the formalities for a contract that comply with either the law of the place from where the notice of offer was dispatched or the law of the place from where the notice of acceptance was dispatched is valid (Article 10).

*93.* Even in cases where the law applicable to the formation and effect of a Consumer contract, as a result of a choice or a change of the applicable law, is a law that is not the law of the consumer's habitual residence, if the consumer has declared his/her intention to the entrepreneur that a specific mandatory provision in the law of the consumer's habitual residence should be applied, such mandatory provision applies to the matters stipulated in the mandatory provision with regard to the formation and effect of the Consumer contract in addition to the chosen applicable law. Notwithstanding Article 8, in the absence of a choice of law under Article 7 with regard to the formation and effect of a Consumer contract, the formation and effect of the Consumer contract is governed by the law of the consumer's habitual residence. Even in cases where a law that is not the law of a consumer's habitual residence is chosen under Article 7 with regard to the formation of a Consumer contract, if the consumer has declared his/her intention to the entrepreneur that a specific mandatory provision from within the law of the consumer's habitual residence should be applied to the formalities for the Consumer contract, such mandatory provision is exclusively applied to the matters stipulated in the mandatory provision with regard to the formalities for the Consumer contract.

*94.* In cases where the law of a consumer's habitual residence is chosen under Article 7 with regard to the formation of a Consumer contract, if the consumer has declared his/her intention to the entrepreneur that the formalities for the Consumer contract should be governed exclusively by the law of the consumer's habitual residence, the formalities for the Consumer contract is governed exclusively by the law of the consumer's habitual residence.

*95.* In the absence of a choice of law under Article 7 with regard to the formation of a Consumer contract, the formalities for the Consumer contract is governed by the law of the consumer's habitual residence.

*96.* The rules for Consumer contracts do not, however, apply in cases:

(a) where an entrepreneur's place of business that is connected with a Consumer contract is located in a place governed by a different law from the law of a consumer's habitual residence, and the consumer visits a place governed by the same law as the law of the entrepreneur's place of business and concludes the Consumer contract there unless the consumer had been, in the place of his/her habitual residence, solicited by the entrepreneur to conclude the Consumer contract in a place governed by the same law as the law of the entrepreneur's place of business;
(b) where an entrepreneur's place of business that is connected with a Consumer contract is located in a place governed by a different law from the law of a consumer's habitual residence, and the consumer has received or has been supposed to receive the entire performance of the obligation under the Consumer contract in a place governed by the same law as the law of the entrepreneur's place of business; unless the consumer had been, in the place of his/her habitual residence, solicited by the business operator to receive the entire performance of the obligation in a place governed by the same law as the law of the entrepreneur's place of business;
(c) where at the time of conclusion of a Consumer contract an entrepreneur did not know a consumer's habitual residence, and had reasonable grounds for not knowing that; or
(d) where at the time of conclusion of a Consumer contract an entrepreneur misidentified the counterparty as not being a consumer, and had reasonable grounds for making such misidentification (Article 11).

*97.* In the context of (b), for example, where the good is delivered to Japan after the consumer purchased on the Internet, the place where the entrepreneur's obligation is performed is in Japan and this exception is not applicable. On the other hand, where a consumer in Japan purchased music data and downloaded them from a foreign website, it might be possible to consider that the entrepreneur's obligation had completely been performed at the moment the music data became downloadable on the server located abroad. It is insisted, however, that the place where the obligation has been performed should be considered to be the place where the consumer is physically located in this case and this exception does not apply as long as the consumer downloads the data to a terminal placed in Japan.

*98.* On the other hand, it is probable that exceptions (c) and (d) apply to transactions on the Internet because the entrepreneur does not necessarily need to know the address of the counterparty, for example, in cases where it fulfils the obligation to supply electronically. In addition, some consumers may give untrue information on the location of their permanent residence or represent themselves as non-consumers.

*99.* The formation and effect of a claim arising from a tort is governed by the law of the place where the result of the wrongful act occurred unless occurrence of the result at the place was ordinarily unforeseeable. In the latter case, the law of the place where the wrongful act was committed governs (Article 17). As an exception to the general rule for torts, where a claim arises from a tort involving injury to life, body or property of others, caused by a defect in a product (good produced or processed) that is delivered, against a producer (a person who has produced, processed, imported, exported, distributed or sold a product in the course of trade) or a person who has provided a representation on the product in a manner which allows the others to recognize such person as its producer, the formation and effect of such claim is governed by the law of the place where the victim received the delivery of the product unless the delivery of the product at the place was ordinarily unforeseeable. In the latter case, the law of the principal place of business of the producer, etc. (in cases where the producer, etc. has no place of business, the law of his/her habitual residence) governs (Article 18).

*100.* 'The place where the victim received the delivery' is interpreted as the place the legal possession of the product is obtained. Where a product is purchased by a sale over the Internet, it is normally understood the 'place where the victim receives the delivery' is the place where the consumer's permanent residence is located, designated to be shipped to.

*101.* As the exception to the rules for torts above, the formation and effect of a claim arising from a tort shall be governed by the law of the place with which the tort is obviously more closely connected than the place designated in Articles 17, 18 or 19, taking into consideration that the parties had their habitual residence in the places governed by the same law at the time of the occurrence of the tort, that the tort was committed in breach of the obligation under a contract between the parties, or any other circumstances concerned (Article 20).

*102.* Even in cases where a tort shall be governed by a foreign law, if the facts do not constitute a tort under Japanese law, no claim under the foreign law can be made for damages or any other remedies in Japan. Moreover, even in cases where the facts constitute a tort both under the foreign law and Japanese law, the victim may make a claim only for damages or any other remedies that are acceptable under Japanese law (Article 22).

# Chapter 4. Competition Law Applied to the Digital Market

## §1. Overview of Competition Regulation in Japan

### I. Unreasonable Restraint of Trade and Private Monopolization

*103.* The Act Concerning the Prohibition of Private Monopolization and the Maintenance of Fair Trade (Law No. 54 of 14 April 1947) (hereinafter cited as the Anti-Monopoly Act) provides that no entrepreneur should effect private monopolization or unreasonable restraint of trade (Article 3).

*104.* The term 'private monopolization' is defined as 'such business activities, by which any entrepreneur, individually or by combination or conspiracy with other entrepreneurs, or in any other manner, excludes or controls the business activities of other entrepreneurs, thereby causing, contrary to the public interest, a substantial restraint of competition in any particular field of trade' (Article 2, paragraph 5).

*105.* 'Unreasonable restraint of trade' is defined as 'business activities by which any entrepreneur, by contract, agreement or any other concerted actions, irrespective of its name, with other entrepreneurs, mutually restrict or conduct their business activities in such a manner as to fix, maintain, or increase prices, or to limit production, technology, products, facilities, or customers or suppliers, thereby causing, contrary to the public interest, a substantial restraint of competition in any particular field of trade' (Article 2, paragraph 6). If the Fair Trade Commission observes that there exists an unreasonable restraint of trade, the Commission may order the entrepreneur concerned to cease and desist from such acts, to transfer a part of his business, or to take any other measures necessary to eliminate the violating acts. The Commission may also, when it deems it particularly necessary, even when a violating act has already ceased to exist, order the entrepreneurs concerned to take measures to publicize that the said act has been discontinued and order any other measures necessary to ensure elimination of the said act (Article 7).

*106.* In case an entrepreneur effects an unreasonable restraint of trade or enters into an international agreement or an international contract containing such matters as constitute an unreasonable restraint of trade, which pertains to the price of goods or services or in effect results in affecting the price of such goods or services by curtailing the volume of the supply thereof, the Fair Trade Commission should order the entrepreneur concerned to pay the Treasury a surcharge of an amount equivalent to that arrived at by multiplying the sales amount of such goods or services, computed in accordance with the method prescribed by a Cabinet Ordinance, for the period from the date on which the entrepreneur was engaged in business activities as constituting such conduct to the date on which the entrepreneur ceased to engage in business activities constituting such conduct (in case such a period exceeds three years, the period is determined three years retroactively from the date on which the entrepreneur ceased to engage in business activities as implementation of such conduct; hereinafter referred to as a 'period of such implementation') by prescribed percentage (Article 7*bis*).

## II. Unfair Trade Practices

*107.* Unfair trade practices are also prohibited (Article 19) and are defined as any act falling under any one of following paragraphs, which tends to impede fair competition and which is designated by the Fair Trade Commission as such:

(1) unjustly discriminating against other entrepreneurs;
(2) dealing at unjust prices;
(3) unjustly inducing or coercing customers of a competitor to deal with itself;
(4) dealing with another party on such terms as will unjustly restrict the business activities of the said party;
(5) dealing with another party through unjust use of one's bargaining position; and
(6) unjustly interfering with a transaction between an entrepreneur who in Japan competes with oneself or with the company of which oneself is a shareholder or an officer and the other transacting party; or, in case such an entrepreneur is a company, unjustly inducing, instigating, or coercing a shareholder or an officer of such a company to act against the interest of such a company (Article 2, paragraph 9).

*108.* In accordance with the provisions of Article 2, paragraph 9 of the Anti-Monopoly Act, the Fair Trade Commission released 'Unfair trade practices' (Fair Trade Commission Notification No. 15, 18 June 1982) (hereinafter cited as the General Designation). The release specified sixteen types of trade practices as unfair.

### A. *Concerted Refusal to Deal*

*109.* Without proper justification, taking one of the following specified acts concertedly with another entrepreneur who is in a competitive relationship with oneself ('competitor'):

(a) refusing to deal with a certain entrepreneur or restricting the quantity or substance of a commodity or service involved in the transaction with a certain entrepreneur; or
(b) causing another entrepreneur to take such an act.

### B. *Other Refusal to Deal*

*110.* Unjustly refusing to deal, or restricting the quantity or substance of a commodity or service involved in the transaction with a certain entrepreneur, or causing another entrepreneur to take any action which comes under one of these categories.

*C. Discriminatory Pricing*

*111.* Unjustly supplying or accepting a commodity or service at prices that discriminate between regions or between the other parties.

*D. Discriminatory Treatment on Transaction Terms*

*112.* Unjustly affording favourable or unfavourable treatment to a certain entrepreneur with regard to the terms of execution of a transaction.

*E. Discriminatory Treatment in a Trade Association*

*113.* Unjustly excluding a specific entrepreneur from a trade association or from a concerted activity, or unjustly discriminating against a specific entrepreneur in a trade association or a concerted activity, thereby causing difficulties in the business activities of the said entrepreneur.

*F. Unjust Low Price Sales*

*114.* Without proper justification, supplying a commodity or service continuously at a price that is excessively below the costs incurred in the said supply, or otherwise unjustly supplying a commodity or service at a low price, thereby tending to cause difficulties to the business activities of other entrepreneurs.

*G. Unjust High Price Purchase*

*115.* Unjustly purchasing a commodity or service at a high price, thereby tending to cause difficulties to the business activities of other entrepreneurs.

*H. Deceptive Customer Inducement*

*116.* Unjustly inducing customers of a competitor to deal with oneself by causing them to misunderstand that the substance of a commodity or service supplied by oneself, or terms of the transaction, or other matters relating to such transaction, are much better or much more favourable than the actual ones or than those relating to the competitor.

### *I. Customer Inducement by Unjust Benefits*

*117.* Inducing the customers of a competitor to deal with oneself by offering unjust benefits in the light of normal business practices.

### *J. Tie-In Sales*

*118.* Unjustly causing the other party to purchase a commodity or service from oneself or from an entrepreneur designated by oneself by tying it to the supply of another commodity or service, or otherwise coercing the said party to deal with itself or with an entrepreneur designated by itself.

### *K. Dealing on Exclusive Terms*

*119.* Unjustly dealing with another party on condition that the said party should not deal with a competitor, thereby tending to reduce transaction opportunities for the said competitor.

### *L. Resale Price Restriction*

*120.* Supplying a commodity to another party who purchases the said commodity from oneself while imposing, without proper justification, one of the restrictive terms specified below:

(a) causing the said party to maintain the sales price of the commodity that one has determined, or otherwise restricting the said party's free decision on sales price of the commodity; or
(b) having the said party cause an entrepreneur who purchases the commodity from the said party to maintain the sales price of the commodity that one has determined, or otherwise causing the said party to restrict the said entrepreneur's free decision on the sales price of the commodity.

### *M. Dealing on Restrictive Terms*

*121.* Other than any act specified under the preceding two paragraphs, dealing with another party on conditions that unjustly restrict any transaction between the said party and other transacting parties or other business activities of the said party.

*N. Abuse of Dominant Bargaining Position*

*122.* Taking any act specified in one of the following paragraphs, unjustly in the light of the normal business practices by making use of its dominant bargaining position over the other party:

(a) causing the other party in a continuous transaction to purchase a commodity or service other than commodities or services involved in the transaction;
(b) causing the other in a continuous transaction to provide for money, service or other economic benefits to it;
(c) setting or changing transaction terms in a way disadvantageous to the other party;
(d) in addition to any act regarding dealing on exclusive terms, resale price restriction and dealing on restrictive terms, imposing a disadvantage on the other regarding terms or execution of transaction; or
(e) causing the other party to follow its direction in advance, or to get its approval, regarding the appointment of officers of the other (meaning those as defined by Article 3(2) of the Anti-Monopoly Act).

*O. Interference with a Competitor's Transaction*

*123.* Unjustly interfering with a transaction between another entrepreneur who is in a domestic competitive relationship with oneself or with the company of which one is a shareholder or an officer and its other party in such transaction, by preventing the formation of a contract, or by inducing the breach of a contract, or by any other means whatsoever.

*P. Interference with Internal Operation of a Competing Company*

*124.* Unjustly inducing, abetting, or coercing a shareholder or an officer of a company which is in a domestic competitive relationship with oneself or with a company of which one is a shareholder or an officer, to take an act disadvantageous to said company by the exercise of voting rights, transfer of stock, divulgence of secrets, or any other means whatsoever.

*125.* When the Fair Trade Commission finds that there exists any unfair trade practice, the Commission may order the entrepreneur concerned to cease and desist from the said act, to delete the clauses concerned from the contract and to take any other measures necessary to eliminate the said act (Article 20).

### III. Injunction and Damages

*126.* A person, whose interests are infringed or likely to be infringed by any act of unfair trade practice and thereby suffering or likely to suffer serious damages, is entitled to demand the suspension or prevention of such infringements from an entrepreneur or a trade association who infringes or is likely to infringe such interests (Article 24).

*127.* Any entrepreneur who has effected unreasonable restraint of trade or employed unfair trade practices is liable to compensate the person injured. No entrepreneur may be exempted from the liability even if he has proven that wilfulness or negligence did not exist on his part (Article 25).

## §2. Exemptions

*128.* The Anti-Monopoly Act provides several exemptions. The most important exemption with respect to the ICT Market is the intellectual property right exemption. Article 21 provides that the provisions of the Anti-Monopoly Act shall not apply to such acts recognizable as the exercise of rights under the Copyright Act, the Patent Act, the Utility Model Act, the Design Act or the Trademark Act. However, there are some problems in interpreting 'acts recognizable as the exercise of rights under the Copyright Act, etc.'.

## §3. Designated Facilities

*129.* After the 1997 amendments, the Telecommunications Business Act stipulates that the Ministry of Internal Affairs and Communications/Minister of Internal Affairs and Communications (MIC) may designate telecommunications facilities (fixed local loop facilities in excess of 50% of the total number of subscriber lines at prefectural levels and intra-prefectural switching facilities installed as one system with those local loop facilities) to assure timely, non-discriminatory and transparent interconnection between the telecommunications carriers that own designated facilities and other carriers. The following obligations are imposed on the designated carriers:

(a) introduction of an interconnection tariff system that includes interconnection charges and technical requirements;
(b) preparation and disclosure of accounting reports concerning interconnection; and
(c) preparation and disclosure of plans to revise or expand facility features or functions.

*130.* Moreover, the Implementing Regulation for the Telecommunications Business Act was amended to require justifiable reasons for refusing application for interconnection to telecommunications facilities.

*131.* Furthermore, the Regulation for Interconnection Accounting requires the separation of accounting between the department that manages and operates the designated telecommunications facilities and the department that exploits the facilities to provide services. The Regulation for Cost Calculation provides an adequate cost calculation method based on the Regulation for Interconnection Accounting.

*132.* The MIC (former Minister of Posts and Telecommunications) in 1997 designated Nippon Telephone & Telegram Co. Ltd's (NTT's) local communications networks as designated telecommunications facilities which are indispensable for other carriers to interconnect, and obliged NTT to introduce an interconnection tariff system including interconnection charges and an accounting system concerning interconnection.

## §4. Provision of Technological Information on Platform Software

*133.* According to the Government's Three-Year Plan for Promotion of Regulation Reform (Cabinet Decision, 30 March 2001), the Fair Trade Commission set up the Study Group on Software and Competition Policy. The Study Group published its interim report, 'Views on Software Licensing Agreements, etc. under the Anti-Monopoly Act' (March 2002) (the final report is unlikely to be prepared and published), which referred to the views presented in the *Guidelines for Patent and Know-how Licensing Agreements under the Anti-Monopoly Act* (as of July 1999), which was superseded by the Guidelines for the Use of Intellectual Property under the Anti-Monopoly Act (28 September 2007) (hereinafter referred to as the 'Guidelines' in this chapter).

*134.* According to the report, in cases where an operating system maker provides hardware and application software makers with technological information, if the operating system maker:

(1) discriminates, for example, by delaying the provision of technological information, any hardware or application software makers that supply products compatible with other, competing operating systems;
(2) makes it a condition that the provision of technological information on recipients' not developing products compatible with other operating systems, and does not provide technological information for hardware or application software makers that do not comply with those conditions;
(3) discriminates, for example, by delaying the provision of technological information, any application software makers that supply products competing with application software that the operating system maker supplies; or
(4) makes it a condition that the provision of technological information on recipients' not supplying products competing with application software or hardware that the operating system maker supplies, and does not provide technological information for application software or hardware makers that do not comply with those conditions;

and if these acts are likely to impede fair competition in a market for products such as operating systems, hardware, or application software or for technologies, such as by deterring these hardware or application software makers from developing products for other, competing operating systems or depriving makers supplying application software competing with the application software supplied by the operating system maker of the opportunities to make transactions with end users, thereby making it difficult for the makers of competing software to find alternative customers, then it is considered that these acts will fall within the category of unfair trade practices and be in violation of the Anti-Monopoly Act (General Designation, Items 2, 4 and 13, etc.).

*135.* Where an operating system maker has added new functions through an update, if the maker does not provide application software makers with technological information or delays its provision, even though the application software makers have to be provided with the technological information by the operating system maker in order to supply application software that competes with the new functions, then it is considered that these acts will also fall within the category of unfair trade practices and be in violation of the Anti-Monopoly Act, provided that the acts are likely to impede fair competition in a market for products such as application software related to the new functions or for relevant technologies, such as by depriving the application software makers of the opportunities to deal with end users or making it difficult for them to find alternative customers (General Designation, Items 2 and 4).

*136.* Where the operating system maker not only obligates the hardware and application software makers to feed back to it the technological information that may be obtained in the process of developing products compatible with the new version but also:

(1) puts those makers under an obligation to have the rights and know-how concerning the technologies they may independently develop belong to it or licence it to make exclusive use of the rights and know-how; or
(2) prohibits them to utilize those technologies for the development of products compatible with competing operating systems or to licence third parties to use the rights and know-how;

then it is considered that these acts fall within the category of unfair trade practices and are in violation of the Anti-Monopoly Act, provided that the acts are likely to impede fair competition in a market for products such as operating systems, hardware, or application software or for technologies, such as by deterring the hardware and application software makers from freely developing products or from developing hardware or application software for competing operating systems (General Designation, Items 11 and 13).

*137.* If the operating system maker:

(1) unjustly expands the scope of the technological information whose secrecy is to be protected and thus applies the obligations to technological information that is not secret; or
(2) applies the obligations to protect secrecy to technological information that is developed independently by hardware or application software makers without using the technological information provided by the operating system maker, then it is considered that these acts will fall within the category of unfair trade practices and be in violation of the Anti-Monopoly Act, provided that the acts are likely to impede fair competition in a market for products such as operating systems, hardware, or application software or for technologies, such as by deterring the hardware and application software makers from freely developing products or from developing hardware or application software for competing operating systems (General Designation, Item 13).

*138.* The report also points out that it is illegal under the Anti-Monopoly Act as private monopolization to perform such acts so that the maker of an operating system that has become a de facto standard may eliminate or control the business activities of makers of other operating systems, application software, hardware, etc., and thereby substantially restrict competition in a market for products such as operating systems, hardware, or application software or for technologies.

*139.* The Guidelines take a view that due consideration should be given to facilitate competition in cases where a particular technology provides a function which other products and services offer on the basis of the specifications and standards of the technology ('platform function') and where many different applied technologies have been developed on the basis of the platform function. If the licensor of this technology introduces new licensing that incorporates some of the functions supported by the existing applied technologies into its platform function under the circumstances presumed above, the new licensing has the effect of preventing the licensees from using other applied technologies and of depriving other firms offering the applied technologies of trading opportunities, given that licensee cannot help but be granted the new licence. It constitutes unfair trade practice if it possesses the tendency to impede fair competition (Items 10 and 13 of the General Designation).

## §5. Software Licensing Agreements

*140.* The interim report of the Study Group on Software and Competition Policy and the Study Group, 'Views on Software Licensing Agreements, etc. under the Anti-Monopoly Act' presents some views on software licensing agreements.

*141.* First, the report points out that an act may actually be considered to be part of or a means of unjust restriction of trade or private monopolization if it is not really an act 'recognizable as the exercise of rights' under the Copyright Act and is therefore subject to the application of the Anti-Monopoly Act even if such an act is externally or formally recognizable as the exercise of rights under the Copyright Act.

*142.* Second, the report suggests that whether the imposition of restrictions on reproduction should not be recognized as the exercise of rights under the Copyright Act, and therefore subject to the application of the Anti-Monopoly Act, must be judged individually and based concretely on the purpose and condition of the act and the magnitude of its effect on competition in the market in question in accordance with the purpose of the copyright system. For example, in cases where the following reproduction restrictions are imposed on hardware makers and distributors, if they are used as a means of impeding fair competition in a market for software and hardware products or for technologies, it is considered that they are not recognizable as the exercise of rights under the Copyright Act and are subject to the application of the Anti-Monopoly Act:

(1) In cases where licensing fees payable by hardware makers and distributors are calculated, if the licensing fees are calculated based not solely on the shipments of products in which the software pertaining to the relevant agreements is reproduced, but on the total shipments of those products and products in which other software competing with the software in question is reproduced, then it is considered that the act will fall within the category of unfair trade practices and be in violation of the Anti-Monopoly Act, provided that the act is likely to impede fair competition in a market for software products, such as by forcing the hardware makers and distributors to adopt the software in question instead of competing software and thereby depriving the competing software makers of the opportunity to deal with the hardware makers and distributors and making it difficult for the competing software makers to find alternative customers (General Designation, Item 13).

(2) If a software maker imposes such a restriction on hardware makers and distributors as setting an upper limit to the number of reproduction times, it is considered that the act will fall within the category of unfair trade practices and be in violation of the Anti-Monopoly Act, provided, for example, that the act consequently causes a supply and demand adjustment effect on a market for hardware or software products (General Designation, Item 13).

*143.* It is also considered that the act will fall within the category of unfair trade practices and be in violation of the Anti-Monopoly Act, provided that the act is likely to impede fair competition in a market for software products, such as by depriving competing software makers of the opportunities to deal with the hardware makers and distributors and making it difficult for the competing software makers to find alternative customers where a software maker imposes such a restriction on the number of times of reproduction by distributors and hardware makers for the purpose of deterring distributors and hardware makers from handling competing software products (General Designation, Item 13).

*144.* Third, where the forbidden alteration of software exceeds the extent necessary for the software maker to provide the guarantee and the maintenance service, such as the cases where the software provider forbids end users:(1) to debug or customize the software; or (2) to connect or incorporate the software with or into other software or hardware personally or through third parties (such as system integrators) for the purpose of making a more efficient use of the software, then it is considered that the act is not recognized as the exercise of rights under the Copyright Act, and falls within the category of unfair trade practices and is in violation of the Anti-Monopoly Act, provided that the act impedes the licensees' research and development activities in a market for software products or for technologies and is thus likely to impede fair competition in a market for software or hardware products that can be used on the software or a market for such services related to the software as are provided by the system integrators and others (General Designation, Item 13).

*145.* Fourth, a licensee's obligation to assign the results of software alteration to the licensor, or to grant to the licensor a licence for exclusive use of the rights and know-how pertaining to the results of software alteration performed by the licensee could result in the enhancement of the position of the licensor in a relevant software technology market by unjustly pooling the rights and know-how pertaining to the results of alteration by the licensee in the hands of the licensor software maker or will impede the development of new software by the licensee, etc., by restricting the use by the licensee itself, or the licensing by the licensee to third parties of the knowledge, experience, and results of alteration, and therefore may have an adverse effect on competition in the market for software products or technologies. In addition, since it is considered that there is no reasonable justification for the licensor to impose such a requirement, the act is highly likely to fall within the category of unfair trade practices and be in violation of the Anti-Monopoly Act (General Designation, Item 13).

*146.* Fifth, where reverse engineering is forbidden in the case of software with platform functions, for example, in cases where: (1) interface information about the software is required in order to develop software or hardware that has interoperability with the software; (2) the interface information is not provided by the licensor; and (3) for the licensee, reverse engineering is an indispensable means for developing software or hardware for the software in question.

*147.* Such prohibition of reverse engineering is not an act recognizable as the exercise of rights under the Copyright Act and is therefore subject to the application of the Anti-Monopoly Act, even if the software may contain know-how and is an act externally or formally recognizable as the exercise of rights under the Copyright Act. Therefore, it is an unfair trade practice for the licensor to forbid the licensee to reverse engineer the software, provided that the licensor's act impedes the licensees' research and development activities in a market for software products or for technologies and thus impedes fair competition in a market for software or hardware products that can be used on the software or a market for such services related to the software as are provided by system integrators and others (General Designation, Item 13).

*148.* Sixth, in cases in which it is an important means of competition in the hardware market for hardware makers to sell certain influential pre-installed software, if at the time of concluding pre-installation agreements with hardware makers, the maker of the software obligates the hardware makers to pre-instal the software maker's other software products as well for tie-in sale of the software pertaining to the agreements, it is considered that the act falls within the category of unfair trade practices and is in violation of the Anti-Monopoly Act, provided that by utilizing the market influence of the software in question, the act is likely to impede the hardware makers' freedom of choosing software and hence fair competition in a market for tied-in software products. It is considered that the same holds true for cases in which these restrictions are imposed on distributors (General Designation, Item 10).

*149.* Seventh, in cases where it is an important means of competition in the hardware and software markets for hardware makers and distributors to sell certain influential software, if the maker of the software forbids hardware makers and distributors to handle software competing with the software provided by the software maker, it is considered that the act falls within the category of unfair trade practices and is in violation of the Anti-Monopoly Act, provided that the act is likely to impede fair competition in a market for software products, such as by depriving the competing software makers of the opportunity to deal with the hardware makers and making it difficult for the competing software makers to find alternative customers. It is considered that the same holds true for cases in which these restrictions are imposed on distributors (General Designation, Item 11).

# Chapter 5. Regulation of the Electronic Communication Market

## §1. Telecommunications Business Act

*150.* Telecommunication service businesses are governed by the Telecommunications Business Act (Law No. 86 of 1984). 'Telecommunications business' is defined as business that provides telecommunications services in order to meet the demands of others (excluding business related to a facility for (wireless) broadcasting, wire radio broadcasting, wire broadcast telephone service, wire television broadcasting service and cable television broadcasting). 'Telecommunications service' is defined as intermediating communications of others through the use of telecommunications facilities, or any other acts of providing telecommunications facilities for the use of communications of others. 'Telecommunications facilities' are defined as machines, equipment, wires, and cables or other electrical facilities for the operation of telecommunications and 'telecommunications' as transmitting, relaying or receiving codes, sounds or images by wire, radio or any other electromagnetic method.

### I. Registration Requirement

#### A. Registration

*151.* The Act requires telecommunications business operators to register at the MIC in principle (Article 9). A small telecommunication business operator is not, however, required to be registered but to notify (proviso to Article 9).

#### B. Application and Registration

*152.* Article 10 of Telecommunications Business Act stipulates that any person who intends to obtain registration for a telecommunication business should file an application with the MIC in accordance with the provisions of the applicable ordinance of the MIC (Implementing Regulation for the Telecommunications Business Act, Ministerial Ordinance of Post, No. 25 of 1985). Where an application for the registration is made, the Minister must register the applicant on the telecommunications carriers' registration book, unless the MIC refuses the registration in accordance with the provisions of paragraph 1 of Article 12 (Telecommunications Business Act, Article 11, paragraph 1).

*153.* A written declaration stating that the applicant is not subject to the reasons for disqualifications, and other documents specified in the applicable ordinance of the MIC (Implementing Regulation for the Telecommunications Business Act, Article 4, paragraph 3) must be attached to the application (Telecommunications Business Act, Article 10, paragraph 2).

Other required documents are as follows:

(1) layout diagrams of network in accordance with Form 3;
(2) documents describing the telecommunications services to be offered by the applicant in accordance with Form 4;
(3) an outline of the business in which the applicant is engaged, other than the telecommunications business;
(4) where the applicant is an existing legal person:
  (a) a certified copy of the articles of association or of the act of endowment and of the register; and
  (b) a list of officers or employees and their curricula vitae.
(5) where the applicant intends to establish a legal entity:
  (a) a certified copy of the articles of association or of the act of endowment; and
  (b) a list of promoters, members or founders, their curricula vitae, and the documents certifying their names, addresses and birthdays.
(6) where the applicant is an association without the status of a legal person:
  (a) a certified copy of the documents on the purpose, organization and operation, etc., such as the articles of association and the agreements; and
  (b) a list of members, their curricula vitae and the documents certifying their names, addresses and birthdays.
(7) where the applicant is an individual:
  (a) a document certifying the name, address and birthday of the applicant; and
  (b) the curriculum vitae.
(8) a table of telecommunications circuit settings.

### *C. Refusal to Register*

*154.* Where the applicant falls under any of the following reasons, or where the application or any document attached thereto includes any false entries on any important matter or fails to describe any important information, the MIC refuses the registration (Telecommunications Business Act, Article 12, paragraph 1):

(1) the applicant has been sentenced to a fine or a more severe penalty in accordance with the provisions of the Telecommunications Business Act, the Wire Telecommunications Act (Law No. 96 of 1953) or the Radio Act (Law No. 131 of 1950) and two years has not yet elapsed since the day on which the penalty was finished or he was exempted from penalty;
(2) the applicant's registration was revoked in accordance with paragraph 1, Article 14 of the Telecommunications Business Act and two years have not yet elapsed since the day of revocation;
(3) any legal person or association, which has as an officer anyone who falls under (2) or (3); or
(4) the launch of telecommunications service by the applicant is deemed as inappropriate for the sound development of telecommunications.

The MIC must, where it refused registration, notify the interested person, in writing, stating the grounds for the refusal (Telecommunications Business Act, Article 12, paragraph 2).

### *D. Revocation of Registration*

*155.* The MIC may revoke registration if a registrant falls within any of the following categories (Telecommunications Business Act, Article 14):

(1) a registrant has violated the provisions of the Telecommunications Business Act, or any orders or administrative rules for the Telecommunications Business Act so that the public interest is being hindered;
(2) a registrant obtained registration or registration of change through dishonest means; or
(3) a registrant has come to fall under any categories for disqualification stipulated in paragraph 1 of Article 12.

### *E. Striking Out the Record*

*156.* Where notice of the discontinuation of all of the operations of a telecommunications business or the dissolution of a telecommunications business has been given, or when the MIC has revoked registration, the MIC strikes out the registration record of the registrant (Telecommunications Business Act, Article 15).

### *F. Succession*

*157.* Where transfer of all of the operations of a telecommunications business, or merger, division (limited to those succeeding to all of the operations of telecommunications business) or inheritance with respect to a telecommunications carrier has been completed, the transferee who has taken over all of the operations of that business, or the legal person who continues to exist after merger or who has been established as a result of merger, or the legal person who has succeeded to all of the operations of said business after division or the inheritor (where there are two or more inheritors, one who has succeeded to the telecommunications carrier after negotiations among inheritors concerned) should succeed to the telecommunications carrier status. This does not, however, apply to the case where the telecommunications carrier is a registrant and the transferee who has taken over all of the operations of the telecommunications business, or the legal person who continues to exist after merger or who has been established as a result of a merger, or the legal person who has succeeded to all of the operations of the telecommunications business after division or the inheritor falls under any categories of disqualified persons (Telecommunications Business Act, Article 17, paragraph 1). Any person who has succeeded to the telecommunications carrier status must submit, without delay, a notification to the MIC (Telecommunications Business Act, Article 18, paragraph 1).

### G. *Suspension and Discontinuation of Business*

*158.* Where a telecommunications carrier has suspended or discontinued a part or all of the operations of its telecommunications business, the telecommunications carrier shall submit, without delay, a notification to the MIC. Where a legal person who is a telecommunications carrier has been dissolved due to reasons other than merger, the liquidator in charge (or the trustee in bankruptcy in the case of dissolution due to bankruptcy) should also submit, without delay, a notification to the Minister (Telecommunications Business Act, Article 18). In addition, where a telecommunications carrier intends to suspend or discontinue a part or all of the operations of its telecommunications business, as specified in the applicable ordinance of the MIC (Implementing Regulation for the Telecommunications Business Act, Article 12), it should inform its users (persons having concluded contracts with a telecommunications carrier to receive telecommunications services) of the telecommunications business that the business is to be suspended and discontinued. However, it does not have to inform where it intends to suspend or discontinue a telecommunications business having a comparatively small influence on the users' benefit in accordance with the applicable ordinance of the MIC (Telecommunications Business Act, Article 18, paragraph 3, Implementing Regulation for the Telecommunications Business Act, Article 13, paragraph 2).

## II. Notification Requirement

*159.* Where the scale of telecommunications circuit facilities (telecommunications circuit facilities connecting transmitting points with receiving points, switching facilities installed as inseparable units therefrom, and other facilities accessory to such facilities) as installed by the person, and the scope of areas where the telecommunications circuit facilities are installed do not exceed the standards specified in the applicable ordinance of the MIC (Implementing Regulation for the Telecommunications Business Act, Article 3, paragraph 1), the telecommunication business operator is not required to be registered but to notify (Telecommunications Business Act, Proviso to Article 9). The telecommunications business operator should, as specified in the applicable ordinance of the MIC (Implementing Regulation for the Telecommunications Business Act, Article 9), submit a notification to that effect to the Minister with documents that describe the name and address of the applicant and, in the cases where the applicant is a legal person, name of the representative, the service areas and the outline of telecommunications facilities (Telecommunications Business Act, Article 16, paragraph 1).

## III. Tariffs and Interconnection

### A. *Tariffs*

*160.* A telecommunications carrier providing universal telecommunications services (telecommunications services that are stipulated in the applicable ordinance of the MIC in order to ensure the provision of such telecommunications services nationwide which are indispensable for people's daily lives) must establish tariffs concerning terms and conditions, including charges relating to the carrier's universal telecommunications services, and submit the tariffs to the MIC prior to application thereof, as specified in the applicable ordinance of the MIC. Where a telecommunications carrier providing universal telecommunications services amends its tariffs, it must submit the amended tariffs to the MIC before it applies the tariffs (Telecommunications Business Act, Article 19, paragraph 1).

*161.* The MIC may, where it is deemed that the tariffs filed fall under any of the following items, order the telecommunications carrier to change the tariffs within a reasonable time period (Telecommunications Business Act, Article 19, paragraph 2):

(1) the calculation methods of charges are not stipulated properly and clearly;
(2) the tariffs related to the responsibilities to be assumed by a telecommunications carrier and its users, and allocation methods of costs related to installation and other works of telecommunications facilities are not properly and clearly stipulated;
(3) the tariffs unreasonably restrict utilization conditions of the telecommunications circuit facilities;
(4) the tariffs include the provisions that unfairly discriminate against specified persons;
(5) due consideration is not paid to the matters relating to essential communications; or
(6) the tariffs impair the users' benefit, leading to illicit competition with other telecommunications carriers, or the tariffs are extremely improper in light of socioeconomic conditions.

*162.* With respect to terms and conditions including charges to be specified in tariffs, any telecommunications carrier providing universal telecommunications services should provide the universal telecommunications services pursuant to the tariffs notified. However, a telecommunications carrier providing universal telecommunications services may, in accordance with the standards specified in the applicable ordinance of the MIC (Implementing Regulation for the Telecommunications Business Act, Article 17), reduce or exempt charges for the universal telecommunications services specified in the tariffs notified (Telecommunications Business Act, Article 19, paragraphs 3 and 4).

*163.* The Telecommunications Business Act provides that 'designated telecommunications services' are telecommunications services which are provided by a telecommunications carrier installing Category I designated telecommunications facilities (Telecommunications Business Act, Article 33 paragraph 2). Through use of Category I designated telecommunications facilities and in consideration of circumstances that other telecommunications services substitute the telecommunications services not sufficiently provided by other telecommunications carriers, they secure the provision of telecommunications services based on proper terms and conditions including charges through use of said Category I designated telecommunications facilities of the telecommunications carrier by installing Category I designated telecommunications facilities. They are specified as telecommunications services especially necessary for protecting the users' benefit in the applicable ordinance of the MIC (*see* Implementing Regulation for the Telecommunications Business Act, Article 18).

*164.* A telecommunications carrier providing designated telecommunications services must establish tariffs concerning terms and conditions including charges relating to the carrier's designated telecommunications services and submit the tariffs (including amended tariffs) to the MIC prior to application thereof, as specified in the applicable ordinance of the MIC (Telecommunications Business Act, Article 20, paragraph 1, Implementing Regulation for the Telecommunications Business Act, Article 19). The MIC may, where it is deemed that the tariffs (guaranteed tariffs) filed fall under any of the following items, order the telecommunications carrier providing designated telecommunications services to change the guaranteed tariffs within a reasonable time period (Telecommunications Business Act, Article 20, paragraph 3):

(1) the calculation methods of charges are not stipulated properly and clearly;
(2) the tariffs related to the responsibilities to be assumed by a telecommunications carrier and its users, and allocation methods of costs related to installation and other works of telecommunications facilities are not properly and clearly stipulated;
(3) the tariffs unreasonably restrict utilization conditions of the telecommunications circuit facilities;
(4) the tariffs include the provisions that unfairly discriminate against specified persons;
(5) due consideration is not paid to the matters relating to essential communications; or
(6) the tariffs impair the users' benefit, leading to illicit competition with other telecommunications carriers, or the tariffs are extremely improper in light of socioeconomic conditions.

*165.* A telecommunications carrier providing designated telecommunications services must provide the designated telecommunications services pursuant to terms and conditions including charges specified in the guaranteed tariffs unless it agreed upon terms and conditions including charges with the other parties or charges for the designated telecommunications services specified in the guaranteed tariffs are reduced or exempted in accordance with the standards specified in the applicable ordinance of the MIC (Implementing Regulation for the Telecommunications Business Act, Article 19-2-2), reduce or exempt charges for the designated telecommunications services specified in the guaranteed tariffs (Telecommunications Business Act, Article 20, paragraphs 5 and 6).

*166.* The MIC, at least once a year, as specified in the applicable ordinance of the MIC, specifies the level of charges that may be normally realized in consideration of reasonable cost based upon managerial efficiency, commodity prices and other economic conditions with the use of the charge index (figures that represent the level of charges for individual categories of telecommunications services, which are calculated with the methods specified in the applicable ordinance of the MIC based upon charges that depend on the distance and speed of communications or other classifications, and based upon the amount of traffic, number of circuits, etc., to which these charges are applied) for telecommunications services (specified telecommunications services being designated telecommunications services, which are specified in the applicable ordinance of the MIC as those having a significant influence on the users' benefit from the perspective of its content, the scope of users, etc.) concerning individual categories of the specified telecommunications services specified in the applicable ordinance of the MIC, and notifies telecommunications carriers providing the specified telecommunications services of the charge index (standard charge index) within the number of days before the day of application thereof specified in the applicable ordinance of the MIC (Telecommunications Business Act, Article 21, paragraph 1, Implementing Regulation for the Telecommunications Business Act, Article 19*ter* through 19*septies*). A telecommunications carrier providing specified telecommunications services must obtain authorization by the MIC where it intends to change charges concerning specified telecommunications services and if the charge index after the change exceeds the standard charge index pertaining to the specified telecommunications services (Telecommunications Business Act, Article 21, paragraph 2, Implementing Regulation for the Telecommunications Business Act, Article 19*octies*). Upon receipt of an application for authorization, the Minister should grant authorization if it is deemed that there are specific reasons making it difficult to comply with the charges of a charge index being equivalent to or below the standard charge index, and that the charges after the change pertaining to the application do not fall under any of the following items (Telecommunications Business Act, Article 21, paragraph 3):

(1) calculating methods of charges are not stipulated properly and clearly;
(2) the charges after the change unfairly discriminate against a particular person; or
(3) the charges after the change impair the users' benefit because the charges lead to illicit competition with other telecommunications carriers, or the charges are extremely improper in light of socioeconomic conditions.

*167.* A telecommunications carrier providing specified telecommunications services must keep records of the amount of traffic, number of circuits, etc., of its specified telecommunications services in accordance with the methods specified in the applicable ordinance of the MIC (Telecommunications Business Act, Article 22,

Implementing Regulation for the Telecommunications Business Act, Article 20*bis*). A telecommunications carrier providing universal telecommunications services, designated telecommunications services or specified telecommunications services must, as specified in the applicable ordinance of the MIC(Implementing Regulation for the Telecommunications Business Act, Article 22*bis*), publish tariffs notified or charges authorized as well as post thereof at its business offices and other workplaces in a manner in which such tariffs and charges can easily be seen by the general public (Telecommunications Business Act, Article 23, paragraph 1). A telecommunications carrier providing universal telecommunications services or designated telecommunications services should put accounts in order in accordance with the account headings and accounting practices specified in the applicable ordinance of the MIC (Telecommunications Business Accounting Regulation, Ministerial Ordinance of Post, No. 26 of 1985), with the purpose of facilitating the proper calculation of charges relating to the universal telecommunications services or the designated telecommunications services provided by the telecommunications carrier (Telecommunications Business Act, Article 24).

### *B. Duty to Provide Services*

*168.* A telecommunications carrier providing universal telecommunications services should not, without due reason, refuse to provide universal telecommunications services within its service areas (Telecommunications Business Act, Article 25, paragraph 1). However, a telecommunications carrier providing designated telecommunications services may not, except as may be otherwise agreed upon in terms and conditions including charges for said designated telecommunications services with the other parties, without due reason, refuse to provide the designated telecommunications services pursuant to terms and conditions including charges specified in the guaranteed tariffs within its service areas (Telecommunications Business Act, Article 25, paragraph 2).

*169.* A telecommunications carrier should agree to the request for interconnection of its telecommunications circuit facilities being installed by the telecommunications carrier from other telecommunications carriers with telecommunications facilities of the other telecommunications carriers, unless (Telecommunications Business Act, Article 32):

(1) there is a risk of hindering the smooth provision of telecommunications services;
(2) there is a risk that the interconnection may unfairly impair the interest of the telecommunications carrier; or
(3) there are due reasons specified in the applicable ordinance of the MIC (Implementing Regulation for the Telecommunications Business Act, Article 23) in addition to (1) and (2).

*C. Category I Designated Telecommunications Facilities*

*170.* The MIC may, as specified in the applicable ordinance of the MIC, designate telecommunications facilities as Category I telecommunications facilities for each area which is specified in the applicable ordinance. The MIC designates from the viewpoint of the area of prefectures and of the actual usage of telecommunications services. The Category I designated telecommunications facilities are the transmission line facilities installed by one telecommunications carrier, one end of which is connected to the users' telecommunications facilities (except for mobile terminal facilities), where the ratio of the number of telecommunications circuits of the transmission line facilities to the number of telecommunications circuits in all transmission line facilities of the same kind installed in the same area exceeds the ratio specified in the applicable ordinance of the MIC, and the telecommunications facilities installed in the area by the telecommunications carrier as an integral part of the facilities and which is specified in the applicable ordinance of the MIC, as the telecommunications facilities which interconnection with the telecommunications facilities of other telecommunications carriers is essential for the enhancement of the users' benefit and the comprehensive and rational development of telecommunications (Telecommunications Business Act, Article 33, paragraph 1, Implementing Regulation for the Telecommunications Business Act, Article 23*bis*).

*171.* For the time being, only a part of facilities held by the NTT East Japan and the NTT West Japan are designated as Category I telecommunications facilities.

*172.* A telecommunications carrier installing Category I designated telecommunications facilities must establish Conditions of Interconnection which specify the amount of money it will receive (interconnection charges) and other terms and conditions of interconnections, including: (i) technical requirements at interconnection points with telecommunications facilities of other telecommunications carriers; (ii) distinctions as to the type of telecommunications carriers for which telecommunications services charges are specified in terms of the interconnection of the Category I designated telecommunications facilities with the telecommunications facilities of other telecommunications carriers; and (iii) obtain authorization from the MIC. The same shall also apply where the Conditions of Interconnection are to be amended (Telecommunications Business Act, Article 33, paragraph 2, Implementing Regulation for the Telecommunications Business Act, Article 23*ter*).

*173.* The Minister shall grant authorization if the application is deemed to meet the following requirements (Telecommunications Business Act, Article 33, paragraph 4):

(1) the following sub-items are specified properly and clearly:
   (a) technical requirements at those points which are specified as standard in the applicable ordinance of the MIC (Implementing Regulation for the Telecommunications Business Act, Article 23*quater*, paragraph 1)

among those interconnection points where the interconnection of telecommunications facilities with other telecommunications carriers is technically and economically feasible;
(b) interconnection charges by individual function are specified in the applicable ordinance of the MIC (Regulations on Interconnection Charges, Ministerial Ordinance of Post, No. 64 of 2000);
(c) the responsibilities of a telecommunications carrier installing Category I designated telecommunications facilities and those of other telecommunications carriers who establish interconnection with them;
(d) distinctions as to type of telecommunications carriers for which charges of telecommunications services are specified; and
(e) in addition to (a) through (d), the matters specified in the applicable ordinance of the MIC (Implementing Regulation for the Telecommunications Business Act, Article 23*quater*, paragraph 2) as necessary to accomplish smooth interconnection with Category I designated telecommunications facilities.

(2) the interconnection charges should be fair and justifiable in light of the costs calculated in accordance with the methods specified in the applicable ordinance of the MIC (Regulations on Interconnection Charges) as a fair amount based on efficient management cost;
(3) the terms and conditions of interconnections shall be no less favourable than those applicable where a telecommunications carrier installing Category I designated telecommunications facilities accomplishes interconnection between the Category I designated telecommunications facilities and the telecommunications facilities of its own; and
(4) it should not be unduly discriminating to particular telecommunications carriers.

*174.* Interconnection charges and terms and conditions of interconnections specified in the Conditions of Interconnection, which are specified in the applicable ordinance of the MIC (Implementing Regulation for the Telecommunications Business Act, Article 23*sexies*) as those having a comparatively small influence on the enhancement of the users' benefit as well as comprehensive and rational development of telecommunications are not, however, required to obtain authorization thereof (Telecommunications Business Act, Article 33, paragraph 3).

### *D. Category II Designated Telecommunications Facilities*

*175.* The MIC may, as specified in the applicable ordinance of the MIC, designate telecommunications facilities as Category II telecommunications facilities. The Category II telecommunications facilities are transmission line facilities installed by one telecommunications carrier, one end of which is connected to the specified mobile terminal facilities (mobile terminal facilities specified in the applicable ordinance of the MIC), where the ratio of the number of the specified mobile terminal facilities connected to all the transmission line facilities of the same kind installed in that same area pertaining to telecommunications services utilizing said transmission line facilities exceeds the ratio specified in the applicable ordinance of the MIC, and the telecommunications facilities installed by the telecommunications carrier in order to provide the telecommunications services specified in the applicable ordinance of the MIC as the designated telecommunications facilities that shall ensure appropriate and smooth interconnections with the telecommunications facilities of other telecommunications carriers (Telecommunications Business Act, Article 34, paragraph 1, Implementing Regulation for the Telecommunications Business Act, Article 23-9-2).

*176.* A telecommunications carrier installing Category II designated telecommunications facilities must establish Conditions of Interconnection on the amount of money it will receive and the terms and conditions of interconnections, and submit a notification prior to application thereof to the MIC, as specified in the applicable ordinance of the MIC (Implementing Regulation for the Telecommunications Business Act, Article 23-9-3). The same also applies where the Conditions of Interconnection are to be amended (Telecommunications Business Act, Article 34, paragraph 2).

The Minister may order the telecommunications carrier installing said Category II telecommunications facilities to amend the Conditions of Interconnection within a reasonable time period where it is deemed that in the Conditions of Interconnection submitted as the notice specified (Telecommunications Business Act, Article 34, paragraph 3):

(1) the following matters are not properly and clearly stipulated:
  (a) the technical requirements at interconnection points with telecommunications facilities of other telecommunications carriers where the applicable ordinance of the MIC specified as standard for technically and economically possible interconnection;
  (b) the amount of money to be received by the telecommunications carrier installing Category II telecommunications facilities for each function specified by the applicable ordinance of the MIC;
  (c) the responsibilities of telecommunications carriers installing Category II telecommunications facilities and other telecommunications carriers that interconnect their telecommunications facilities with the Category II telecommunications facilities;
  (d) the distinctions as to the type of telecommunications carriers for which charges of telecommunications services are specified; and
  (e) other matters that the applicable ordinance of the MIC specified as necessary for smooth interconnection with Category II telecommunications facilities.

(2) the amount of money to be received by the telecommunications carrier installing Category II telecommunications facilities surpasses the sum that is calculated by the methods specified in the applicable ordinance of the MIC for calculation of reasonable costs and reasonable profit under efficient management;

(3) the conditions are less advantageous than those that would be applied in the cases where the telecommunication carrier installing Category II telecommunications facilities itself should interconnect its telecommunication facilities to the Category II telecommunications facilities; or
(4) the Conditions of Interconnection unfairly discriminate particular telecommunications carriers.

### *E. Order to Reopen Negotiations for Interconnection or Interconnect*

*177.* Where a telecommunications carrier, in spite of another telecommunications carrier's proposal to enter into an agreement to interconnect telecommunications facilities of said telecommunications carrier with telecommunications facilities of said other telecommunications carrier, does not accept entering into a negotiation or where said negotiation fails to come to an agreement, the MIC should, upon petition of the telecommunications carrier who proposed the agreement, order the other telecommunications carrier to start or reopen the negotiation, except in cases where it is deemed that such interconnections fall under any cases stipulated in Article 32 and an application for arbitration has been filed (Telecommunications Business Act, Article 35, paragraph 1).

*178.* In addition, if despite one's proposal to enter into an agreement to interconnect telecommunications facilities between telecommunications carriers, the other party does not accept entering into a negotiation or where the negotiation fails to come to an agreement, the Minister may, upon request of one of the telecommunications carriers, order the other telecommunications carrier to start or reopen the negotiation when it is deemed the interconnection is especially necessary and appropriate to promote the public interest except for cases where an application for arbitration has been filed (Telecommunications Business Act, Article 35, paragraph 2).

*179.* Where a negotiation between the parties concerned about the interconnections to telecommunications facilities of a telecommunications carrier fail to come to an agreement with respect to the details such as the amount of money to be received and paid by them or the terms and conditions of interconnections, a telecommunications carrier who instals telecommunications facilities to be connected to the telecommunications facilities of the telecommunications carrier may apply for an award to the Minister unless the parties have filed an application for arbitration (Telecommunications Business Act, Article 35, paragraph 3).

### *F. Prohibited Acts*

*180.* Any telecommunications carrier that has installed Category I telecommunications facilities must not conduct any acts as follows (Article 30, paragraph 4):

(1) Making use of or providing proprietary information on other telecommunications carriers or their users, which came to its knowledge with respect to

business activities to interconnect with the telecommunications facilities of the telecommunications carriers, for purposes other than such business activities.

(2) Applying unreasonable preferential treatment or conferring benefits, or applying unreasonable disadvantageous treatment or causing disadvantages, to certain telecommunications carriers, with regard to its telecommunications activities.

(3) Unreasonably disciplining or intervening in the business activities of other telecommunications carriers (including those who operate any of the telecommunications business listed in Items of Article 164 paragraph 1), or manufacturers or sellers of telecommunications facilities.

*181.* In cases where the total profits that a telecommunications carrier that has installed Category II telecommunications facilities has earned from its telecommunications services using the Category II telecommunications facilities in the most recent year as a percentage of the total profit earned from all telecommunications services of the same kind in the most recent year in the same area as the service area pertaining to the telecommunications services exceeds the percentage specified by the applicable ordinance of the MIC (Implementing Regulation for the Telecommunications Business Act, Article 22*ter*, paragraph 2), the MIC may, as specified by the applicable ordinance of the MIC (Implementing Regulation for the Telecommunications Business Act, Article 22*ter*, paragraph 1), designate the telecommunications carrier as a telecommunications carrier to whom the provisions of paragraphs 3, 5 and 6 of Article 30 shall apply, where the Minister finds it necessary to ensure proper competition with other telecommunications carriers in consideration of changes in the percentage and other circumstances (Article 30, paragraph 1). Where the MIC finds the designation pursuant to the provision of paragraph 1 is no longer necessary, the Minister shall repeal the designation (Article 30, paragraph 2).

*182.* The telecommunications carrier designated in accordance with paragraph 1 must not conduct any acts as follows (Article 30, paragraph 3):

(1) Making use of or providing proprietary information on other telecommunications carriers or their users, which came to its knowledge with respect to business activities to interconnect with the telecommunications facilities of the telecommunications carriers, for purposes other than such business activities.

(2) In cases where the telecommunications carrier is a legal person, applying unreasonable preferential treatment or conferring benefits with regard to its telecommunications activities to its specific related legal persons (Telecommunications Business Act, Article 12*bis*, paragraph 4, Item 1; Implementing Order for the telecommunications Business Act, Article 1) that is a telecommunication carrier and has been designated by the MIC.'

*183.* Where the MIC finds that an act committed by any telecommunications carrier who has been designated pursuant to the provision of paragraph 1 or any telecommunications carrier who has installed Category I telecommunications facilities has violated the provision of paragraph 3 or 4, the Minister may order the telecommunications carrier to suspend or alter the act (Article 30, paragraph 5).

## IV. Telecommunications Facilities

### *A. Maintenance of Technical Conditions*

*184.* A telecommunications carrier installing telecommunications circuit facilities must maintain its telecommunications facilities, except for those used for the telecommunication business exclusively to provide domain name telecommunications services (Telecommunications Business Act, Article 164, paragraph 2, Item 1; Implementing Regulation for the Telecommunications Business Act, Article 59*bis*) and those specified in the applicable ordinance of the MIC (Implementing Regulation for the Telecommunications Business Act, Article 27*bis*) as those having a minor influence on the users' benefit in the cases of damage or failure, etc. thereof, for use of its telecommunications business in compliance with the technical conditions specified in the applicable ordinance of the MIC (Telecommunications Business Act, Article 41, paragraph 1).

*185.* A telecommunications carrier providing universal telecommunications services must maintain its telecommunications facilities (except telecommunications facilities stipulated in paragraph 1 and those used for the telecommunication business exclusively to provide domain name telecommunications services) for use of its telecommunications business to provide the universal telecommunications services in compliance with the technical conditions specified in the applicable ordinance of the MIC (Telecommunications Business Act, Article 41, paragraph 2).

*186.* MIC, pursuant to the provisions in an ordinance of the MIC, may designate a telecommunications carrier providing the telecommunications services (except for universal telecommunication services and domain name telecommunications services) specified in the applicable Ordinance of MIC (Implementing Regulation for the Telecommunications Business Act, Article 27-2-2) as those have a large impact on the benefits of the user in view of the content and the range of user telecommunications as the telecommunications carrier that properly manages the telecommunications facilities for the telecommunications business (Telecommunications Business Act, Article 41, paragraph 3). The designated telecommunications carrier should keep the telecommunications facilities for the telecommunications business to provide the telecommunications services specified in the applicable ordinance of MIC (except for the telecommunications facilities provided for in paragraph 1) in conformity with the technical standards prescribed by the ordinance of MIC (Telecommunications Business Act, Article 41, paragraph 4).

*187.* The technical conditions should be so specified to ensure the following requirements (Telecommunications Business Act, Article 41, paragraph 5):

(1) the provision of telecommunications service shall not be extremely hindered by damage or failure of telecommunications facilities;
(2) the quality of telecommunications services shall maintain an appropriate level;
(3) the secrecy of communications shall not be violated;
(4) telecommunications facilities of users or other telecommunications carriers connected shall not be damaged or impaired, nor shall functions thereof be impaired; and
(5) the demarcation of responsibilities between the telecommunications facilities of a telecommunications carrier and those of others shall be clearly stipulated.

*188.* A telecommunications carrier providing domain name telecommunications services (Article 164, paragraph 2, Item 1; Implementing Regulation for the Telecommunications Business Act, Article 59*bis*) must maintain its telecommunications facilities for use of its telecommunications business to provide the domain name telecommunications services in compliance with the international standards relating to the management of the telecommunication facilities (Article 41*bis*).

*189.* A telecommunications carrier installing telecommunications circuit facilities should, as specified in the applicable ordinance of the MIC, when intending to start operating telecommunications facilities, confirm that the telecommunications facilities (except for those specified in the applicable ordinance of the MIC) are in compliance with the technical conditions specified in the applicable ordinance of the MIC (Telecommunications Business Act, Article 42, paragraph 1, Implementing Regulation for the Telecommunications Business Act, Article 27*ter*).

*190.* The Minister may, when it is deemed that the telecommunications facilities fail to comply with the technical conditions stipulated in the applicable ordinance of the MIC, order a telecommunications carrier installing the telecommunications facilities to repair or improve said telecommunications facilities so as to make them comply with the technical conditions, or may restrict the use thereof (Telecommunications Business Act, Article 43, paragraph 1).

### *B. Administrative Rules of Telecommunications Facilities for Telecommunications Business*

*191.* A telecommunications carrier must, as specified in the applicable ordinance of the MIC, establish administrative rules governing telecommunications facilities for telecommunications business as stipulated in Article 41 paragraph 1, 2 or 4 (telecommunications facilities for telecommunications business). This is done in order to ensure the reliable and stable provision of telecommunications services.

It must submit notice of the administrative rules to the Minister prior to the commencement of its telecommunications business (Telecommunications Business Act, Article 44, paragraph 1). Where a telecommunications carrier has amended its administrative rules, it must submit, without delay, notification of the amendments to the Minister (Telecommunications Business Act, Article 44, paragraph 3).

*192.* A carrier must provide in accordance with the applicable ordinance of the MIC (Implementing Regulation for the Telecommunications Business Act, Article 29) the following in the administrative rules (Telecommunications Business Act, Article 44, paragraph 2):

(1) matters related to the policy of the management of the telecommunications facilities for the business in order to ensure the reliable and stable provision of telecommunications services;
(2) matters related to the system of managing the telecommunications facilities for the business in order to ensure the reliable and stable provision of telecommunications services;
(3) matters related to the ways to manage the telecommunications facilities for the business in order to ensure the reliable and stable provision of telecommunications services; and
(4) matters related to the appointment of telecommunications facilities supervising administrator as prescribed in paragraph 1 of Article 44*ter*.

*193.* In cases where MIC finds that the administrative rules submitted by a telecommunications carrier do not conform to the provisions of paragraph 2 of Article 44, he/she may order the carrier to amend them. He/she may also order a carrier to comply with the administrative rules to the extent necessary in order to ensure a reliable and stable provision of telecommunications services in case where he/she admits that the telecommunications carriers are not in compliance with the administrative rules (Telecommunications Business Act, Article 44*bis*).

### *C. Telecommunications Facilities Supervising Administrator*

*194.* A telecommunications carrier shall, pursuant to the provisions of ordinance of MIC (Implementing Regulation for the Telecommunications Business Act, Article 29*bis*, paragraph 2), appoint the telecommunications facilities supervising administrator from persons who are in administrative positions to participate in the important decisions of business operations and meet the requirements prescribed by the applicable MIC ordinance (Implementing Regulation for the Telecommunications Business Act, Article 29*bis*, paragraph 1), including experience in certain practices related to the management of telecommunications facilities. When a telecommunications carrier has appointed or dismissed a telecommunications facilities supervising administrator, it shall, pursuant to the provisions of ordinance of MIC (Implementing Regulation for the Telecommunications Business Act, Article 29*ter*), without delay, notify to that effect to the MIC (Telecommunications Business Act, Article 44*ter*).

*195.* A telecommunications facilities supervising administrator must conscientiously perform his/her duties. In order to ensure a reliable and stable provision of telecommunications services, a telecommunications carrier must respect the opinion of the telecommunications facilities supervising administrator in performing his/her duties (Telecommunications Business Act, Article 44*quater*).

*196.* The MIC may order a telecommunications carrier to dismiss a telecommunications facilities supervising administrator in cases where the telecommunications facilities supervising administrator has neglected his/her duties and the Minister deems that it is likely to cause significant hindrance to ensure a reliable and stable provision of telecommunications services to allow the telecommunications facilities supervising administrator to continue to perform the duties (Telecommunications Business Act, Article 44*quinquies*).

### *D. Chief Telecommunications Engineer*

*197.* A telecommunications carrier must, as specified in the applicable ordinance of the MIC, appoint chief telecommunications engineers selected from persons who have chief telecommunications engineer's licences and place them in charge of the supervision of matters specified in the applicable ordinance of the MIC (Chief Telecommunications Engineer Regulations, Article 3) that are related to the installation, maintenance and operation of telecommunications facilities for the telecommunications business unless the telecommunications facilities for the telecommunications business are small-scale ones or otherwise specified in the applicable ordinance of the MIC (Telecommunications Business Act, Article 45, paragraph 1; Chief Telecommunications Engineer Regulations, Article 3*bis*).

*198.* When a telecommunications carrier has appointed chief telecommunications engineers, it must submit, without delay, notification to that effect to the MIC (Chief Telecommunications Engineer Regulations, Article 4). A carrier must, as well, notify the Minister of the dismissal of any of its chief telecommunications engineers (Telecommunications Business Act, Article 45, paragraph 2).

*199.* A chief telecommunications engineer should be appointed at each worksite from the persons that work at the site and have a chief telecommunications engineer's licence (Chief Telecommunications Engineer Regulation, Article 3). However, the chief telecommunications engineer appointed at one site can serve concurrently as the chief telecommunications engineer at other sites if the latter site satisfies all the following requirements in accordance with 'On the Appointment of Chief Telecommunications Engineers' (MPT Notice No. 231 of 1985):

(1) if necessary, the chief telecommunications engineer can reach the site quickly;
(2) in case of failure of the telecommunications facilities at the site, emergency measures must be taken immediately such as switching to a backup system;

(3) if necessary, the chief telecommunications engineer can be informed easily on matters related to the installation, maintenance and operation of telecommunications facilities at the site;
(4) the result of inspection and testing at the site must be reported to the chief telecommunications engineer; and
(5) the chief telecommunications engineer can perform his functions regarding the supervision of the site without any difficulties.

*200.* Chief telecommunications engineer shall conscientiously perform the duty of supervising construction maintenance and operation of telecommunications facilities for the business. A telecommunications carrier must be given the necessary powers in fulfilling his/her duties to the chief telecommunications engineer. A telecommunications carrier must respect the advice of the chief telecommunications engineer for the construction, maintenance or operation of telecommunications facilities for the business at the workplace where the chief telecommunications engineer fulfils his/her duties. Those who are engaged in the construction, maintenance or operation of telecommunications facilities for the business must follow the instructions of the chief telecommunications engineer that the chief telecommunications engineer deems it necessary to carry out his/her duties. A telecommunications carrier must, for each period specified in the applicable Ordinance of MIC (Chief Telecommunications Engineer Regulations, Article 43*ter*), make the chief telecommunications engineer take courses given by a registered training institution (Telecommunications Business Act, Article 85*bis*, paragraph 1; Chief Telecommunications Engineer Regulations, Articles 58 through 68) relating to the supervision of construction, maintenance and operation of telecommunications facilities for the business (Telecommunications Business Act, Article 49). The Japan Data Communications Association is registered as a registered training institution.

### *E. Standards for Telecommunications Numbers*

*201.* A telecommunications carrier should, where the telecommunications carrier provides telecommunications services through use of telecommunications numbers (numbers, signs or other codes which a telecommunications carrier, upon the provision of telecommunications services, uses for the identification of telecommunications facilities in order to connect between the place of transmission and the place of reception, or for the identification of the type or content of transmission the telecommunications facilities are to deliver), ensure that the telecommunications numbers shall comply with the standards specified in the applicable ordinance of the MIC (Telecommunications Numbers Regulation), except for domain names, IP addresses and other telecommunication numbers that are specified in the applicable ordinance of MIC (Telecommunications Business Act, Article 50, paragraph 1; Implementing Regulation for the Telecommunications Business Act, Article 29*quater*). The standards must be set so that the following requirements are met (Telecommunications Business Act, Article 50, paragraph 2):

(1) by using the telecommunications numbers, telecommunications carriers and the user should clearly and easily identify telecommunications facilities or the type or content of the telecommunications service;
(2) necessary telecommunications numbers needed for the provision of telecommunications services are retained;
(3) change of telecommunications numbers should be avoided as much as possible; and
(4) fair and efficient use of telecommunications numbers is secured.

*202.* Where it is deemed that the telecommunications numbers that a telecommunications carrier uses in making connection of its telecommunications facilities with those of other telecommunications carriers, or which the telecommunications carrier uses for handling urgent communications in light of the public interest, do not comply with the standards specified in the applicable ordinance of the MIC (Telecommunications Numbers Regulation), the Minister may order that telecommunications carrier to change said telecommunications numbers to comply with the standards, or may prohibit usage thereof (Telecommunications Business Act, Article 51).

## §2. Radio Act

### I. Licence

*203.* For the construction of a network using radio equipment by a telecommunications carrier, in addition to obtaining business permission and meeting other provisions, said carrier must meet requirements concerning the radio station licence, radio equipment, radio operator and operation of a radio station prescribed in the Radio Act.

Any person who intends to establish a radio station should obtain in advance of such establishment a licence from the MIC (Radio Act, Article 4). To establish a radio station means to instal radio equipment and to have it operated by persons who are capable of emitting radio waves, thereby constituting a radio station.

### II. Application for a Licence for Specified Radio Stations

*204.* In applying for a licence for a Specified Radio Station, submission of the following documents is required:

(1) Specified Radio Station licence application form;
(2) Specified Radio Station operation plans; and
(3) Radio station construction design.

*205.* Low-power radio equipment, such as cordless phones and Personal Handyphone System (PHS) terminals, certified by the System for Certification of Conformity with the Technical Regulations for Specified Radio Equipment (SRE) will be exempt from the licence for equipment.

## III. Application for a Licence for Radio Stations

*206.* In applying for a licence for a radio station, the following documents should be submitted:

(1) a radio station licence application form;
(2) radio station operation plans; and
(3) radio station construction plans.

## IV. Licence and Examination

### A. *Provisional Licence*

*207.* The MIC, in addition to determining that an application for a licence does not fall under the disqualification category:

(1) ensures that the construction plan conforms to the technical regulations as specified by the Radio Act;
(2) ascertains whether the assignment of a radio frequency is deemed as possible;
(3) determines that the application meets the fundamental standards for establishment of radio stations as stipulated in the MIC ordinance.

A provisional licence will be issued after the Minister has confirmed the above.

### B. *Examination Standards*

*208.* The standards used to determine if a radio station is licensable will be used as examination standards as well.

### C. *Disqualification*

*209.* In principle, no licence is granted to any person who is a foreign national. However, the licence for the following radio stations is an exception:

(1) experimental radio stations, specified ship radio stations, specified aircraft radio stations, amateur radio stations;

(2) fixed radio stations for the diplomatic use of foreign embassies or organizations (based on the principle of diplomatic reciprocity);
(3) land mobile radio stations, portable radio stations and base radio stations communicating with those radio stations; and
(4) radio stations for the purpose of conducting telecommunications activities.

*210.* A licence may nevertheless not be granted to any person or entity that has been punished for a crime against the Radio Act or the Broadcast Act, or any person whose radio station licence was revoked and a period of two years has not yet elapsed since the day the sentence was served or the stay to execution was granted.

### *D. Inspection after Provisional Licensing*

*211.* A full licence will be provided to those with provisional licences upon passing inspection of radio equipment, and operators after completion of the radio station.

However, for inspections of radio equipment and such items where a record of inspection results, written by an attested (foreign) examiner authorized by the MIC, is submitted, the MIC can use a system that partially curtails the inspection process (Attested Inspector System), which has become available for use.

### *E. Simplified Licensing Procedure*

*212.* When using radio equipment, such as cellular phones, that have received the confirmation from the Minister or the designated certification body as meeting the technical regulations' requirements, a licence can be obtained through a simplified licensing procedure that bypasses the need for provisional licensing and the inspection thereafter.

As for the certification of conformity with technical regulations (for radio equipment other than amateur radio stations), this is provided through the Telecom Engineering Centre, a designated certification body.

### *F. Other Required Procedures*

#### 1. Procedure Required to Meet Radio Regulations of the International Telecommunication Union

*213.* When constructing and operating a satellite communications network, international coordination and notification procedures in accordance with the Radio Regulations (RR) are necessary. Upon application for licensing of satellite and earth stations, the coordination status with existing or planned satellite networks of relating administrations must be confirmed. When the territory of other administrations rests within the coordination area of an earth station, coordination with such administrations is also needed.

## 2. Qualification of a Radio Operator

*214.* As a rule, a radio operator or a person under the supervision of a radio operator in full charge should operate radio equipment of radio stations.

## 3. Certification of Conformity with Technical Regulations for SRE

*215.* The 'Certification of Conformity with Technical Regulations for Specified Radio Equipment' is the system for certifying that an 'SRE', such as cellular, automobile and cordless phones, conforms to the Radio Act and the applicable MIC ordinances. ('SRE' refers to transmitters and transceivers used under the applicable MIC ordinances at most types of small radio stations.)

*216.* There are major benefits for licensees if they use SRE certified under this system: licensing procedures are simplified and such cordless phones are exempt from licensing:

(1) System for Technical Regulations Conformity Certifications of SRE: the system in which each SRE model is examined and certified under the Technical Regulations for Conformity Certification.
(2) Type Certification System for Technical Regulations Conformity Certifications of SRE: the certification system in which each model design (type) of SRE is examined. If the model design is certified, every specified radio facility or unit, with marking stipulated in the applicable ministerial ordinance, made with this design is regarded as certified SRE.

# Chapter 6. Regulation of Broadcasting Activities

## §1. Broadcasting Act

*217.* The Broadcasting Act (Law No. 132 of 1950) classifies broadcasting as a key broadcast (which uses a specific spectrum assigned exclusively or preferentially to a broadcasting station in accordance with the Radio Act) and a general broadcast, which is any broadcast other than a key broadcast.

### I. Key Broadcaster

*218.* A key broadcaster (a terrestrial-based television broadcaster or a satellite-based television broadcaster) needs authorization from the Minister for broadcasting in accordance with the Broadcasting Act and a licence for establishing radio stations from the Minister in accordance with the Radio Act.

*219.* An authorization to be a key broadcaster will not be granted to: any person who does not have Japanese nationality; any foreign government or its representative; any foreign juridical person or entity; and other persons or entities, 20% or more of whose shares are held directly or indirectly by foreign persons or entities. Moreover, if foreign ownership in a key broadcasting company exceeds 20%, the Minister must revoke the authorization of the company. Accordingly, a key broadcasting company may reject a record of share transfer to a foreign person or entity into the shareholders' list where such transfer would result in foreign ownership of over 20%.

*220.* The Broadcasting Act prohibits the centralization of media, and the MIC ordinances prohibit a key broadcaster, its owner or its subsidiary from obtaining another authorization as a key broadcaster from the Minister though some exceptions exist and there are media groups that own television, radio and newspapers.

*221.* The Broadcasting Act requires broadcasters not to harm public safety or good morals; not to distort the facts; to take a neutral political position; and to raise points at issue from various perspectives as possible on a divisive issue (Article 4). A broadcaster must draw up and publicly disclose its standards for its television programs, and follow the standards in producing programs (Article 5). The Broadcasting Act prohibits the Japan Broadcasting Corporation (NHK), the only public broadcaster in Japan, from broadcasting any advertising for other businesses.

*222.* The Japan Commercial Broadcasters Association has prepared a template for those standards, which the member commercial broadcasting companies usually incorporate or refer to in their own standards. The standards provide for, for example, restrictions on advertising, including requirements for broadcasters to make it clear that advertising is for commercial purposes, to ensure viewers do not feel uncomfortable on account of the duration of the advertisement, and to ensure that the hours of advertising is not more than 18% of the total broadcasting hours per week.

*223.* Moreover, the standards provide for the general principles in making television programs. Broadcasters should respect legal requirements and human rights, be careful about the content (e.g., violence or unlawful behaviour) of programs prepared for children and young people, and consider a suitable slot for a program, taking into consideration which period of time children and young people may be watching. In addition, a key broadcasting company may not broadcast any advertising that may disturb education by schools when the company broadcasts an educational program for schools under the Broadcasting Act.

*224.* A key broadcasting company must endeavour to make broadcasts to prevent or mitigate any disasters such as a storm, heavy rain, flood, earthquake or conflagration.

## II. General Broadcaster

*225.* A general broadcast requires registration in principle in accordance with the Broadcasting Act while it requires submission of a report for small broadcasting (e.g., cable television or cable radio). Regulations on general broadcasts and other media are less strict than those for key broadcasts that must deliver well-balanced programs (cultural and educational programs, news and entertainment and so on).

## §2. Radio Act

*226.* The Radio Act regulates the use of radio waves and applies to both telecommunications and broadcasting using radio waves. Under the Radio Act, any person or entity planning to start a radio station must be granted a licence from the MIC. However, certain types of radio stations that emit weak radio waves (as designated by the Implementing Regulation for the Radio Act), such as phone handsets for home use and wireless card systems, are exempt from licensing under the Radio Act.

*227.* In order to obtain a radio station licence, an applicant must submit to the MIC a standard application form containing information such as the purpose of the radio station, its facilities' locations, and the type and frequency of radio waves to be used. If the radio station plans to provide broadcasting services, certain other information, such as a business plan, items for broadcasting and the area for broadcasting, must also be provided.

*228.* The MIC examines the application from a viewpoint of adequate financial base to operate the planned business and conformity with the standards provided in the relevant MIC ministerial ordinance. In the case of the radio station providing broadcasting services, conformity to broadcast content and broadcast area requirements is considered as well. Approval of a radio station licence will be subject to the radio frequency planning because available radio frequency is necessary for radio wave broadcasting. The Radio Act grants the MIC the authority to allocate frequency spectrum to private bodies at its discretion after consultation with the Radio Regulatory Council and consideration of the plans submitted by the applicants.

*229.* Application fees for a licence to start radio stations under the Radio Act vary depending on the emission power of the radio station. The registration fee for a broadcasting station is JPY 150,000 and annual fees for using frequency spectrum vary from less than JPY 1,000 to more than JPY 100,000,000, depending on the type of radio station (e.g., mobiles, satellites or others), the emission power of the radio station and the operating area of the radio station.

# Chapter 7. Regulation of Online Interactive Services

## §1. Act on Special Commercial Practices

*230.* The Special Commercial Practices Act has provisions on administrative regulations. Administrative regulations set a number of obligations and prohibitions applicable to businesses that sell goods or provide services to consumers within respect to sales transactions that fall within seven categories (door-to-door sales, mail-order sales, telemarketing sales, multilevel marketing transactions, designated long-term service, business opportunity related sales and door-to-door purchase). Where a competent Minister or a prefectural governor finds that a business has violated the regulation, he/she may issue orders, including those to suspend its business. A business is required to furnish information and deliver a document. The Act also has provisions to prevent unfair commercial practices.

*231.* Online sales and internet auction fall within mail-order sales since mail-order sales for the purpose of the Special Commercial Practices Act are transactions in which a business distributes advertisements via newspapers, magazines, websites, or other media, and receives an offer via postal mail or using communication devices (including telephone and facsimile apparatus) or devices for information processing (Implementing Regulation for the Special Commercial Practices Act, Article 2).

*232.* The Special Commercial Practices Act governs in cases where sellers or service providers (hereinafter sellers) engage in the sale of goods or the provision of services as a business. 'Engaging as a business' means that transactions are performed repeatedly and continuously with the intention of making a profit. Whether such intention exists or not will be judged objectively regardless of the person's subjective intention. 'Intention of making a profit' and 'repeatedly and continuously' are comprehensively judged, also taking into account transactions performed at places other than internet sites. For example, if a person who conducts business at a place other than internet auction sites (regardless of whether it is on the Internet or at a physical place) lists goods that it deals in on an auction site, he/she in principle is considered to sell goods as a business regardless of the quantity or amount of the listed goods.

*233.* Sellers must advertise in compliance with the regulations on advertisement in the Special Commercial Practices Act (Articles 11, 12, 12*ter*, 12*quater*). If they violate the regulations, they will be subject to administrative or other penalties.

*234.* Sellers must include in the advertisement the information as follows (Special Commercial Practices Act, Article 11, Implementing Regulation for the Special Commercial Practices Act, Article 8): Sales price, delivery charge, etc. of the good, service, etc.; time and method of payment for the good or service, etc.; time of delivery of the good, service, etc.; matters related with rescission and cancellation of the sales contract of the good and/or designated right (including a special contract, if any); name, address and telephone number of the seller (and the name of the representative or the responsible person if the seller is a juridical person and uses a data-processing system for advertising); date of expiry of the effective period of an offer, if any; description and the amount of any money that the purchaser has to pay in addition to the price of the good, service, etc.; contents of the clauses, if any, of the seller's responsibility for any latent defect in the good; the requisite operating environments for the software, etc., if the transaction is related to software, etc.; contents of special sales conditions, if any, of the product, service, etc., such as a limited sales quantity; shipping cost to be paid by a person requesting documents of the information omitted on the advertisement, if any; e-mail address, if advertising is made by e-mail.

*235.* As including all the information above in an advertisement is sometimes unrealistic, some information can be omitted if a note to the effect that a document (or e-mail in the case of Mail-Order Sales on the Internet) describing omitted information will be provided 'without delay' upon a consumer's request is given in the advertisement, and measures are taken so as to actually provide it 'without delay' upon request (Special Commercial Practices Act, proviso to Article 11; Implementing Regulation for the Special Commercial Practices Act, Article 10).

*236.* 'Without delay' requires that the information be provided with sufficient time before customers make up their minds to make an offer, reflecting the actual situation of transactions such as selling methods or offer expiration date. For example, in internet auctions, offer expiration dates are normally expedited, and many people often vie to make their offers before the dates, and thus it is considered to be difficult to provide such documents 'without delay'.

*237.* Information on rescission and cancellation of the sales contract of the products and/or designated rights (including a special contract, if any) should be clearly posted in a prominent place where the customer can easily find it so that the customer can recognize it without difficulty (Implementing Regulation for the Special Commercial Practices Act, Article 9).

*238.* Sellers must not present in an advertisement the information as follows in a manner which is substantially different from what they are in actuality or in a manner which will cause a consumer to believe that the subject of the advertisement is better or more advantageous than it really is (Special Commercial Practices Act, Article 12, Implementing Regulation for the Special Commercial Practices Act, Article 11): Performance, quality and efficacy of a product; contents and effectiveness of a service; contents of rights, and effectiveness of the service pertaining to rights; matters related with rescission and cancellation of the sales contract of the products and/or designated rights (including a special contract, if any); involvement of the national government, local governments and other public entities in products, rights, services; in sellers and service providers; in the business conducted by sellers and service providers; country of origin, place of production and manufacturer; and other matters that are required to be shown in an advertisement in compliance with the regulations in the Special Commercial Practices Act.

*239.* In principle, a business is prohibited from sending e-mail advertising unless the consumer gave his or her consent in advance (opt-in). This regulation is applied not only to a business of mail-order sales, but also to those whom the business entrusted with e-mail that advertises their mail-order sales. Where a consent to, or a request for the provision of e-mail advertising has been received from a consumer, it is necessary to keep a record of the consent or the request for three years from the date when the last e-mail advertising was sent.

*240.* The regulation on unsolicited e-mails does not apply, however, to:

(1) advertisements included as part of an e-mail making notification of material information such as 'conclusion of contract', 'confirmation of order', 'notification of shipment', etc.;
(2) advertisements included as part of the e-mail advertising which is sent with the request or consent of the consumer; or
(3) advertisements included as part of the e-mail sent from an e-mail account created for free on the Internet for services in which a free e-mail account is given on the condition that advertisements will be automatically included in every e-mail sent from that account (Special Commercial Practices Act, Articles 12*ter* and 12*quater*).

*241.* In the case of 'prepaid' mail-order sales in the payment is made by a customer in whole or in part prior to the delivery of the goods (the transfer of the rights, the provision of the services) to the consumer, where it will take time until goods are delivered after the payment, a business has to deliver a document that shows:

(1) the acceptance or non-acceptance of the offer (if the business does not accept the offer, he/she must clarify that the received payment will be immediately refunded, and how the money will be refunded.);
(2) where the acceptance or non-acceptance of the offer was notified before the payment is received, a notice to that effect;
(3) name, address, and telephone number of the business;
(4) the amount of the payment received (if any payments have been received previously, the total amount);
(5) date on which the payment was received;
(6) goods for which the offer was received, and their quantity (types of rights and services); and
(7) where the offer has been accepted, the time at which the goods are expected to be delivered (time at which the rights will be transferred, or the time at which the services will be provided) (a specific period or date must be given) (Special Commercial Practices Act, Article 13).

*242.* If the METI Minister finds that a conduct is likely to prejudice the fairness of transactions in mail-order sales and the interests of the purchaser or the service recipient, he/she may instruct a seller or a service provider to take measures for correcting any violation or conduct, measures to protect the interests of the purchaser or the service recipient, and any other necessary measures, in cases where the seller or the service provider has violated any of the provisions of Article 11, 12, or 12*ter* (excluding paragraph 5), Article 12*quinquies*, or Article 13, paragraph 1 or has:

(a) refused to perform or unjustly delaying the performance of the obligations under a sales contract or a service contract for mail-order sales or the obligations that had occurred through the cancellation of a sales contract or a service contract arising from mail-order sales in whole or in part;
(b) engaged in any conduct that which is specified by a METI ordinance as conduct through which the relevant person sought to cause a customer to offer a sales contract or a service contract during mail-order sales against the customer's will; and
(c) engaged in any conduct connected with mail-order sales that is specified by a METI ordinance as being likely to prejudice the fairness of a transaction in mail-order sales and the interests of the purchaser or the service recipient, including not displaying appropriately so as to enable consumers to easily recognize that the operation of the computer related to an electronic contract is an offer for the electronic contract and not taking measures so as to enable consumers to easily confirm and modify their offer (Special Commercial Practices Act, Article 14).

## §2. Act to Improve Transparency and Fairness of Digital Platform

*243.* The Act to Improve Transparency and Fairness of Digital Platforms (TFDPA) (Law No.38 of 2020) governs the transparency and fairness of digital platforms.

*244.* The TFDPA stipulates necessary measures for digital platforms, including requirements for 'specified digital platform providers', whether they are domestic or overseas businesses. For the purpose of this Act, 'digital platforms' are defined in terms of the characteristics as follows: (a) they provide places (multi-sided markets) to connect product providers and consumers using digital technology; (b) they provide services via the internet; and (c) they provide services utilizing network effects (through, for example, relationships where mutual benefits for product providers and consumers increase, thereby increasing the number of both providers and consumers).

*245.* In setting the genres and scale criteria for specified digital platform providers, the following factors are taken into consideration:

(a) the degree of that genre's impact on the lives of the people and the national economy;
(b) the degree of concentration of use of certain digital platforms in that genres;
(c) the necessity for the protection of product providers based on actual conditions and circumstances;
(d) current situation of other regulations or measures and policies; and
(e) certain scale (e.g., sales) has been reached within that genre.

*246.* Accordingly, the Cabinet Order for Stipulating the Business Category and Scale under Article 4, paragraph 1 of the stipulates the category and scale of the business to be designated as a 'specified digital platform provider', which is subject to TFDPA:

(1) businesses operating comprehensive online shopping malls selling goods: Those having sales of JPY 300 billion or more per FY in Japan; and
(2) businesses operating application stores: Those having sales of JPY 200 billion or more per FY in Japan.

*247.* METI designated digital platform providers as 'specified digital platform providers' as follows:

(1) Digital platform providers of comprehensive online shopping malls selling goods

| Designated digital platform provider | Comprehensive online shopping malls selling goods |
|---|---|
| Amazon Japan Godo kaisha | Amazon.co.jp |
| Rakuten Group, Inc. | Rakuten Ichiba |
| Yahoo Japan Corporation | Yahoo! Shopping |

(2) Digital platform providers of application stores

| Designated digital platform provider | Application stores provided by the relevant provider |
|---|---|
| Apple Inc. and iTunes Kabushiki kaisha | App Store |
| Google LLC | Google Play Store |

*248.* Specified digital platform providers have to notify the terms and conditions and other information and give prior notices of any change thereof to the METI Minister, making use of a gBizID (gBiz is an account service created by Japan's central government available to corporations and sole proprietors, allowing you to log in to various government services with a single ID [gBizID] and password), and to the platform users, for example:

(a) Criteria for rejecting transactions;
(b) In the case of requesting the use of other services, that effect and the reasons;
(c) In the case of requesting amendment of a contract or operations that are not included in the contract, prior notification of the details thereof and the reasons;

(d) In the case of rejecting transactions, prior notification of that effect and the reasons;
(e) Matters regarding handling of inquiries, complaints, etc. (whom to contact, process flow, etc.)
(f) Basic matters for deciding search rankings (not algorithms)
(g) Subject of and conditions for the data obtained and used by the specified digital platform provider
(h) Whether product providers may obtain and use data, and if so, the extent thereof, the method of doing so, etc.

(f) and (g) should be disclosed to the public (consumer) as well.

*249.* The METI Minister issues recommendations and public announcements where notification is not made and administrative orders where necessary correction is not made without justifiable grounds.

*250.* The TFDPA requests such platform providers to develop in a voluntary manner procedures and systems, including systems and procedures for dealing appropriately with product providers and for settling and resolving complaints and disputes, as well as those for securing fairness in operating digital platforms in accordance with the guidelines specified by the Minister of Economy, Trade and Industry. *The Guidelines for Measures Taken by Specified Digital Platform Providers to Facilitate Mutual Understanding with Platform Users* is published by the METI. The Guidelines stipulate the fundamental principles and examples of specific measures that specified digital platform providers should take to facilitate mutual understanding with their customers. The Guidelines are to be taken into consideration in monitoring reviews by the government.

*251.* Specified digital platform providers should appoint a manager to manage communication within Japan and take other measures necessary for taking into consideration customer situations.

*252.* Specified digital platform providers have to conduct self-assessments on the current situation of business operation and submit a yearly report on the state of affairs of the business operation with the results of self-assessment. The Implementing Regulation for the TFDPA stipulates requirements for specified digital platform providers, including methods for disclosing terms and conditions and other information to their customers, information that such providers are required to disclose in addition to those explicitly required under the TFDPA, grounds for exceptions to the disclosure requirements to their customers regarding notification of reasons, and information to be included in the annual report and formats for those information.

*253.* The METI Minister reviews under the TFDPA the business operation of the platform based on the yearly report and other information with involvement of business users, consumers and academics, and publishes the results of the assessment.

*254.* The TFDPA is to require the METI to establish a system in which the METI should request the Fair Trade Commission to take measures under the Anti-monopoly Act if the METI finds any suspected violation of the Anti-monopoly Act.

*255.* In addition, the TFDPA requests the government to encourage digital platform providers and their customers to facilitate mutual understanding based on digital platform providers' voluntary and proactive efforts but with minimum required commitments by the government.

## §3. ACT FOR THE PROTECTION OF CONSUMERS WHO USE DIGITAL PLATFORMS

*256.* The Act for the protection of consumers who use digital platforms (Law No.32 of 2021) provides obligations to digital platform providers.

*257.* In order to improve mail-order transactions (business to customer transactions) conducted using digital platforms and promote dispute resolutions, digital platform providers must endeavour to implement measures as follows: measures to enable smooth communication between sellers and consumers; measures necessary for ensuring proper indication of sales conditions including implementation of investigations when a complaint regarding the indication on the platform has been brought; and requesting sellers to provide information on their identity as necessary. They are requested to disclose an outline of the measures they have implemented. The Prime Minister draws up guidelines for implementation and disclosure of the measures by digital platform providers (Article 3).

*258.* The Prime Minister may request digital platform providers to remove listings of any products, etc., with extremely false or misleading indications on important particulars (those regarding product safety and so on) and it is unlikely to rectify by the seller because, for example, the seller or his/her address cannot be specified. The digital platform provider is exempted from liability for damages to the seller arising from response to the request (Article 4).

*259.* A consumer who used a digital platform has the right to request the platform provider to disclose seller information as necessary in cases where he/she makes a claim for damages and so on. This is not applicable, however, if the amount of damages claimed is less than a certain amount or the claim has been brought with an abusive purpose. The digital platform providers are not liable to sellers for response to requests in accordance with appropriate procedures (Article 5).

*260.* A public-private council, which consists of the Prime Minister, relevant central government agencies, organizations of digital platform providers, the National Consumer Affairs Center of Japan, local public authorities and consumer organizations, will be organized. The council exchanges necessary information and discusses measures to protect consumers who use digital platforms. It gives its opinion to the Prime Minister on measures to improve transactions and promote dispute resolution related to mail-order sales using digital platforms. Based on the results of the discussion, the members of the public-private council will take necessary measures to protect consumers who use digital platforms (Articles 6–9).

*261.* If anyone finds that the interests of consumers using the trading digital platform may be harmed, he/she may lodge the Prime Minister (the Consumer Affairs Agency) to that effect and request that appropriate measures be taken. Where the request has been made to the Prime Minister, he/she must conduct necessary investigations, and if he/she finds that the content of the request is true, he/she should take measures provided in the Act for the Protection of Consumers who use Digital Platforms and other appropriate measures (Article 10).

# Chapter 8. Regulation of Cryptography and Other Dual-Use Goods

*262.* Though there are no domestic laws and regulations restricting the use of cryptography, export regulations are designed to implement the (pre-December 1998) Wassenaar Arrangement, including the General Software Note. Decisions are made on an individual basis. Businesses must acquire approval for a cryptography export order larger than JPY 50,000.

*263.* The Ministry of International Trade and Industry (MITI) (now the METI) published a draft policy paper, 'Towards the Age of the Digital Economy', in May 1997. To ensure security, encryption, and authentication, technologies should be sophisticated through market competition. Development of cryptography and experiments of projects should be promoted, and network users should be provided with much more information about these, according to the draft.

# Part II. Online Public Services

## Chapter 1. e-Government Legal Framework

### §1. Act on Promotion of Administration Utilizing Information and Communication Technology

*264.* Law No.16 of 2018 amended and renamed the Act Concerning the Use of Information and Communication Technology in Administrative Procedures, etc. (Law No. 151 of 2002) as the Act on Promotion of Administration Utilizing Information and Communication Technology.

*265.* First, Article 2 provides the fundamental principles for promotion of administration utilizing information and communication technology:

(a) carrying out a series of processes related to procedures, etc., office work of government agencies, etc. related to this, and processing of business of private businesses, using information and communication technology so as to remove restrictions on time, place and other related to the procedures, etc., to automate and standardize the office work and operations so that the procedures, etc. can be carried out promptly and accurately by an easy-to-use method;
(b) cooperating with each other and sharing the information provided to government agencies, etc. by private businesses and other persons, making use of information systems so that the information with the same content once provided need not be provided;
(c) enabling to carry out collectively a large number of procedures, etc. (including the notification made to or made by any private business operator in relation to these procedures, etc.) usually required to the same opportunities due to social life or business activities, using information and communication technology with the cooperation between the administrative agencies, etc. and private businesses.

*266.* Second, the central government must set a plan to organize information systems in order to implement comprehensively and systematically information systems of national government agencies, etc. related to administrative procedures which make use of information and communication technology (Article 4, paragraph 1).

*267.* Third, national government agencies, etc. must develop information systems in accordance with the information system development plan. When developing an information system, they should take necessary measures to ensure the safety and reliability of the information system. In addition, they must endeavour to simplify, streamline or review the procedures, etc. performed using the information system and the administrative work of the administrative agencies, etc. related thereto. (Article 5).

*268.* Fourth, 'application, etc.' which is required to be done in writing or by other methods in other laws and regulations related to the application, etc. can be done by the method using the electronic information processing system (electronic information processing system in which computers (including input/output devices) used by government agencies, etc. and computers used by the other party in the procedures, etc. are connected by a telecommunication line) specified by an ordinance of the competent Ministry, regardless of the provisions of the relevant laws and regulations (Article 6, paragraph 1).

*269.* Fifth, 'notice of administrative actions, etc.' which is required to be done in writing or by other methods in other laws and regulations related to the notice, etc. can be done by the method using the electronic information processing system specified by an ordinance of the competent Ministry, regardless of the provisions of the relevant laws and regulations, so long as the recipient of the notice, etc. declares by any method specified in the ordinance of the competent Ministry to the effect that he/she receives the notice, etc., using the electronic information processing system (Article 7, paragraph 1).

*270.* Sixth, 'public inspections, etc.' which are required to be done in writing, etc. in other laws and regulations related to the public inspections, etc. (excluding those based on applications, etc.) can be done by documents that describe the matters recorded in the electromagnetic record pertaining to the document, etc. or the matter, in accordance with an ordinance of the competent Ministry, regardless of the provisions of the relevant laws and regulations describing the matters (Article 8, paragraph 1).

*271.* Seventh, 'preparations, etc.' which are required to be done in writing, etc. in other laws and regulations related to the preparation, etc., can be done by making an electromagnetic record in accordance with an ordinance of the competent Ministry, regardless of the provisions of the relevant laws and regulations (Article 9, paragraph 1).

*272.* Eighth, a copy of the resident's record, a certificate of registered information, and other documents, etc. specified by a Cabinet Ordinance pertaining to the person making the application, etc., which are stipulated in the other laws and regulations related to the application, etc. need not be attached, in cases where, regardless of the provisions of the relevant laws and regulations, it is possible for a government agency to obtain or refer to the information related to the matters to be confirmed by the relevant documents, etc., directly or by using an electronic information processing system, making use of the personal number card or other measures by the person making the application, etc. using the electronic information processing system, etc. as specified by the Cabinet ordinance (Article 11).

*273.* Ninth, local public authorities must endeavour to take the necessary measures so that the procedures required by the local ordinances or regulations can be carried out, making use of electronic information processing systems and other information and communication technologies in order to promote administration utilizing information and communication technology. The central government shall endeavour to provide information and take other necessary measures in order to support the measures taken by local governments (Article 13).

## §2. Framework Act for Formation of a Digital Society

*274.* The Framework Act for Formation of a Digital Society (Law No.135 of 2021) is the successor to the Framework Act for Formation of an Advanced Information and Communication Network Society (Law No. 144 of 2000).

*275.* For the purpose of this Act, 'digital society' is defined as a society in which creative and vigorous development is enabled in all fields by obtaining, sharing or transmitting a wide variety of information or knowledge globally in a free and safe manner via the Internet and other advanced information and telecommunications networks, and by using information and telecommunications technologies and other advanced technologies to appropriately and effectively utilize the wide variety and large amount of information recorded as an electromagnetic record.

*276.* This Act specifies the basic principles with respect to the formation of a digital society: Realization of a society where all citizens can enjoy the benefits of information and communication technology; Promotion of economic structural reform and strengthening of industrial international competitiveness; Realization of a vibrant community, etc.; Realization of a society where people can live safely and with peace of mind; Correction of disparities in usage opportunities, etc.; Role sharing between national and local governments and the private sector; Protection of rights and interests of individuals and corporations, etc.; Correspondence to the progress of information and communication technology; and Responding to new issues associated with changes in socioeconomic structure.

*277.* The Act also specifies the role of the central government, local public authorities and business operators with respect to the formation of a digital society.

*278.* The national government is responsible for formulating and implementing measures for the formation of a digital society in accordance with the basic principles for the formation of a digital society (Article 13). Local governments should formulate and implement voluntary measures that take advantage of the characteristics of the area of the local governments, based on the basic principles and the appropriate division of roles with the national government regarding the formation of a digital society (Article 14). The national and local governments must cooperate with each other so that measures for the formation of a digital society can be implemented promptly and with priority (Article 15). Businesses must endeavour to actively promote the formation of a digital society in their business activities in accordance with the basic philosophy, and cooperate with the measures for the formation of a digital society implemented by the national or local governments. I shall endeavour (Article 16).

*279.* The national government must take legal or financial measures and other measures necessary to implement measures related to the formation of a digital society (Article 17).

*280.* It specifies that in the development of strategies to form a digital society, the necessary measures must be taken to ensure the smooth circulation of information by diverse actors (standardization of data, etc.), ensure opportunities for use of advanced information and telecommunications networks and utilization of information using information and telecommunications technologies, develop human resources, improve the productivity and the convenience of everyday life, ensure utilization by citizens of information held by the national government and local public authorities, develop a public basic information database (Base Registries), secure cybersecurity, and protect personal information

## §3. The Act to Create the Digital Agency

*281.* The Digital Agency is created in the Cabinet under the Act to Create the Digital Agency (Law No. 36 of 2021) in order to promote measures for the formation of a digital society in a prompt and focused manner. It assists the Cabinet in carrying out the Cabinet's function in the formation of a digital society together with the Cabinet Secretariat and carries out the relevant administrative functions in the formation of a digital society in a prompt and focused manner.

*282.* The main function of the Digital Agency is to assist the Cabinet in planning and comprehensive coordination of basic policies on measures for the formation of a digital society. In addition, the Digital Agency shares the functions with other relevant government agencies: to develop and implement priority plans for the formation of a digital society; to do comprehensive and basic policy planning, etc. regarding individual identification numbers; to make good use of My Number, My Number cards and corporate numbers as well as to instal and manage network systems to provide information; to formulate comprehensive and basic policies on verifying identity using information and communication technology, etc.; to deal with the affairs concerning electronic certification of commercial registration (through verifying identity using information and communication technology), electronic signatures, public personal authentication (related to verifiers), electronic power of attorney; to do comprehensive and basic policy planning for data standardization, external cooperating function s and a database on basic public information (basic registry), etc.; to develop and implement basic policies for developing and managing the information systems of national and local governments as well as private businesses in the quasi-public sectors; and to supervise the development and management of information systems by the national government, lump sum budget, and execute all or part of those affairs by itself.

*283.* While the head and Chief Minister of the Digital Agency is the Prime Minister, the Minister of Digital Agency assists the Prime Minister and supervises the affairs of the Agency, and may recommend to the heads of relevant administrative organs in order to carry out the functions of the Agency. Not only a Vice Minister and a Parliamentary Secretary but also a Chief Digital Officer will be appointed by the Cabinet, to give advice to the Minister of Digital Agency, organize the Agency's affairs, and supervise the affairs of each department of the Agency.

*284.* The Digital Society Promotion Council, composed of all the Ministers of State, is responsible for promoting the implementation of measures for the formation of a digital society.

## §4. Other Amendments to Relevant Laws for the Formation of a Digital Society

*285.* The Act to amend relevant laws for the formation of a digital society (Law No. 37 of 2021) was enacted in line with the Framework Act for Formation of a Digital Society.

*286.* First, the Act on the Protection of Personal Information (APPI), the Act on the Protection of Personal Information Held by Administrative Organs, and the Act on the Protection of Personal Information Held by Incorporated Administrative Agencies were consolidated into the APPI. The APPI also stipulates common nationwide rules for local governments' personal information protection systems and the Personal Information Protection Commission the jurisdiction over personal information protection in both public and private sectors. The definition of personal information is standardized and the rules are clarified for the handling of anonymously processed information by government agencies.

*287.* Second, the My Number Act and relevant laws were amended to allow the use of My Number and information sharing in affairs related to national qualifications, etc. and the provision of specific personal information of an employee among the employers for administrative procedures where the employee move, if the employee gives a consent.

*288.* Third, the Act on Handling at Post Offices Act, the Public Personal Authentication Act, the Act on Base Registration of Residents, the My Number Act, the Japan Agency for Local Authority Information Systems Act and other Acts were revised to improve the usability and functionality of My Number cards, and the system for its issuance. For example, it will become possible to apply to issue and renew digital certificates of the Japanese Public Key Infrastructure at post offices designated by cities, wards, towns and villages. It will be allowed to provide the name, date of birth, sex and address of a person under the Japanese Public Key Infrastructure if he/she gives consent. It will be possible for My Number card holders to instal digital certificates on their smartphones (mobile terminal equipment). The government will develop a system to give information about change of address of My Number card holders to move-in municipality in advance.

*289.* The national government will set the goal, approve the plans, and take fiscal measures regarding individual number card related affairs handled by the Japan Agency for Local Authority Information Systems (J-LIS). The issuance of digital certificates by local government becomes a statutory entrusted function.

*290.* Fourth, forty-eight Acts were amended to repeal seal requirements in administrative and private procedures and allow to digitalize paper-based proceedings and transactions.

# Chapter 2. Legal Framework for eHealth

## §1. Online Medical Care

*291.* Article 20 of the Medical Practitioners Act provides that 'no medical practitioner shall provide medical care or issue a medical certificate or prescription without performing an examination in person, nor shall he/she issue a birth certificate or certificate of stillbirth without being in attendance at the birth in person, nor shall he/she issue an autopsy certificate without performing the autopsy in person'.

*292.* In 1997, the Ministry of Health and Welfare (at that time) issued a notice, 'On medical treatment using information and communication equipment (so-called telemedicine)', which stated that 'even if it is not equivalent to direct face-to-face medical treatment, in cases where useful information on the physical and mental condition of the patient can be obtained, telemedicine does not immediately violate Article 20 of the Medical Practitioners Act'.

*293.* Online medical treatment is the act of examining and diagnosing patients through information and communication equipment between doctors and patients and performing medical treatment such as transmission of diagnosis results and prescriptions in real time. Traditionally, Article 20 of the Medical Practitioners Act imposes a 'medical examination' obligation on doctors, and it has been interpreted that this medical examination must be face-to-face in principle. This face-to-face consultation obligation has been gradually deregulated since 2015. Finally, in March 2018, the Ministry of Health, Labor and Welfare issued the 'Guidelines for Proper Implementation of Online Medical Care' (hereinafter the Guidelines), which made clear that online medical care without face-to-face contact is widely available and partially revised in July 2019.

*294.* According to the Guidelines, first, the doctor explicitly makes sure that the patient prefers online medical care.

*295.* Second, the doctor explains to the patient: (a) that it is necessary to combine online medical care with face-to-face medical care because the information that can be obtained from the patient is limited in online medical treatment; (b) that the doctor decides whether or not to take online medical care each time; and (c) the details of the medical care plan.

*296.* Third, the doctor and the patient agree to carry out online medical care.

*297.* Fourth, each time a doctor provides online medical care, he/she decides whether or not to carry out online medical care from a medical point of view. If the doctor finds that the online medical care is not appropriate, he/she will stop the online medical care and promptly switch to the appropriate face-to-face medical care.

*298.* As a general rule, the first patient contact should be done face-to-face. Moreover, for patients with sudden illness or sudden changes in illness, face-to-face medical care is the principle regardless of whether it is the first medical examination. It is, however, possible to consider offering online medical care after the condition of the patient stabilizes.

*299.* As an exception to the principle of face-to-face meeting at the first contact, in cases where the patient is in a situation where appropriate medical care cannot be received immediately, a doctor can make judgment based on the necessity and effectiveness of online medical care as well as the risks of online medical care and decide to provide online medical care even for the first contact. However, even in this case, face-to-face medical care is required in principle after the online medical treatment.

*300.* Online medical treatment is allowed even for the first patient contact as well in cases where the patient is with another doctor who provides sufficient information.

*301.* When a doctor plans to offer online medical care, he/she diagnoses the patient's physical and mental condition in direct face-to-face medical care in advance. He/she should establish a medical treatment plan on the details of the specific medical care (disease name, details of treatment, etc.) to be provided with in the online medical care, the conditions for judging that he/she will not take online medical care and so on. The medical treatment plan should be kept for two years.

*302.* In principle, both the doctor and the patient must use identification documents to verify each other's identity. It is not, however, necessary to confirm the identity of each patient if the person can be recognized as the person himself/herself according to social conventions. Doctor's identification documents include HPKI (Healthcare Public Key Infrastructure) card and doctor's licence certificate while patient's identification documents include health insurance card, My Number card and driver's licence.

*303.* As a general rule, when a doctor prescribes a drug for a new disease, he must do based on direct face-to-face medical care.

*304.* However, as an exception to this rule, prescribing medicines for changes in symptoms that are easily predicted to occur for patients who have difficulty in prompt consultation, because of home medical care, remote islands or remote areas is accepted so long as the disease name and the possibility of such medicine prescription is stated in the medical care plan in advance. In this case, it is necessary to confirm the progress of changes in new symptoms at the occasion of face-to-face medical care.

*305.* In cases where a doctor is not convinced that sufficient information about the patient's condition has been obtained during online medical care, it is necessary to promptly discontinue online medical care and offer direct face-to-face medical care.

*306.* In addition, in order to provide online medical care, it is necessary to use information and communication means to receive real-time visual and auditory information. While it is possible to make use of the exchange of information such as images and characters using chat function as an auxiliary means, online medical care should not be completed by exchanging only characters, photos and recorded videos.

## §2. Online Medication Guidance

*307.* Medication guidance is to provide necessary information and guidance based on pharmaceutical knowledge by a pharmacist when a pharmacy sells a drug to a patient based on a prescription from a doctor. Article 9ter, paragraph 1 of the Act on Securing Quality, Efficacy and Safety of Products Including Pharmaceuticals and Medical Devices (PMD Act) required to give medication guidance face-to-face. This regulation made it difficult for a patient to receive drug prescriptions remotely by out-of-hospital prescription, the in-hospital prescription method has been widely used in the prescription of drugs in online medical treatment. However, since the above-mentioned deregulation of online medical care has increased the need for remote prescription and delivery of drugs, the revised PMD Act lifted under certain requirements the ban on online medication guidance given absence of face-to-face contact.

*308.* It is now allowed to give medication guidance by 'the method that enables talks while mutually recognizing the state of the other party by transmitting and receiving video and audio' and other methods recognized as being able to ensure the proper use of drugs and specified by the ordinance of the Ministry of Health, Labor and Welfare.

*309.* The requirements for online medication guidance are generally similar to the requirements for online medical care as follows (Revised Implementing Regulation for the PMD Act, Articles 15–13, paragraph 2).

*310.* First, for drugs dispensed with the same prescription, in advance, face-to-face medication guidance must be given.

*311.* Second, each medication guidance should be provided with in accordance with the medication guidance plan that stipulates: matters concerning the types of drugs handled in online medication guidance and the method of giving and receiving the drugs; matters concerning the combination of online medication guidance and face-to-face medication guidance; matters concerning cases where online medication guidance cannot be provided; matters concerning the communication system and response procedures with the hospital, clinic or other related medical institutions where the doctor or dentist who issued the prescription in an emergency works; and other matters necessary for online medication guidance.

*312.* Third, online medication guidance can be offered only when selling or giving drugs dispensed in accordance with a prescription issued in online medical treatment or home-visit medical treatment.

*313.* Furthermore, in implementing online medication guidance, it is also necessary to consult an administrative notice issued by the Ministry of Health, Labor and Welfare, 'On partial enforcement of the PMD Act (Online Medication Guidance)' (31 March 2020) .

## §3. Provisional Rules in Response to COVID-19

*314.* Apart from the deregulation above, restrictions on non-face-to-face medical care and medication guidance were eased in the wake of the spread of the COVID-19 infection. This temporary measure further relaxes the requirements for online medical care prescribed in the *Guidelines for Proper Implementation of Online Medical Care* and allows online medication guidance prior to the effectuation of the revised PMD Act (1 September 2020).

*315.* First, when a request from a patient is received and a doctor determines that medical care/prescription is possible through online or telephone, the first medical examination by online medical care or by telephone medical care is permitted. The requirements for this case are as follows: (a) the doctor must provide sufficient information and explanation to the patient about the disadvantages that may occur and the response policy in the event of a sudden illness or a sudden change in illness and so on, and record it in the medical record; (b) the doctor determines that face-to-face medical care is necessary, the medical institution that provided the online medical care or telephone medical care should promptly provide face-to-face medical care or refer to another medical institution with prior consent; and (c) in order to identify both the doctor and the patient, the health insurance card for the patient and an identification card with a face photo for the doctor should be confirmed by screen, facsimile or verbally and so on.

*316.* Before making diagnosis and prescription in online or telephone medical care, the doctor should grasp information on the patient's underlying disease from past medical records, medical information provision forms, regional medical information cooperation networks, health examination results, etc. as much as possible and understand them.

*317.* Second, when a patient wishes to receive online medication guidance, the doctor writes '0410 compatible' in the remarks column of the prescription form. With the consent of the patient, the medical institution sends the prescription information by fax or other means to the pharmacy chosen by the patient. This allows patients to receive medical care, prescription of drugs, and medication guidance without having to go to a medical institution or pharmacy. In addition, when prescribing in-hospital, it is possible to deliver the drug to the patient by direct delivery from the medical institution after having consulted with the patient. If information on the patient's underlying illness cannot be grasped from medical records, etc., the maximum prescription length is seven days, and it is not possible to prescribe drugs that require special safety management as well as narcotics and psychotropic drugs.

*318.* Third, prescribing the previously prescribed medicines to the patients who are treated by medical care using telephones or online even if a medical treatment plan is not created in advance. It is also permissible to prescribe previously unprescribed medicines for changes in the patient's symptoms that are easily predicted to develop due to the known disease so long as certain requirements including the patient's consent be met.

*319.* Fourth, a pharmacy that received prescription information by facsimile, etc. from a medical institution may dispense drugs in accordance with the information until the original prescription is obtained from the medical institution.

*320.* Fifth, a pharmacist may provide online medication guidance even in first patient contact so long as he/she obtains information on the patient, his/her medication status, etc., and determines that online medication guidance can be given appropriately. Some requirements for this case are as follows: (a) providing sufficient information and explanations and making records at the medical institutions that sends prescription information; (b) prompt switching to face-to-face contact as necessary; (c) thorough identity verification; (d) understanding the drug compliance/side effects; and (e) feedback to doctors.

## Chapter 3. Online Voting

*321.* The Special Act on Voting Method by Means of Electromagnetic Votes Recording Devices in Election of Local Assembly Members and Heads of Local Governments (Law No.147 of 2001; E-voting Act) was enacted in 2001 in order to allow ballots by means of electromagnetic recording voting devices (e-voting) at polling stations, though it does not allow ballots by e-mail and so on. It is necessary for a local government to lay down its own local ordinance before allowing any e-voting. Between 2002 and 2016, ten local governments held twenty-five elections in which e-voting was available while no local government does for the time being mainly because of financial challenge. In addition, of particular concern are the instability of the electronic voting system and the malfunction of terminals. In the July 2003 election for city council members of Kani City, the data storage system for the electronic voting was suspended due to overheating. As restrictions were imposed on voting, and even a disagreement in the number of votes took place on that occasion, the election was declared invalid in the Nagoya High Court's judgment of 9 March 2005 (1914 *Hanrei Jiho* 54).

*322.* The Study Group on Election Systems Using Electronic Devices at the Ministry of Internal Affairs published the final report in 2002. According to the report, the introduction of e-voting has three phases: the first phase in which electors may vote using an electronic voting device at a designated polling station; the second phase in which electors may vote at any polling station; and the third phase is which voting at a polling station is no longer required and electors may cast ballots using a privately owned computer terminal. The E-voting Act allows the e-voting at the first phase. Electronic voting devices are not connected to any network; they are individually installed both in designated polling stations and vote-counting stations.

*323.* The recording medium that stores data has been physically delivered by the staffs from designated polling stations to the vote-counting station because sending the data via a network connecting the polling station and vote-counting site involves various issues, including security issues.

*324.* In 2005, the Ministry of Internal Affairs set up the Research Committee on E-voting System as a permanent research body that provides advice from the perspective of experts regarding methods of an e-voting system, creating new structure to improve reliability of the system. The Committee submitted in 2006 a report, *Basic Policy Regarding a Measure for Improving Reliability of E-voting System*, which presented measures for preventing troubles in e-voting, in particular, technical requirements of electronic voting devices as well as systems for certifying technical requirements.

*325.* The report recommended to introduce a system of confirming compliance by third parties in order to prevent further occurrence of mechanical troubles and ensuring the reliability of e-voting system. Based on the report, the MIC issued in

2006 the revised technical requirements and the Implementation Guideline for Confirming Compliance regarding the Technical Requirements of E-voting System.

*326.* In 2007, in order to allow e-voting in national elections, the Bill to amend the Special Act on Voting Method by Means of Electromagnetic Votes Recording Devices in Election of Local Assembly Members and Heads of Local Governments and the Act on Review of the Supreme Court Judges was introduced to the Diet (Bill sponsored by members of the House of Representatives No.47 of the 166th Session). While it was approved in the House of Representatives in December 2007, it was dead as an unfinished matter in the House of Councillors. This was because concerns about the measures against the failure of voting devices were raised.

*327.* The Japanese nationals abroad are currently allowed to cast votes through Japanese embassies and consulates or by mailing their ballots if they have resided in a place for over three months and are registered as voters abroad. However, the voter turnout has been low because visiting embassies and consulates or preparing postal votes might be time-consuming or complex. Accordingly, an expert panel at the MIC discussed ways to improve the voting environment for Japanese nationals and proposed in August 2018 that voters overseas be allowed to cast their ballots online for elections in Japan. Under the online voting system proposed, voters will be able to log into an online voting site using the My Number identification system implemented in Japan so long as they are registered with the last place they resided in Japan.

*328.* While it is necessary to relevant laws such as the Public Offices Election Act and the Act Concerning Public Personal Certification in order to introduce such a system, no bill has been prepared and introduced so far. In 2020, Mr Akamatsu, Director of Election Department, Home Affair Bureau, Ministry of Internal Affairs and Communications, responded, however, at the meeting of the Internal Affairs Committee, the House of Councillors, that the MIC was solving various issues regarding the introduction of the Internet voting for overseas voters. He pointed out that when introducing Internet voting, there are a lot of challenges such as ensuring identity verification, preventing double voting, ensuring the confidentiality of voting on the system (Debates and Minutes No. 15, 15 May 2020, p.14).

*329.* In addition, the panel report requested that online voting for domestic voters be discussed after the validity of the overseas system is confirmed.

*330.* In June 2021, some members of the Constitutional Democratic Party submitted the Bill to Promote Introduction of Internet Voting (Bill sponsored by members of the House of Representatives No.41 of the 204th Session) to the House of Representatives. The Bill sets the target time and the basic policy for the introduction of Internet voting as well as the conditions that Internet voting must meet. It also provides that a forum to promote the introduction of Internet voting be created.

# Chapter 4. Other e-Government Services

## §1. Electronic Certification Services Based on the Commercial Registry

*331*. In addition to private electronic certification services providers, there is an official certification system based on the commercial registration system in Japan. The commercial registry has played a role as an electronic certification service provider for the companies.

*332*. In Japan, certain matters related to merchants, including companies, are registered in the commercial register. As for companies, important particulars such as the purpose, the name, the principal office, branches and directors must be registered. The public may access the register (Commercial Registration Act, Article 10) and certified copies of the commercial register are issued (Commercial Registration Act, Article 11).

*333*. In this system, an impression of a seal (*inkan*) of an applicant for registration is submitted in advance to the commercial registry to identify the applicant for registration (Commercial Registration Act, Article 20), and the commercial registry issues a certificate of an impression of a seal to one who submits a seal to the commercial registry (Commercial Registration Act, Article 12).

*334*. For a long time, a corporation's certified copy of the commercial register, certification of qualifications and a certificate of an impression of a seal, all of which are based on the information registered in the commercial register, have been widely used as a means to confirm the counterparty and the power of representation.

*335*. Accordingly, it is both inexpensive and natural to establish an electronic certification system based on the commercial registration system. Japanese people place trust in the commercial registration system because the reliability is ensured by the legal system which has skills in registration and publication of information on companies. There exists a legal system ensuring reliability of operations of the commercial registry and skills in registration and publication of information. Thus, an electronic certificate issued by the commercial register will be treated as reliable as a corporation's exemplified copy of the commercial register, a certificate of qualification and a certificate of an impression of a seal.

*336*. Upon request, the commercial registry issues an electronic certificate on the public key of the electronic signature of an applicant (Commercial Registration Act, Article 12*bis*). The commercial registry uses asymmetric cryptography, whose details are prescribed in ordinances.

## §2. ELECTRONIC CERTIFICATION SERVICES BASED ON THE BASIC RESIDENT REGISTER ACT

*337.* The Act on Certification Service for Electronic Signatures by the Japan Agency for Local Authority Information Systems (Act on the Public Certification for Individuals) (Law No.153 of 2002) stipulates the system and other necessary matters related to the certification service by the Japan Agency for Local Authority Information Systems (J-LIS) related to electronic signatures and electronic user certifications (Public Certification Service for Individuals). The purpose of the service is to promote the smooth use of certification, thereby improving the convenience of citizens and contributing to the simplification and efficiency of administrative operations of the national and local governments.

*338.* The Public Certification Service for Individuals provides citizens with an electronic certificate to prevent identity fraud or falsification, enabling them to make safe and secure administrative procedures online.

*339.* Under the Act, 'electronic user certification service' and 'signature certification service' are provided by the J-LIS. The former certifies that a verification code for user certification belongs to the applicant while the latter certifies that a verification code for signer belongs to the applicant. For using the services, an electronic certificate for user certification and/or an electronic certificate for signature certification are issued based on the Basic Resident Register upon request.

*340.* While the J-LIS was established in April 2014 and jointly operated by local public authorities, the involvement of the central government in the J-LIS was strengthened with the launch of the Digital Agency on 1 September 2021 and the J-LIS is now a body corporate jointly managed by the central and local governments.

## §3. GBIZ SYSTEM

*341.* In 2020, the Japanese central government implemented the gBiz system in order to eliminate repeated submissions of documents required for verification. The gBiz is an account service available to companies and sole proprietors, allowing them to log in to various government services with a single ID and password. Businesses can apply for a gBizID and gain access to such as jGrants, METI's subsidy application site, and other useful government sites. They no longer need to affix seals on documents and can complete procedures without submitting paper documents. No fees are imposed associated with getting a gBizID account.

*342.* Though it is not mandatory for businesses to have a gBizID, it will be convenient for them to have one since government processes will become more digitized and with less paperwork. For the time being, having a gBizID is a prerequisite for applying for certain subsidies, which are no longer available to apply for in-person or by postal mail but must be applied for online.

# Part III. Online Transactions

## Chapter 1. Electronic Contracting

*343.* In order to form a contract, there must in principle be an offer made by one party and an acceptance thereof by the other (Civil Code, Article 522, paragraph 1).

*344.* Where displaying of goods and/or services is not for a specific person, it is understood as an invitation to make offers unless it states, for example, 'We will send anyone who accepts'.

*345.* An e-mail message is not considered a notice of acceptance when it states that 'this e-mail is only for confirming the receipt of your offer and does not constitute an acceptance of your offer. We will send you an official notice of acceptance when your order is accepted after we check the inventory', which acknowledges that acceptance of the offer will be given separately.

*346.* As a declaration of intention becomes effective from the time when the notice thereof has reached the other party (Civil Code, Article 97, paragraph 1), an offer is effective from the time when the offer reaches the other party. For this purpose, the Supreme Court has interpreted that a declaration of intention reaches a party when the message is available for the party (Judgment, Supreme Court, 20 April 1961, 15 *Minshu* 774). For example, a declaration of intention via e-mail arrives at the time when the e-mail has been recorded in the mailbox of the designated mail server or in the mailbox usually used by the intended recipient and the e-mail is legible. A party's declaration of intention arrives at the time when his declaration has been displayed on the monitor screen of the other party in cases where the other party uses internet browser windows.

*347.* An offer which specifies a period for acceptance may not be withdrawn unless the offeror reserves the right to withdraw (Civil Code, Article 523, paragraph 1). Where the offeror does not receive notice of acceptance of the offer within the specified period for acceptance, the offer ceases to be effective (Civil Code, Article 523, paragraph 2) while the offeror may deem a delayed acceptance to be a new offer (Civil Code, Article 524).

*348.* An offer made without specifying a period for acceptance may not be withdrawn for a reasonable period of time to receive a notice of acceptance unless the offeror reserves the right to withdraw (Civil Code, Article 525, paragraph 1) while an offer made *inter praesentes* may be withdrawn at any time until the end of the dialogue (Civil Code, Article 525, paragraph 1).

*349.* If no notice of acceptance is required due to the offeror's declaration of intention or the custom applicable to the transaction, a contract is formed upon the occurrence of any fact which should be regarded as a declaration of intention of acceptance (Civil Code, Article 527).

*350.* Unless otherwise provided for in laws and regulations, it is not required to satisfy any formalities such as preparation of a written document in order to form a contract (Civil Code, Article 522, paragraph 2). There have been several statutes requiring a 'writing' (*shomen*), mainly for protecting consumers, investors or a party who has less bargaining power than the other party (e.g., the Act on Special Commercial Practices, the Travel Agency Act and the Financial Instruments and Exchange Act). These statutes provide the particulars to be shown in writing in principle.

*351.* The Act Amending Several Statutes Requiring the Delivery of Writing (Law No. 126 of 2000) amended, however, fifty statutes in order to allow businesses to deliver an electronic document instead of a paper-based document ('writing'), provided that the customer or member has agreed to be delivered documents in electromagnetic form. In other words, these amendments allow using electronic documents in cases where both the producer and the recipient of the documentation have agreed to do so. It has been interpreted that the parties are allowed to use e-mail, facsimiles, websites (cellular telephones may also be included if necessary) as well as the physical delivery of CD-ROMs, floppy disks or other equivalent electromagnetic memory devices.

## Chapter 2. Electronic Signatures

*352.* The Act Concerning Electronic Signatures and Electronic Certification Services (Law No. 102 of 2000) provides the legal effect of an electronic signature to some extent. An electromagnetic record which is made in order to provide information, except for that produced by a public official in the course of his official functions, is presumed to be authentic if an electronic signature is performed by the principal in relation to information recorded in the electromagnetic record, provided that such an electronic signature is made under the proper control of the codes and objects necessary to produce the signature under the exclusive control of the signatory (Article 3).

*353.* For the purpose of this law, 'electronic signature' is defined as a measure taken with regard to information that can be recorded in an electromagnetic record (any record which is produced by electronic, magnetic or any other means unrecognizable by natural perceptive function, and is used for data-processing by a computer). At the same time, an electronic signature must be a measure capable of identifying the signatory and linked to the data to which it relates in such a manner that any subsequent change of the data is detectable (Article 2, paragraph 1).

# Chapter 3. Trust Services

## §1. Regulation of Electronic Certification Services

### I. Act Concerning Electronic Signatures and Certification Services

*354.* Though there is no restriction on providing electronic certification services in Japan, the Act Concerning Electronic Signatures and Certification Services (hereinafter cited as the Electronic Signature Act) provides an accreditation scheme for electronic certification providers. A person seeking to perform or who has been performing designated certification services may receive an accreditation from the competent Ministers (Article 4, paragraph 1).

*355.* For the purpose of this Act, 'certification service' is defined as a service that, in compliance with either the request of a person who uses such a service (hereinafter referred to as 'user') with regard to the electronic signature that he himself performs or with the request of another person, certifies that an item used to confirm that the user performed an electronic signature belongs to the user (Article 2, paragraph 2). An 'accredited certification service' is defined as a certification service that is performed with regard to those electronic signatures that conform to the standards prescribed by the ordinance of the competent ministries as ones that, according to the method thereof, can only be substantially performed by that person (Article 2, paragraph 3). The Implementing Regulation for the Act Concerning Electronic Signatures and Certification Services (Ordinance of the MIC, the Ministry of Justice and the METI, No. 2 of 2001) provides the standard (Article 2). The security of an electronic signature must be based on the difficulty of one of the following computations:

(1) factoring an integer that is the product of two distinct odd primes and not less than 1,024 bits long;
(2) finding discrete logs in the multiplicative group in a finite field not less than 1,024 bits;
(3) finding discrete logs in a group on an elliptic curve not less than 160 bits;
(4) another computation that the competent Ministers deem to be as difficult as the preceding three computation methods.

### II. Application for Accreditation

*356.* A person seeking to receive such an accreditation must, in accordance with the prescriptions of the ordinance of the competent ministries, file with the competent Ministers an application form that states the following facts, as well as other documents prescribed by the ordinance of the competent ministries (Ordinance of the MIC, the Ministry of Justice and the METI, No. 2 of 2001):

(1) the name and address, and if an organization, the name of its representative; and
(2) an outline of the facilities used for the service applied for accreditation, and the method of implementation of the service applied for accreditation (Article 4, paragraph 2).

When the competent Ministers have been granted the accreditation, they must make a public announcement of that fact (Article 4, paragraph 3).

## III. Disqualification

*357.* Article 5 of the law stipulates that an accreditation may not be granted to:

(1) a person who has been sentenced to a penalty of imprisonment or to a more serious penalty (including an equivalent penalty pursuant to the laws and regulations of a foreign country) or who has been sentenced to a penalty pursuant to the Electronic Signature Act, unless two years have passed since the day on which either the enforcement of the penalty finished or the person came to be no longer subject thereto;
(2) a person whose accreditation has been revoked pursuant to the provisions of either paragraph 1 of Article 14 or paragraph 1 of Article 16, unless two years have passed since the day of the revocation; or
(3) an organization, any of whose directors performing the service falls within (1) or (2).

## IV. Requirements for Accreditation

*358.* The competent Ministers must grant an accreditation only when they find that the application for accreditation conforms to all of the following requirements:

(1) the facilities, including hardware and software, used for the service applied for accreditation conform to requirements prescribed by the ordinance of the competent ministries;
(2) the confirmation in the service applied for accreditation of the identity of the user is performed through a method prescribed by the ordinance of the competent ministries; and in addition to the facts listed in the preceding numbered items, the service applied for accreditation is performed through a method that conforms with requirements prescribed by the ordinance of the competent ministries (Article 6, paragraph 1).

*359.* In conducting the review for the purposes of the accreditation, the competent Ministers must, in accordance with the prescriptions of the ordinance of the competent ministries (Ordinance of the MIC, the Ministry of Justice and the METI,

No. 2 of 2001), perform an on-site investigation of the system involved in the implementation of the service applied for accreditation (Electronic Signature Act, Article 6, paragraph 2).

## V. Renewal of Accreditation

*360.* If the accreditation is not renewed for each term of no less than one year prescribed by Cabinet Order,[5] the accreditation becomes null and void upon the elapse of the term (Article 7, paragraph 1).

*361.* The provisions concerning application for accreditation, disqualification and requirements are applied, *mutatis mutandis*, to the renewal of accreditation (Article 7, paragraph 2).

## VI. Succession

*362.* If a person who has received the accreditation ('accredited certification service provider') transfers all of the business performing that accredited certification service, or if there is a succession or merger with respect to the accredited certification service provider, the person who obtains all of that business by transfer, the successor (the person chosen by agreement among such successors to succeed to the business in case there are two or more successors), or the organization that continues to exist after the merger or the organization established by the merger will succeed to the standing of such accredited certification service provider. However, where the person who obtained all of such business by transfer, the successor, or the organization that continues to exist after the merger or the organization established by the merger is a disqualified person according to Article 5, such a person will not succeed to the standing of such an accredited certification service provider.

## VII. Business Closing

*363.* If an accredited certification service provider seeks to discontinue its accredited service, it must, in accordance with the prescriptions of the ordinance of the competent ministries (Ordinance of the MIC, the Ministry of Justice and the METI, No. 2 of 2001), give advance notice of the intention to the competent Ministers without delay (Electronic Signature Act, Article 10, paragraph 1). When the competent Ministers have received the notice, they must make a public announcement of that fact (Article 10, paragraph 1).

5. The Implementing Order Concerning the Act Concerning Electronic Signatures and Certification Services (Cabinet Ordinance No. 41 of 2001) provides that the accreditation is effective for one year (Art. 1).

## VIII. Duty of an Accredited Certification Service Provider

*364.* An accredited certification service provider must, in accordance with the prescriptions of the ordinance of the competent ministries (Ordinance of the MIC, the Ministry of Justice and the METI, No. 2 of 2001), prepare and maintain books and records relating to its accredited service (Article 11).

*365.* An accredited certification service provider must not use the information it learns in the course of confirming the identity of users for its accredited service for any purpose other than those necessary for the provision of the accredited service (Article 12).

## IX. Mark

*366.* An accredited certification service provider may, in accordance with the prescriptions of the ordinance of the competent ministries (Ordinance of the MIC, the Ministry of Justice and the METI, No. 2 of 2001), place a mark to the effect that its service has received accreditation on an electronic certificate, etc., which means an electromagnetic record or other means prescribed by the ordinance of the competent ministries as one used for the sake of the certification service, created to verify that an item used to confirm that a user performed an electronic signature belongs to the user. No person may place such a mark, or any mark not clearly distinguishable therefrom, on any electronic certificate, etc., unless he is an accredited certification service provider (Electronic Signature Act, Article 13).

## X. Revocation of Accreditation

*367.* If an accredited certification service provider or, if the accredited certification service provider is an organization, any director, performing the service has been sentenced to a penalty of imprisonment or more serious penalty (including an equivalent penalty pursuant to the laws and regulations of a foreign country) or has been sentenced to a penalty pursuant to the Electronic Signature Act, then unless two years have passed since the day on which either the enforcement of the penalty finished or the person no longer came to be subject thereto, or if an accredited certification service provider fails to meet the requirements, violates any provision of paragraph 1 of Article 9, Article 11, Article 12 or paragraph 2 of Article 13, or receives the accreditation or the accreditation of change through improper means, the competent Ministers may revoke such accreditation. When competent Ministers have revoked an accreditation, they must make a public announcement of that fact (Electronic Signature Act, Article 14).

## XI. Accreditation of a Foreign Certification Service

*368.* A person seeking to perform the designated certification service by means of an office located in a foreign country may receive the accreditation from the competent Ministers (Article 15, paragraph 1).

*369.* If the competent Ministers find that a person seeking to receive the accreditation, a renewal thereof or the accreditation of change is a person who is performing the certification service by means of offices in a foreign country pursuant to provisions concerning a certification service based on the laws and regulations of that foreign country that are similar to the provisions for accreditation stipulated in Article 4, paragraph 1, and it is necessary to faithfully perform a treaty that Japan has entered into with said foreign country or another international agreement (including administrative agreement), they may require such persons to file documents that state the facts prescribed by the ordinance of the competent ministries instead of the investigation. In such a case, where the documents are received from such persons, the competent Ministers should, taking the documents into account, perform an examination for the purpose of the accreditation, a renewal thereof or the accreditation of change (Electronic Signature Act, Article 15, paragraphs 3 and 4).

## XII. Designated Investigating Organization

*370.* The competent Ministers may have the person they designate ('designated investigating organization') conduct the whole or part of the investigation. If competent Ministers have the designated investigating organization conduct the whole or part of the investigation, they should not conduct the whole or part of said investigation. In such a case, the competent Ministers must perform an examination, taking the results of the investigation carried out by the designated investigating organization into consideration (Electronic Signature Act, Article 17).

*371.* When the designated investigating organization is requested to conduct an investigation, it must conduct the investigation without delay unless there is a valid reason not to conduct it (Electronic Signature Act, Article 24).

*372.* The designated investigating organization should prescribe rules concerning the investigation service ('investigation service rules') and obtain the authorization of the competent Ministers. The same procedure applies to amendments to the investigation service rules. Matters to be prescribed in the investigation service rules are prescribed by the ordinance of the competent ministries (The Ministerial Ordinance concerning Designated Investigating Organization under the Act Concerning Electronic Signatures and Certification Services (Ordinance of the MIC, the Ministry of Justice and the METI, No. 1 of 2001)). If the competent Ministers find that existing authorized investigation service rules have become inappropriate for the fair implementation of investigations, they may order that such investigation service rules be amended (Article 25).

*373.* A person who has been sentenced to a penalty of imprisonment or who has been sentenced to a penalty pursuant to the Electronic Signature Act and with respect to whom less than two years have passed since the day on which either the enforcement of the penalty finished or the person came to be no longer subject thereto, a person whose designation has been revoked or whose approval has been revoked and with respect to whom less than two years have passed since the day of said revocation, or an organization whose director performing said service falls in the disqualification criteria, may not be designated as a designated investigating organization (Article 19).

*374.* The criteria for designation are as follows:

(1) the applicant possesses the financial resources and technological ability sufficient to competently and smoothly implement the investigation service;
(2) where the applicant is an organization, there is no risk that its board members or the makeup of the constituents prescribed by the ordinance of the competent ministries in accordance with organization type will interfere with the fair implementation of the investigation;
(3) where the applicant performs a service other than the investigation service, there is no risk that the investigation will become unfair through the performance of such a service; and
(4) a proper and smooth implementation of the investigation upon the application will not be impeded as a result of designation (Article 20).

*375.* When the competent Ministers have made a designation, they must announce the name and address of the designated investigating organization and the location of its office performing the investigation service (Article 21, paragraph 1).

*376.* If the designation is not renewed for each term of five years or more but less than ten years prescribed by a Cabinet Order,[6] the designation will become null and void upon the passing of said term (Article 22, paragraph 1).

*377.* The board members (where the designated investigating organization is not an organization, the person who received said designation) and staff members of the designated investigating organization, as well as persons who formerly held such positions, must not disclose any secrets that they learned in connection with the investigation service (Article 23, paragraph 1). For the purposes of the application of the Penal Code (Law No. 45 of 1907) and other penalties, the directors and staff members of a designated investigating organization engaging in the investigation service are deemed as public officials pursuant to laws and regulations (Article 23, paragraph 2).

6. The Implementing Order Concerning the Act Concerning Electronic Signatures and Certification Services (Cabinet Ordinance No. 41 of 2001) provides that the designation is effective for five years (Art. 2).

*378.* If competent Ministers find that a designated investigating organization is not in conformity with Article 20, numbered items 1 through 3, they may order that such designated investigating organization take such measures necessary to conform to these provisions (Article 27).

*379.* Unless it receives the authorization of competent Ministers, a designated investigating organization may not suspend or abrogate the whole or a part of its investigation service (Article 28). If the competent Ministers find that a designated investigating organization has violated any provisions in the Electronic Signature Act or any order of the competent Ministers, has fallen in the disqualification criteria, has performed an investigation service in violation of the investigation service regulations authorized, or the designation is received by any improper means, they may revoke such designation, or they may order that the whole or part of the investigation service be suspended for a prescribed period. Where they have revoked a designation or ordered that the whole or a part of the investigation service be suspended for a prescribed period, the competent Ministers must make a public announcement of that fact (Article 29).

*380.* If the designated investigating organization suspends the whole or a part of the investigation service pursuant to the provisions of Article 28, the designated investigating organization is ordered to suspend the whole or a part of the investigation service or the designated investigating organization becomes unable to conduct the whole or a part of the investigation service due to a natural disaster or other ground, the competent Ministers must conduct the whole or part of the investigation service when they find it necessary (Article 30).

*381.* As of September 2021, the Japan Information Processing Development Centre has been designated as an investigating organization.[7]

## XIII. Liability

*382.* There is no special legislation concerning the liability of certification service providers and the general rules stipulated in the Civil Code apply to certification service providers.

*383.* In ordinary cases, as there is no contractual relationship between the certification service provider and the plaintiff, the certification service provider, in principle, might be liable under tort law. In cases where an electronic signature certification service provider issues an electronic certificate without carrying out adequate personal identification, if another party receives and relies on the certificate but suffers damage because the effects of this transaction with the spoofer do not belong to the principal (the name of the electronic signature), the certification

7. For details of the activities of the designated investigation organization, *see* N. Ando, *Activities of Designated Certification Services under the e-Signature Law*, 3 ECOM J. 68–70 (2002).

service provider is liable to the recipient of the certificate. In this case, the recipient bears the burden of proof as to the negligence of the certification service provider.

*384.* Where there is a contractual relationship between the plaintiff, who reasonably relied on that certificate and suffered loss, and the certification service providers, the plaintiff may freely choose between contract law and tort law. On the grounds of contract law, the obligor is liable for the failure to perform the obligation in accordance with its purport and meaning (Civil Code, Article 415). Article 709 of the Civil Code provides that a person who intentionally or negligently violates another's rights shall be liable for the losses caused by the act (torts).

*385.* Some argue that a contractual relationship may already be established between the certification service provider and the recipient when the former shows its certification practice standards (CPS) and the latter acknowledges it. If a contractual relationship is established, the certification service provider is obliged to follow the CPS. In such a case, the burden of proof lies upon the certification authority as to the absence of fault on his side.

*386.* In cases where no contractual relationship is established between the recipient of the certificate and the certification service provider, the recipient is not bound by the limitation clause at all. However, the parties concerned are bound, in principle, by the exemption clause in cases where a contractual relationship is established. However, in consumer contracts, such a clause in CPS will be judged invalid if it totally exempts or partly exempts the certification service provider from the liability to compensate for damages resulting from the non-performance of an obligation or from a tort committed during the performance of an obligation (Consumer Contracts Act, Article 8). According to the prevailing view, an exemption clause, which totally exempts or partly exempts the certification service provider from the liability to compensate for damage arising from his misconduct in bad faith or gross negligence, is invalid.

## §2. Electronic Notary

*387.* In Japan, the Notary Act (Law No. 53 of 1908) governs the notarization system and notaries provide the notary service. Notaries can attach an officially stamped date to certain documents to certify the date when a document is prepared (Implementing Act for the Civil Code (Law No. 11 of 1898), Article 5, paragraph 2 and Article 6) and can examine the contents of certain documents to notarize certain private documents to certify the existence and the contents of documents to prevent future disputes (Notary Act, Article 1). In addition, notaries can prepare notarial documents to certify the execution of contracts and legitimacy of their contents.

*388.* Under the Notary Act (Article 1, No. 4), a designated notary[8] must attach an electronic officially stamped date and his/her electronic signature to an electronic document (electronic official date stamping). A designated notary also notarizes an electronic private document. Such a notary inspects the contents and effectiveness of an electronic private document and attaches a certification statement and his/her electronic signature to the document (Notarization of an Electronic Private Document). In addition, such a notary must store, in accordance with the provisions in an ordinance of the Ministry of Justice, the information necessary for verifying the identity of the information recorded in the notarized electromagnetic document. Upon request of the applicant, such a notary must store electromagnetic notarized documents and electronic officially stamped documents and certify the existence and the contents of the electronic documents (Commercial Registration Act, Article 62*septies*).[9]

## §3. Time Stamp

*389.* Article 10(3) of the Framework Act on Advancing Public and Private Sector Data Utilization (Law No. 103 of 2016) provides as follows:

*390.* The state is to implement legislative and other necessary measures to ensure that a person that was delegated with mandate by a representative of a corporation is able to implement an offer of a contract or any other procedure by exclusively using an electronic data-processing system.

*391.* In addition, the Act on Promotion of Dissemination of Electronic Power of Attorney (Law No. 64 of 2017) promotes the dissemination of electronic power of attorney, which displays the authorization of representation given by corporate representatives to others, such as their employees. The Act stipulates basic guidelines for promoting the dissemination of electronic power of attorney and sets out an accreditation system for handling electronic power of attorney, in which electronic power of attorney is to be kept under the consignment of corporations and presented to the parties concerned.

*392.* Based on Article 3, paragraph 1 of the Act, the METI and the MIC issued in 2017 and revised in 2020 the Basic Guidelines for Promoting the Dissemination of Electronic Power of Attorney in order to promote the utilization of electronic power of attorney in administrative procedures. The 2020 revision makes it possible to handle electronic power of attorney by using the individual number card as

8. The Minister of Justice appoints and supervises notaries who have professional knowledge of and careers in legal affairs. Notaries should act in a disinterested and public fashion (in relation to this, there are restrictions on notaries holding other jobs (Notary Act, Art. 5)). The disinterested operations of notaries are ensured by the Penal Code (Art. 156) and other statutes. Finally, the State Redress Law is applied in case of inappropriate operations of notaries.
9. Electronic public notary services are offered solely by the notaries designated for such services by the Ministry of Justice (Notary Act, Art. 7*bis*).

one of the methods of recording electronic power of attorney. Moreover, using electronic power of attorney became possible in the Government Electronic Procurement System from May 2021.

*393.* Moreover, the Act Concerning the Use of Information and Communication Technology for the Storage of Documents by Private Business, etc. (Law No.149 of 2004) permits private companies electronic storage of both electronic documents (documents originally electronically prepared) and computerized documents (documents computerized by scanning paper documents) in order to fulfil the duty to store the documents as evidence while only paper documents were accepted as evidence before this Act. This Act covers many kinds of documents and provides detailed requirements for electronic storage. Electronic signatures and time stamps are required to assure the integrity of e-documents in electronic storage.

*394.* The Special Act Concerning the Method to Store National Tax-related Records Prepared with Computers (Law No. 25 of 1998) (hereinafter cited as the 'Electronic Ledger Storage Act') and the Local Tax Act (Law No. 226 of 1950) permit taxpayers to store transaction and accounting records electromagnetically in order to meet the requirements of having paper-based ledgers and documents stored or placed at the offices. The Implementing Regulation for the Electronic Ledger Storage Act (Ordinance of Ministry of Finance No. 43 of 1998) lays down requirements that qualified electronic signatures and the time stamps accredited are mandatory for electronic storage of national tax-related documents, respectively. For local tax-related documents, the same requirements are applicable. The guideline on e-Documents of the Ministry of Health, Labor and Welfare concerning 'Trusted administration of medical IT system' provides similar obligation for electronic storage of medical documents.

*395.* From February 2005 to March 2021, the Japan Data Communications Association (JADAC), a juridical foundation and its competent authority is the MIC, had run a voluntary accreditation program for time-stamping services.

*396.* The JADAC was the accreditation body, which operates, maintains and manages the overall accreditation program. The advisory committee authorized the policy and operation related to the program while the screening committee gives advice to the JADAC on technical assessments for accreditation.

*397.* The National Institute of Information and Communications Technology (NICT) offers information about GPS common view measurements and the Coordinated Universal Time (UTC). The JADAC cooperates with the Time Business Forum and NICT in making new criteria. The Time Business Forum is a council composed of members from industries, academia and the government. The accreditation program was under the guidance of the MIC.

*398.* The program was built in accordance with the *Guideline of Time Business* issued by the MIC. The services of a TA (Time Authority) or a TSA (Time-Stamping Authority) would be approved if they meet the required criteria. The criteria consist of those on technical issues; management and operation; facilities; network security; and disclosure and notification. Those criteria are developed in line with ISO/IEC 18014-1 (Information technology-Security techniques-Time-stamping services- Part1: Framework); ISO/IEC 18014-2 (Information technology-Security techniques-Time-stamping services- Part2 Mechanisms producing independent tokens); ISO/IEC 18014-3 (Information technology-Security techniques-Time-stamping services- Part1:Mechanisms producing linked tokens); RFC 3161-Internet X.509 Public Key Infrastructure Time-Stamp Protocol; and ETSI TS 102 023 v1.2.1 (Electronic Signatures and Infrastructures (ESI); Policy requirements for time-stamping authorities).

*399.* The accredited TA or TSA must have business stronghold as well as facilities and equipment for time-stamping business within Japan. Accreditation was valid for two years but renewable on an application for renewal.

*400.* The MIC introduced, however, a national accreditation system for time-stamping services on April 1, 2021 ('Regulation for Accreditation of Time Certification Services', Ministry of Internal Affairs and Communications Notice No. 146). 'Time certification business' is the business to provide the service of putting a 'time stamp', which is information certifying that the electronic data existed at a certain time and that the electronic data has not been tampered with from that time, on the information related to the electronic data. The time certification services that meet the requirements for issuing time stamps reliably and stably are referred to as 'accredited time certification services'.

*401.* Under this system, the applicant applies for accreditation of its service as 'accredited time certification services' to the MIC. The applicant requests a designated investigating organization to evaluate at the same time. The results of the evaluation are notified to the MIC and the Minister accredits the applicant' service based on the results of the evaluation. The MIC designated the JADAC as a designated investigating organization. Accreditation is valid for two years but renewable on an application for renewal.

# Chapter 4. Online Financial Services

## §1. Payment and Settlement System in Japan

*402.* There are four major payment systems for clearing and settling interbank payments in Japan:

(1) Bank of Japan Financial Network System (BOJ-NET).
(2) *Zengin* Data Telecommunications System (*Zengin* System).
(3) Foreign Exchange Yen Clearing System (FEYCS).
(4) Bill and check clearing system.[10]

### I. BOJ-NET

*403.* The BOJ-NET is operated by the Bank of Japan (hereinafter referred to as the BOJ). Operations of the BOJ-NET include the settlement of funds transfers across current accounts held by financial institutions at the BOJ; the clearance of yen payments related to the FEYCS; the issuance, registration and book-entry transfer of Japanese government bonds and bills (JGBs); and the delivery-*v.*-payment (DVP) services for JGBs and corporate bonds.

*404.* For the final settlement of funds and JGBs among financial institutions, the BOJ-NET has an online and offline interface with various private payment and settlement systems. With respect to funds transfers, the BOJ has online links with the *Zengin* Data Telecommunications System and the Tokyo Clearing House through its internal host computer systems. It also exchanges data with the Tokyo International Financial Futures Exchange (TIFFE). Furthermore, the BOJ exchanges data with the Tokyo Stock Exchange (TSE), the Osaka Securities Exchange (OSE) and the Japan Bond Settlement Network Co. (JBNet) through BOJ-NET terminals with respect to securities transfers. Accordingly, banks, securities firms and money brokers (*tanshi kaisha*) participate in the BOJ-NET.

*405.* Transfers are settled individually through the participants' current accounts with the BOJ in real-time or at the times designated by the participants. Funds transfers made through BOJ-NET are irrevocable and unconditional. In the case of designated-time settlements, payment instructions can be revoked before they are executed, whereas real-time funds transfers are instantaneously irrevocable.

*406.* The BOJ constructed and introduced the Real-Time Gross Settlement System (RTGS), the only settlement mode for funds and Japanese government securities (JGS) transfers over the BOJ-NET, on 4 January 2001. With the new RTGS system, the BOJ, in principle, can process instructions for funds and JGS transfers

10. There are 179 clearing houses designated by the Minister of Justice in Japan. The Tokyo Clearing House (TCH) is the largest, with 295 participating financial institutions as of the end of September 2021. It is run by the Japanese Bankers Association.

immediately ('real time') upon receipt, and individually without netting them ('gross'). By making RTGS the only settlement mode, each transaction is processed immediately and individually, and thus the risk that a settlement failure of a financial institution might trigger settlement failures at other financial institutions, thereby causing a disruption in the entire payment and settlement system, is minimized compared with that under designated time settlement.

### II. *Zengin* Data Telecommunications System

*407.* The *Zengin* Data Telecommunications System (hereinafter referred to as the Zengin System) is operated by the Japanese Banks' Payment Clearing Network (*Zengin*-net) and its communication network is provided and maintained by NTT Data Corporation. Banks participate directly in the system whereas smaller financial institutions, such as various cooperatives, participate indirectly through the respective umbrella body of such institutions. The *Zengin* System handles domestic funds transfers. The credit and debit positions of participants are calculated within the system. As the *Zengin*-net acts as the central counterparty, the obligations among the participants are replaced with those between the *Zengin*-net and each participant. Each participant is required to deposit a collateral equivalent to its sender net debit cap with the *Zengin*-net. The net positions of participants of the *Zengin* System are, in principle, settled through the BOJ-NET Funds Transfer System on an RTGS basis at 16:15.

### III. Foreign Exchange Yen Clearing System

*408.* The FEYCS is also managed by the Japanese Bankers Association while the automated system is a part of the BOJ-NET. Banks and foreign banks are participants of the system, though five-sixths of the participants are indirect participants who participate in the system through direct participants. This system is designed to handle yen payments resulting from cross-border financial transactions.

*409.* As the Japanese Bankers Association also acts as the central counterparty in this system, the obligations among the participants are replaced with those between the Japanese Bankers Association and each participant. The Japanese Bankers Association requires the participants to deposit collaterals. The net positions of the participants of the FEYCS are settled through the BOJ-NET Funds Transfer System on an RTGS basis.

## §2. Some Issues Concerning Electronic Banking

*410.* With respect to retail payments, electronic funds transfers, including services such as prearranged direct credit for the payment of payrolls and direct debit for the payment of electric, gas, water or telephone bills, are popular among individuals and firms. Credit cards are widely used and the use of electronic money is growing, whereas the use of debit cards is still less. Various retail payment services using the Internet and cell phones are becoming popular.

*411.* Online banking services are offered to firms and individuals.

*412.* As there are no specific Japanese laws specially designed for electronic banking, the legal relationships among parties are determined by private contracts, case law and general provisions in the Civil Code and Commercial Code. It has been common in Japan that a standard contract governs a client's relationship with his bank.

## I. Funds Transfers

*413.* With respect to funds transfers, a purported sender is bound not just by a payment order issued by him or his agent. In addition, he may be liable for an unauthorized payment order issued by an apparent agent (an agency by estoppel or an ostensible agency) (Civil Code, Articles 109, 110 and 112).

*414.* Banks may also be protected under Article 478 of the Civil Code, which provides that a good-faith payment to an apparent creditor discharges the debtor's obligation. According to case law, Article 478 applies to payments against forged or altered checks, notes or bills by a payer bank (Judgment, Tokyo Appeal Court, 22 June 1915, 1042 *Horitsu Shinbun* 28; Judgment, Tokyo High Court, 20 September 1955, 8 *Kosai Minshu* 479 etc.) unless the payer bank was negligent (*see* Judgment, Supreme Court, 8 April 2003, 57 *Minshu* 337).

*415.* However, the Depositors Protection Act (Law No. 94 of 2005) provides that banks should bear a loss arising from unauthorized funds transfers, whose order is made using a stolen cash card at an Automated/Automatic Teller Machine (ATM), in cases where the client is in good faith and is not negligent (Article 5, paragraph 1). Banks should also share three-fourths of a loss arising from unauthorized funds transfers, whose order is made using a stolen cash card at an ATM, in cases where the client is in good faith and negligent but not grossly negligent (Article 5, paragraph 2).

## II. Electronic Banking

*416.* If a person, disguising himself as another person who has an account at a bank, has instructed a funds transfer through Internet banking, the validity of the funds transfer with respect to the named person will be at issue. According to the standard contract between banks and their customers, if a prior agreement is reached on personal identification and if the agreed identification method is used, a funds transfer made according to a spoofer's instructions is treated as valid. The validity of this clause is, however, judged in consideration of the degree of the bank's system security and other factors.

*417.* The Supreme Court has admitted the validity of the banking agreement (Judgment, 19 July 1993, 1489 *Hanrei Jiho* 111). The court held that it is reasonable to consider that the bank is exempted from the responsibility under the exemption clause as long as the withdrawal was effected based on the confirmation of the cash card and the personal identification number (PIN) by the ATM if the genuine cash card delivered by the bank to the depositor was used and the correct PIN number was entered, except for cases where there were special circumstances, such as inadequate management of the PIN number by the bank.

*418.* The court is likely to take similar factors as those considered in this case into consideration in judging the validity of the disclaimer clause concerning funds transfers to an unauthorized person. It should be noted that this judgment refers not only to the exemption clause but also to the security of the payment system adopted by the bank at the time when the accident occurred. Accordingly, the degree of system security at the time an accident takes place will also be considered when judging the validity of the banking clause. Based on the existing technology, it is highly likely that the clause will be judged valid if multiple passwords are used for personal identification and if data is transmitted after being encrypted using Secure Sockets Layer (SSL) (Judgment, Tokyo High Court, 13 July 2006, 1785 *Kin'yu Homu Jijo* 45). However, it is unclear whether the courts will admit the validity of the exemption clause in cases where an unauthorized person has instructed the funds transfer under the current practices.

*419.* However, Article 478 of the Civil Code applies to a payment made to a person with no authority to receive it. According to this provision, the payment is valid if the person appeared to be the creditor and the payer did not know through any fault of his or her own that the payee was not the creditor. This article applies to electronic funds transfers in cases where there is no prior agreement concerning such an accident through standard contracts for electronic banking which have a similar provision to Article 478 of the Civil Code. Though the Depositors Protection Act does not apply to Internet banking transactions, banks have decided voluntarily to bear or share a loss from unauthorized Internet banking transactions if the client is in good faith and not grossly negligent (Resolution of the Japanese Bankers Association, *Measure on Illicit Withdrawals*, 19 February 2008).[11]

11. For body corporate clients, *see* Resolution of the Japanese Bankers Association, *On Approach to Compensation in Case of Illicit Withdrawals in Internet Banking Service for Body Corporate*, 17 Jul. 2014.

## Chapter 5. Law of Evidence in the Digital Environment

*420.* In Japan, since there are no explicit provisions regarding the admissibility of evidence in civil procedures and since the freedom of proof is the general rule, the courts have admitted electromagnetic records. In addition, the courts have a discretionary power, to a reasonable extent, regarding the probative value of the evidence (Civil Procedure Code, Article 247). Moreover, Article 231 of the Civil Procedure Code provides that the provisions concerning documentary evidence shall apply to non-documentary evidence containing information such as drawings, pictures, recording tapes and videotapes. Article 147 of the Civil Procedure Regulation also provides that Articles 137–146 of the Regulation shall apply to the evidence provided in Article 231 of the Code, while Article 143 of the Regulation provides that documentary evidence should be brought into the court and sent to the interested parties in its original or in certified copies (*tohon*). Logically, electromagnetic records (not in writing) may be used as copies in civil proceedings.

*421.* With respect to the evidential value, it is important that the computer equipment used was reliable and that sufficient measures were taken to ensure the accuracy of the data during entry, storage and processing. It is also indispensable to prove that the printouts were prepared to ensure they are identical to the original electromagnetic data. In practice, it may be difficult to prove the terms of a contract if different versions of contracts have been used at different times, and it may be required to prove the integrity of the electronic record system in or by which the data was recorded or stored.

*422.* The Civil Procedure Code contains a general presumption that as against the signatory, signed (either by the principal or by his agent) private documents are authentic unless the signatory produces evidence to counter this presumption (Article 228, paragraph 4). The Electronic Signatures and Electronic Certification Service Act provides that an electromagnetic record, except for that produced by a public official in the course of his official functions, is presumed to be authentic (Article 3).

# Chapter 6. Consumer Protection

## §1. Right to Revoke

### I. Consumer Contracts Act

*423.* The Consumer Contracts Act (Law No. 61 of 2000) applies to contracts between businesses and consumers, including as a matter of course B-to-C e-commerce transactions. This Act intends to protect consumers' interests, taking asymmetrical information and bargaining power between businesses and consumers into consideration.

*424.* The term 'consumer' as used in this Act is defined as an individual (excluding persons who become a party to a contract as a business or for the purpose of business), and the term 'entrepreneur' is defined as a legal person, association or individual that becomes a party to a contract as a business or for the purpose of business (Article 2, paragraph 2). Based on these definitions, the term 'consumer contract' in this Act is defined as a contract concluded between consumers and businesses.

*425.* A consumer may withdraw his declaration of intention to offer or accept a consumer contract when the declaration was induced by fraud or duress (Civil Code, Article 96, paragraph 1) as a matter of course. However, it is not always easy to prove that the declaration was induced by fraud or duress. Accordingly, the Consumer Contracts Act provides some cases in which a consumer may withdraw his declaration of intention, in addition to Article 96 of the Civil Code (Consumer Contracts Act, Article 6).

*426.* A consumer may withdraw his declaration of intention to offer or accept a consumer contract where the consumer has made, at the time when he has been solicited to enter into the consumer contract by business, any of the following specified mistakes resulting from any of the following specified acts by a business (Consumer Contracts Act, Article 4, paragraph 1):

(1) where a business has made a representation that is not true as to a material item, i.e., believing that the content of the representation is true; or
(2) where the business has provided conclusive evaluations on the future prices, the amounts of money to be received by the consumer in the future and other uncertain matters that may change in the future with respect to goods, rights, services and other things that are to be the object of the consumer contract, i.e., believing that the conclusive evaluation so provided is reliable.

*427.* A consumer may withdraw his declaration of intention to offer or accept a consumer contract if made when a business has, at the time it solicited the consumer to enter into the consumer contract, shown to the consumer the advantageous facts regarding material particulars of the object but intentionally failed to advise of the disadvantageous facts regarding material particulars and the consumer has believed by mistake that there have been no such disadvantageous facts. However, this does not apply to cases where the business has tried to explain such facts to the consumer but the consumer has refused such an explanation (Consumer Contracts Act, Article 4, paragraph 2).

*428.* For this purpose, the term 'material items' is defined as the particulars in a consumer contract that would normally influence a consumer's decision to conclude a consumer contract, such as the following (Consumer Contracts Act, Article 4, paragraph 4):

(1) the quality, usage and other contents of the goods, rights, services, and other things that are to be the object of a consumer contract; or
(2) the price and other conditions in a transaction of goods, rights, services, and other things that are to be the object of a consumer contract.

*429.* A consumer may withdraw his declaration of intent to offer or accept a consumer contract where the consumer was distressed at the time he was solicited to enter into the consumer contract by a business, because of any of the following specified acts by the business (Consumer Contracts Act, Article 4, paragraph 3):

(1) if a solicitor has failed to leave the place where the consumer resides or does business in spite of the fact that the consumer has requested the solicitor to leave;
(2) if a solicitor has not allowed the consumer to leave the place where the consumer has been solicited to enter into a consumer contract by that business in spite of the fact that the consumer has shown the intention to leave.

*430.* However, the withdrawal of a declaration of intention to offer or accept subject to paragraphs 1–3 may not prevail against a third party who has acted in good faith (Consumer Contracts Act, Article 4, paragraph 5). In addition, the right to revoke will lapse by prescription if it has been not exercised within six months after the time ratification became possible or after five years have lapsed from the time when a consumer contract was concluded (Consumer Contracts Act, Article 7, paragraph 1).

*431.* A consumer has the right to revoke, which is subject to similar conditions as those mentioned above, in cases where a business has entrusted a third party to be an intermediary to a consumer contract and the entrusted third party (including those who have been entrusted by such a third party) has solicited the consumer (Consumer Contracts Act, Article 5, paragraph 1). Agents of consumers, businesses or those entrusted, etc. to conclude a consumer contract are deemed as consumers, businesses or entrusted, etc., respectively (Consumer Contracts Act, Article 5, paragraph 2).

*432.* Article 8, paragraph 1 of the Consumer Contracts Act provides that some types of clauses exempting businesses from their liability are null and void (*see also* above paragraph 334):

(1) clauses that totally exclude a business from liability to compensate damages to a consumer arising from that business's non-performance;
(2) clauses which partially exclude a business from liability to compensate damages to a consumer arising from that business's non-performance (such non-performance is limited to instances where the same arises by wilful misconduct or gross negligence on the part of the business, the business's representative or an employee);
(3) clauses that totally exclude a business from liability to compensate damages to a consumer arising from a tort provided in the Civil Code, committed on occasion of the business's performance of a consumer contract;
(4) clauses which partially exclude a business from liability to compensate damages to a consumer arising from a tort (such torts are limited to instances where the same arises from gross negligence or wilful misconduct on the part of the business, the business's representative or an employee) provided in the Civil Code committed on occasion of the business's performance of a consumer contract;
(5) clauses which totally exclude a business from liability to compensate for damages to a consumer caused by a defect if a consumer contract is a contract for value and if there exists a latent defect in the material subject to that consumer contract (in case a consumer contract is a contract for work, a defect should exist in the object of the work). However, this clause will not be null and void (Article 8, paragraph 2) to the extent that the consumer contract provides that the business is responsible to deliver substitute goods without defects or repair the subject if any defects exist in the material subject to the consumer contract, or another contract between the consumer and another business entrusted by the business or a contract between the business and another business for the benefit of the consumer, which is concluded before or simultaneously with the consumer contract, provided that the other business is responsible to compensate the whole or a part of the damage caused by the defect, deliver substitute goods without defects or repair the subject if any defect exists in the material, subject to the consumer contract.

Article 8*bis* of the Consumer Contracts Act stipulates other types of clauses deemed as null and void: clauses that a consumer gives up the right to rescind the contract due to non-performance or incomplete performance by the business; clauses that a consumer gives up the right to rescind the contract due to hidden defects in case of a contract for value.

*433.* In addition, clauses to deem that a consumer has indicated his/her intention to offer or accept a new consumer contract by the consumer's non-feasance and other clauses which restrict the rights of consumers or expand the duties of consumers beyond the restrictions and expansions that would otherwise apply by application of the provisions of the Civil Code, the Commercial Code, and other such statutes not concerned with the public order and which, at the same time, unilaterally impair the interests of consumers against the fundamental principle provided in the second paragraph of Article 1 of the Civil Code, are null and void (Consumer Contracts Act, Article 10).

*434.* Moreover, Article 9 of the Consumer Contracts Act stipulates that some types of clauses in a consumer contract are null and void to a limited extent. With respect to clauses stipulating the amount of damages in case of a rescission or to clauses fixing the penalty, part of the clauses is null and void to the extent that the total amount of liquidated damages, in addition to the penalty, exceeds the average amount of damages by the rescission of a contract of the same kind to the business in accordance with the reason, the time of the rescission or other factors. As to clauses stipulating the amount of damages or fixing the penalty in case of total or partial default (in case payments should be made twice or more, every failure of payment is deemed as a default) of a consumer who is overdue, the clauses are null and void to the extent that the total amount of liquidated damages in addition to the penalty exceeds the amount calculated by deducting the amount of money actually paid by the appointed deadline from the amount of money which should have been paid and multiplying it by 14.6% a year in accordance with the number of days from the appointed deadline to the day on which the money is actually paid.

## II. Act Concerning the Exceptions to the Civil Code

*435.* The Law Regarding the Exceptions to the Civil Code with respect to mistakes in consumer contracts and notices of acceptance in electronic commerce was enacted in 2001. This Law is significant for e-commerce in Japan because e-commerce, using the Internet, has become so popular in Japan that it is necessary to ensure the legal stability of transactions over the Internet, on the one hand. On the other hand, increasing B-to-C e-commerce draws attention to consumer protection in e-commerce. The possibility that people might make a mistake as to what they are purchasing or how much they are purchasing seems to be higher when they purchase something on the Internet than when they buy face-to-face or when they use paper-based order forms. *See also Preliminary Report of the Consumer Policy Committee, the Social Policy Council* (January 1998).

*436.* Article 95 of the Civil Code stipulates that a declaration of intention shall be voidable if it is based on either of the following mistakes, and the mistake is material in light of the purpose of the juridical act and common sense in the transaction: (i) a mistake wherein the person lacks the intention that corresponds to the manifestation of intention; or (ii) a mistake wherein the person making the manifestation of intention holds an understanding that does not correspond to the truth with regard to the circumstances which the person has taken as the basis for the juridical act, but the declarant cannot claim himself null when he has made the mistake with gross negligence. However, it is not necessarily clear, either for the seller or for the consumer-purchaser, in what case the courts will find the purchaser grossly negligent in relation to with Article 95 of the Civil Code.

*437.* According to a widely accepted opinion, a seller can insist that a purchaser was grossly negligent, at least if the website was designed to prevent the anticipated purchaser's mistakes and to give the purchaser an opportunity to correct the error (cf. *Report of the Subcommittee on Substantial Law, the Study Group on the Legal*

*System for Electronic Commerce* (chaired by Professor *Kenjiro Egashira*, on behalf of the Director of the Civil Affairs Bureau, Ministry of Justice), December 1999, IV.2(1)(a)). In other words, it is unlikely that a seller will be successful in proving a purchaser's gross negligence, unless the seller's site is designed to display what the purchaser has ordered and how much of it he has ordered in order to enable the purchaser to reconfirm his order. Article 3 is in line with this opinion:

**Article 3**

1. Article 95(3) of the Civil Code shall not apply to the cases in which there have been mistakes in the elements of an electronic consumer contract in respect of a consumer's declaration of intention to offer or accept the contract and the mistakes fall under any one of the following. However, this shall not apply to the cases in which the entrepreneur (including his mandatory; hereinafter the same), who is the other party of the electronic consumer contract, has taken measures to request, on the screen by electromagnetic means, that the consumer confirm that the consumer has an intention to declare his intention to offer or accept when the offer or acceptance is made, or the consumer has declared his intention to the entrepreneur that the entrepreneur will not need to take such measures in cases:
   1. where the consumer was not willing to declare his intent to offer or accept an electronic consumer contract with the entrepreneur as the other party to the electronic consumer contract (including his mandatory; hereinafter the same) when he transmitted a message by the computer used by him; or
   2. where the consumer was willing to declare his intent for something other than an offer or acceptance of the electronic consumer contract when he transmitted a message by the computer used by him.
2. The preceding paragraph shall not apply where the entrepreneur, as the other party to the electronic consumer contract, has taken the following measures on the screen by electromagnetic means when the consumer has declared his intent to offer or accept the electronic consumer contract:
   1. to request a consumer, where the consumer is willing to declare his intent to offer or accept a specified electronic consumer contract, to express his intent;
   2. to display clearly the content of the declaration of intent regarding the expression mentioned at the preceding item;
   3. to request the consumer to edit the content of the declaration of intent mentioned at the preceding item, if necessary, and to confirm there are no errors;
   4. to request the consumer, where the consumer has confirmed in accordance with the preceding item, to declare that he has confirmed;
   5. to request clearly the consumer to choose whether he will declare the intent the same as the declaration mentioned at the preceding paragraph.

This provision makes it clear that a purchaser-consumer may claim the transaction voidable against the seller whenever he had no intention to offer or accept an electronic consumer contract with the entrepreneur unless measures have been taken by the entrepreneur to reconfirm the intention of the consumer.

*438.* For this purpose, the term 'electronic consumer contract' is defined as a contract concluded between a consumer and an entrepreneur (*jigyosha*) on the screen of computers by electromagnetic means, for which the consumer, with the computer he uses, transmits a declaration of his intention to offer or acceptance, following the displayed instructions given by the entrepreneur or his mandatory (Article 2, paragraph 1). At the same time, the term 'electromagnetic means' is defined widely and means any means using an electronic information processing system and other means utilizing information and telecommunication technology.

The definitions of 'consumer' and 'entrepreneur' in this Act are the same as those provided in Article 2 of the Consumer Contracts Act.

## III. Act on Special Commercial Practices

*439.* The Special Commercial Practices Act provides a cooling-off system (not mandatory for mail-order sales), the right of consumers to rescind the contract in case of unfair solicitation and limitation of liability of consumers.

*440.* There is no cooling-off system for mail-order sales under the Special Commercial Practices Act. Consumer's statutory right to return purchased goods is now, however, prescribed in case where the agreement concerning return of goods is not clearly specified on an advertisement in the light of the provisions of the Special Commercial Practices Act (Special Commercial Practices Act, Article 11, Item 4 and Article 15*bis*, Proviso of paragraph 1). The statutory right is not available for a consumer where the agreement on return is shown on an advertisement so that the consumers can easily recognize it (Special Commercial Practices Act, Article 15*bis*). While the agreement shall be presented in an advertisement (Special Commercial Practices Act, Article 11, Item 4, Implementing Regulation for the Special Commercial Practices Act, Article 9, Item 3), it needs to be shown on the final screen for order for any electronic consumer contract (Implementing Regulation for the Special Commercial Practices Act, Article 16*bis*). Under such a circumstance, a consumer may return the purchased goods or designated rights in cases where: (i) The counterparty of the contract must be the seller who has advertised the sales conditions for the products or designated rights; (ii) within eight days from the day on which delivery of the product or transfer of the designated right related with the sales contract in question; and (iii) there must be an expression of intention to rescind or cancel the contract.

*441.* Any cost necessary for withdrawal or returning of the product or the designated right shall be paid by the purchaser (Special Commercial Practices Act, Article 15*bis*, paragraph 2). Except for this, the provisions of the Civil Code apply in case where a consumer has exercised the statutory right to return. Thus, where cancellation or rescission of the contract takes effect, both of the parties must restore to the original state, but if the purchaser seriously damages the subject of the contract or is unable to return by way of his/her intention or negligence, the right to cancel shall be extinguished unless the purchaser does not know that he/she has a right to cancel (Civil Code, Article 548). Different from a case of cooling-off, the seller may claim damages or penalty from the purchaser if the cancellation or rescission of the contract causes damages to the seller.

*442.* The Act requires an e-mail sender to furnish an opt-in requirement (Act Promoting Proper Sending Specific E-Mail (Law No. 26 of 2002) has similar provision) and imposes the business to save the communication log via e-mail. Unsolicited e-mail related to mail order or teleshopping services may only be sent to recipients who have requested advertisements related to sales terms and conditions of the relevant goods or services or entered into a contract (or offered to do so) for the goods or services. However, it does not stipulate any civil liability for breach of the prohibition though administrative and/or criminal sanctions will be imposed on the wrongdoers.

## IV. Telecommunications Business Act

*443.* In 2015, Telecommunications Business Act was amended (Law No. 26 of 2015) to include provisions aiming to secure consumer benefit by ensuring fair provision of services, especially with respect to fundamental public services.

*444.* Where any telecommunications carrier or any person entrusted by the carrier to engage in intermediation, agency or acting as agent (hereinafter referred to as intermediation, etc.) for concluding a contract for the provision of telecommunications services of a telecommunications carrier or ancillary activities (including a person entrusted by such party (further entrustment at the second or higher degree of separation from the original entrustment is also included) hereinafter referred to as entrusted party) intends to conclude a contract, or to act as an intermediary, agency or agent for concluding a contract, with a user (except a telecommunications carrier) who intends to receive telecommunications services on the provision of telecommunications services as follows, they should, as specified by the applicable ordinance of the MIC, explain to the person an outline of the charges and other terms and conditions for the provision of the telecommunications services subject to a few exceptions stipulated in the applicable ordinance of the MIC (Article 26, paragraph 1; Implementing Regulation for the Telecommunications Business Act, Article 22-2-3):

(1) telecommunications services which are provided using transmission line facilities one end of which is connected to mobile terminal facilities (users' telecommunications facilities as radio facilities of mobile radio stations) and designated by the MIC as particularly necessary for the protection of the interests of users in the light of the content, tariff and other conditions for provision as well as the range and volume of users (Item 1);

(2) telecommunications services other than those which are provided using transmission line facilities one end of which is connected to mobile terminal facilities but designated by the MIC as particularly necessary for the protection of the interests of users in the light of the content, tariff and other conditions for provision as well as the range and volume of users (Item 2); and
(3) telecommunications services other than (1) and (2) but designated by the MIC as having non-negligible influence on the interests of users in the light of the content, tariff and other conditions for provision, the range of users and other circumstances (Item 3).

*445.* Those designations are made in a notice of the MIC (Article 26, paragraph 2, MIC Notice No. 106 of 2016, Articles 2 through 4).

*446.* When a telecommunication carrier has concluded a contract to provide the telecommunication service listed in paragraph 1 of Article 26, it should, except for the cases prescribed in the applicable ordinance of the MIC, deliver without delay to the user (except for he/she who is a telecommunication carrier) a document, pursuant to the provisions of the applicable ordinance of MIC (Article 26*bis*, paragraph 1; Implementing Regulation for the Telecommunications Business Act, Article 22-2-4). A telecommunication carrier may, in lieu of delivering a document, provide the information that is required to be detailed in the document through the use of an electronic data-processing system or through any other application of ICT which is specified by the applicable ordinance of the MIC (Implementing Regulation for the Telecommunications Business Act, Article 22-2-5), with the approval of the user and pursuant to the provisions of the applicable Cabinet Order (Implementing Order for the Telecommunications Business Act, Article 2). In such cases, the telecommunication carrier who submitted the application shall be deemed to have given a document under paragraph 1 (Article 26*bis*, paragraph 2). In this case, the provision of the information that is required to be detailed in the document shall be deemed to have arrived at the user when it is recorded onto a file stored in the computer used by the user (Article 26*bis*, paragraph 3).

*447.* Unless the applicable ordinance of the MIC provided otherwise (Implementing Regulation for the Telecommunications Business Act, Article 22-2-7), where a user has concluded a contract on the provision of the telecommunication services stipulated in Item 1 or Item 2, paragraph 1, Article 26, may cancel in writing the contract before eight days have passed since the date on which he/she received the document referred to in Article 26*bis*, paragraph 1 (in cases where the telecommunication service is that stipulated in Item 1, paragraph 1, Article 26, the date of commencement of the service is later than the date of delivery of the document, the former). If the user has not cancelled the contract under this provision by the relevant time limit because he/she misunderstood that information about cancelling since that the telecommunication carrier or its entrusted party had misrepresented to him/her, in violation of the provisions of Article 27*bis*, Item 1, he/she may cancel the contract before eight days have passed since the date on which he/she received a document delivered thereto by the seller, pursuant to the provisions of the applicable ordinance of the MIC (Implementing Regulation for the Telecommunications Business Act, Article 22-2-8), that contains a notice to the effect that he/she may cancel the contract (Article 26*ter*, paragraph 1). The cancellation takes effect at the time the cancellation is set forth in writing (Article 26*ter*, paragraph 2). Where a cancellation prescribed in paragraph 1 has been effected, the telecommunication carrier may not claim the user damages, demand the payment of any penalty, or the payment or delivery of cash or other property in connection with the cancellation. The telecommunication carrier may, however, require the user to pay the amount for the telecommunication service provided to the user during the period up to the cancellation of the contract and the amount that the applicable ordinance of the MIC (Implementing Regulation for the Telecommunications Business Act, Article 22-2-9) stipulates that the user should pay in connection with the contract (Article 26*ter*, paragraph 3). Where a telecommunication service contract has been cancelled under the provisions of paragraph 1, the telecommunication carrier must promptly return any money, other than the amount prescribed in the applicable ordinance of the MIC (Implementing Regulation for the Telecommunications Business Act, Article 22-2-9) as set forth in the proviso to paragraph 4, Article 26*ter* of the Telecommunications Business Act, that it received in connection with the contract to the user.

*448.* Any provisions that run counter to the provisions of paragraphs 1 through 4 and that are disadvantageous to the user are void and null (Article 26*ter*, paragraph 5).

*449.* Any telecommunications carrier must, properly and promptly, process complaints and inquiries from users with regard to the telecommunications carrier's methods of conducting its business activities pertaining to the telecommunications services as set forth in Items in paragraph 1, Article 26 or with regard to the telecommunications services as set forth in Items in paragraph 1, which are provided by the telecommunications carrier (Article 27).

*450.* A telecommunication carrier or its entrusted parties should not:

(1) deliberately fail to disclose or misrepresent to a user material facts that would affect the decision of the user with respect to the information listed in Items, paragraph 1, Article 26; or
(2) solicit the conclusion of a telecommunications service contract from a person (except for if he/she is a telecommunication carrier) who has manifested the intention not to conclude such contract or not to be solicited unless the applicable ordinance of the MIC (Implementing Regulation for the Telecommunications Business Act, Article 22-2-10) permits as it will not hamper the protection of users' interests (Article 27*bis*).

*451.* Where a telecommunication carrier has entrusted another to carry out intermediation, etc. for concluding a contract for the provision of telecommunications services of a telecommunications carrier and ancillary activities, it must take, in accordance with the provisions in the applicable ordinance of the MIC (Implementing Regulation for the Telecommunications Business Act, Article 22-2-11), measures necessary to ensure the proper and sound performance of the entrusted works by the entrusted parties, including guidance to the entrusted parties (Article 27*ter*).

*452.* In cases where a telecommunications carrier or its entrusted party has violated the provisions of paragraph 1 of Article 26 or Article 26*bis*, or Article 27, Article 27*bis* or Article 27*ter*, the MIC may order the telecommunications carrier or the entrusted party to improve the ways to conduct its activities or take other measures, to the extent necessary for ensuring the interests of users (Article 29, paragraph 2).

*453.* In addition, the MIC has published the *Guidelines relating to the Consumers Protection Rules for the purpose of the Telecommunications Business Act* in 2014 and amended in 2016 in line with the 2015 amendments to the Telecommunications Business Act. The *Guidelines* was further revised in 2018 in response to the amendments to Article 26*ter* of the Implementing Regulation for the Telecommunications Business Act[12] and revised again in 2019 in response to the amendments to the Telecommunications Business Act.

12. Revised version is available in Japanese at http://www.soumu.go.jp/main_content/000575755.pdf.

# Chapter 7. Liability of Online Service Providers

## §1. Non-contractual Liability (Torts)

### I. General

*454.* Article 709 of the Civil Code provides that a person who intentionally or negligently violates another's rights shall be liable for the losses caused by the act. This provision is abstract enough to give sufficient discretion to the courts for interpretation. It is said that four elements of tort can be derived from this provision: fault, unlawfulness, victim's loss and causal relationship between the tortious act and the loss.

### II. Fault

*455.* It is a widely accepted opinion that negligence is a breach of duty rather than a state of mind. In other words, one is considered negligent if one fails to take appropriate measures to prevent the loss that was foreseen or should have been foreseen. A breach of duty to foresee and prevent the loss constitutes negligence. In this respect, the required standard of care is that of the reasonable man, taking into account the profession of the defendant and the knowledge, competence, and experience required for a similar class of people as the defendant. If one has satisfied the standards of the ordinary man in the profession to which one belongs, one is not considered negligent.

### III. Unlawfulness

*456.* Though Article 709 does not explicitly require the unlawfulness of the defendant's act, unlawfulness of an act is the key to tort according to the prevailing view (Judgment, Supreme Tribunal, 28 November 1925, 4 *Minshu* 670). This is because the extent of 'right' in Article 709 is not clear and the remedy should not be limited to cases where a right in a strict sense has been violated. It is said that one should take into consideration the nature of the interests which have been infringed and the mode of the tortious act, in order to decide whether an act was unlawful or not.

### IV. Burden of Proof

*457.* Though the burden of proof of all elements lies with the plaintiff, there are some exceptions. First, in some cases, the fault of the defendant can be presumed in accordance with facts if the plaintiff has proven the existence of some relevant factors. In such a case, the defendant should prove that he was not at fault. Second, Article 248 of the Civil Procedure Code provides that the court may award appropriate damages in a case where loss has occurred, though it is very difficult to prove the amount of the damages due to the nature of the damage. Third, it would seem that the courts sometimes find it easy to accept the existence of a causal link between the defendant's act and the loss. In addition, the Supreme Court has adopted the doctrine of indirect counter-proof (Judgment, Supreme Court, 24 October 1975, 29 *Minshu* 1417). According to this doctrine, the existence of a causal link should be acknowledged if the plaintiff has proven the existence of some indirect facts and the causal link between the defendant's act and the loss can be presumed empirically from these indirect facts unless the defendant is successful in proving that there exist opposing facts.

## V. Scope of Loss to Be Compensated

*458.* The scope of the loss to be compensated has been discussed with respect to the causal link between the tortious act and the loss. The courts have held that Article 416 should apply *mutatis mutandis* to tort (cf. Judgment, Supreme Court, 25 April 1974, 28 *Minshu* 447). Article 416 provides that the obligee is entitled to demand the recovery of loss that would normally arise from non-performance of the obligation (normal loss), while the obligee may claim damages for loss that has arisen from special circumstances that the parties had foreseen or should have foreseen. The courts decide whether a loss was in 'adequate causal relation' with the defendant's act.

## VI. Employer's Liability

*459.* An employer is liable for the loss suffered by a third party caused by the tortious act of a business employee in the course of business unless the employer proves that he has taken reasonable care in selecting the employee and overseeing his work, or that the loss could not have been avoided even with reasonable care (Civil Code, Article 715). This liability is considered vicarious liability.

*460.* With respect to this liability, the courts have held that 'business' is not limited to commercial undertakings and that whether an act was done 'in the course of business' is judged by appearance, not by the employee's intention (Judgment, Supreme Court, 16 July 1957, 11 *Minshu* 1254; Judgment, Supreme Court, 2 November 1967, 21 *Minshu* 2278). This criteria applies not only in cases involving business transactions but also in cases other than those involving business transactions (Judgment, Supreme Court, 4 February 1964, 18 *Minshu* 252).

*461.* In addition, it is the prevailing view that the relationship between an 'employee' and an 'employer' does not have to be onerous.

## §2. CONTRACTUAL LIABILITY

*462.* Under the Civil Code, compensation can be pursued either in contract or in tort.

*463.* Obligors are liable for the failure to perform the obligation in accordance with its purport and meaning (Civil Code, Article 415, paragraph 1). A delivery of defective goods falls within this category. As defective performance is not considered valid performance, the obligee may refuse to accept such performance and demand proper performance within a reasonable period. The obligee is also entitled to claim damages, provided that there is fault on the obligor's side in the defective performance (Judgment, Supreme Tribunal, 22 November 1922, 27 *Minroku* 1978). The obligee is in principle entitled to demand the recovery of the loss that would normally arise from non-performance of the obligation (normal loss) (Civil Code, Article 416, paragraph 1). However, the obligee may claim damages for loss that has arisen from special circumstances which the parties had foreseen or should have foreseen (Civil Code, Article 416, paragraph 2). It has been the common understanding that 'adequate causation' between the defective performance and the loss is a prerequisite for establishing the obligor's liability.

*464.* The differences between liability in contract and in tort are as follows:

(1) the plaintiff has to prove fault on the part of the tortfeasor under Article 709, whereas Article 415 lays the burden of proof with the obligor;
(2) the victim may claim damages within three years after he has recognized that such a tort had taken place or twenty years after a tort had taken place, whereas claims based on Article 415 (effective from 1 April 2020) can be exercised for ten years after it has become possible for the obligee to exercise the right or for five years after the obligee has recognized that the performance had been incomplete, which is shorter (Article 166);[13]
(3) contributory negligence is always taken into consideration with respect to contract law action, whereas it is not always taken into consideration with respect to tort law action;
(4) the scope of the compensable may differ between contract law action and tort law action.

*465.* The courts seem to believe that the victim may choose freely between contract law and tort law.

13. Before 1 Apr. 2020, claims based on Art. 415 can be exercised for ten years after it has become possible for the obligee to exercise the right.

## §3. Liability of Service Providers

### I. Liability in Tort-Civil Code

*466.* Though the person who has transmitted illegal and harmful content is the principal party responsible for the damages suffered by the victim, Internet service providers (ISPs) offer subscribers the means to transmit the contents. This implies that ISPs may sometimes be able to control the transmission of illegal or harmful content.

*467.* However, ISPs have to keep the secret of communication under the Telecommunications Business Act (Law No. 86 of 1984) (Article 104). As a result, in the usual cases, it is impossible – or at least inadequate – for ISPs to be involved with the content of the subscribers. In addition, if ISPs were responsible and liable for illegal or harmful content posted by the subscribers, they could attempt to deter users or violate the subscriber's freedom of speech.

*468.* Of course, there are varying levels of control that can be exercised by ISPs, and the level of ISP liability may vary as well. It has been widely accepted that ISPs are not liable if they have no means to control the content. ISPs are rarely held liable without knowledge of the infringement caused by the content unless they are the providers of the information. In contrast, many have argued that ISPs should be liable when they actually know that the content of the subscribers' sites has been infringing another's right, unless they take reasonable measures to remove the content or block the access to such contents.

*469.* Tokyo District Court (*Niftyserve* (No. 1) case) (Judgment, 26 February 1997, 1610 *Hanrei Jiho* 22) once held that Y1 – the system operator of the '*Gendai Shiso* Forum' – and Y2 – the Nifty, the ISP that had entrusted Y1 as a system operator – were liable for the damages of the plaintiff whose reputation had been injured by statements in the forum, on the grounds that Y1 had the duty to take appropriate measures to stop libel in the forum when Y1 became aware of the fact, but did not take any measures, and Y2 was liable as a de facto employer of Y1 (Civil Code, Article 715). However, the decision was reversed by the Tokyo High Court (Judgment, 5 September 2001, 1786 *Hanrei Jiho* 80) on the grounds that Y1 took the appropriate measures to remove the harmful statements posted by the participants to a reasonable extent and within a reasonable period.

*470.* However, in the *Tokyo Metropolitan University* case (Judgment, 24 September 1999, 1707 *Hanrei Jiho* 139), the Tokyo District Court held that a network operator may be liable in tort only in exceptional cases if he has actual knowledge of a libel and it is obvious to the operator that the manner of such a libel is malicious and that the resulting damages might be serious. In principle, the court does not consider it just to impose the duty on a systems operator of protecting the victim from the damages arising from libel because libel seldom affects the third party's interest, and it might be difficult for the network operator to tell whether a statement qualifies as libel or not.

*471.* The judicial precedents remain split and are largely divided into: (a) those held that an ISP owes a broad duty to delete illegal information immediately once the ISP becomes or should become aware of the dissemination of such illegal information (*Animal hospital* Case (Judgment, Tokyo District Court, 26 June 2002, 1810 *Hanrei Jiho* 78; Judgment, Tokyo High Court, 25 December 2002, 1816 *Hanrei Jiho* 52), *DHC* Case (Judgment, Tokyo District Court, 17 July 2003, 1869 *Hanrei Jiho* 46)) and (b) those held that an ISP owes a duty to delete illegal information under limited circumstances such as that the ISP itself transmitted such information or that the infringement of rights is obvious (*Shogakkan* Case (Judgment, Tokyo District Court, 11 March 2004, 1893 *Hanrei Jiho* 126; Judgment, Tokyo High Court, 3 March 2005, 1893 *Hanrei Jiho* 126)).

*472.* In cases where there is a contractual relationship between the ISP and the sender of the information, what kind of information may be deleted by the ISP depends primarily on the provisions of the contract. In case where an ISP that provides hosting services to the sender of the information based on a membership agreement, for example, deletes certain lawful information at another person's request, the ISP will not bc considered to be performing its contractual obligations to provide hosting services. Thus, the ISP may be liable for damages for the non-performance while disclaimer or limitation of liability clause may apply (the validity of such clauses might be denied under the Consumer Contract Act).

*473.* On the other hand, even in cases where there is no contractual relationship between the ISP and the sender of the information, the ISP might be held liable in tort for deleting information under special circumstances. The sender who posted the information is not, however, entitled to pursue any liability against the operator where the deletion is reasonable and falls within the scope of the message board operator's rights and power. There are no published judicial precedents where the liability of any ISP for deleting the information became an issue of dispute while a judgment held that an ISP is not liable for deleting images which are thought to be obscene or offensive to public order and morals (Judgment, Tokyo High Court, 13 March 2008, unreported, *cert. denied*, Decision, Supreme Court, 9 September 2008, *unreported*).

*474.* As far as the disclosure of sender data is concerned, a legal scheme has been studied for enabling the disclosure of confidential information so that the sender of the infringing data can be identified under clearly defined conditions and in due process. However, a telecommunications business must keep to the confidentiality of telecommunication (Telecommunications Business Act, Article 104), and an ISP has refused to disclose information identifying a subscriber in the *Niftyserve* (No. 2) case (Judgment, Tokyo District Court, 27 August 2001, 1778 *Hanrei Jiho* 90) so as to comply with the provision in the Telecommunications Business Act and to protect the privacy of the subscriber.

## II. TSP's Liability Limitation and Sender Data Disclosure Act

*475.* The Act on the Limitation on the Liability of Specified Telecommunications Service Providers and the Disclosure of Sender Data (Law No. 137 of 2001) limits the liability of a telecommunication service provider (TSP) to the infringed person and the sender of claimed infringing data unless the TSP is a sender. A sender is defined as a person who has recorded any data in the recording medium of the specified telecommunications facilities used by a specified telecommunications service provider, or who has inputted any data into the transmitting facilities of such specified telecommunications facilities in cases where such data will be transmitted to unspecified persons (the public). Thus, a person who edits or modifies the posted original messages, such as a bulletin board operator, is a sender who may be liable.

*476.* Pursuant to paragraph 1, Article 3 of this Act, a TSP will be liable for damages due to neglecting to delete information only where: (i) deleting the information is technically possible and the TSP knew that the dissemination of information would cause infringement of some rights, (ii) deleting the information is technically possible and the TSP not only is aware of the dissemination of the information, but the infringement of rights arising from such dissemination of information should have been reasonably known to the TSP, or (iii) the TSP itself transmitted the information.

*477.* The Supreme Court approved the claim of a victim who suffered defamation via internet bulletin boards and ordered an internet access provider to disclose information of senders, saying that intermediating internet access provider is responsible to disclose sender's information because posting via the internet is usually made through an internet access provider, who often is the only entity that has information regarding posting entity and a victim of defamation could not get relief at all unless he/she could obtain the information of the sender from the intermediating internet access provider (Judgment, 8 April 2010, 64 *Minshu* 676).

*478.* Article 3, paragraph 1 provides that a TSP is liable for damages suffered by the victim resulting from a distribution of data only in cases where it had – or should have had – actual knowledge of the infringement (Judgment, Tokyo District Court, 26 April 2006, *unreported*) as mentioned above. The Supreme Court also rejected a claim of plaintiff who asked to disclose information about the internet bulletin board sender (Judgment, 13 April 2010, 64 *Minshu* 758), saying that the plaintiff failed to prove gross negligence on the defendant who did not respond to the requirement of disclosure by the reason why it was not apparently for the plaintiff to be injured of his personal rights. This implies that in ordinary cases TSPs do not have to monitor the distribution of data by subscribers. Article 3(2) limits a TSP's liability for the damages suffered by the sender of information that is blocked by the TSP. A TSP is not liable for mistakenly deleting lawful information in cases where: (i) the TSP deleted the information to the extent necessary and there is good reason for it to believe that the dissemination of the information would unduly infringe another person's rights or (ii) the TSP deleted the information to the extent necessary, another person claimed that his/her rights were infringed and the TSP, for the purpose of determining whether or not to consent to the deletion of the information, inquired for the opinion of the sender of the information, who did not express objection to deleting the information within seven days of the date of receipt of inquiry (Article 3, paragraph 2). The TSP should, in principle, make inquiries to the sender as to the blocking. Unless the TSP has good reason to believe that another's right has been infringed, the TSP need not block the distribution of data if the sender makes an objection to the blocking within seven days of the inquiry.

*479.* In the same way, the TSP should, in principle, hear the sender's opinion before disclosing the sender data to the claimant (Article 4, paragraph 2), and is not liable for the damages suffered by the claimant as a result of the refusal to disclose unless it has refused in bad faith or with gross negligence, or it is the sender (Article 4, paragraph 4).

*480.* This Act covers cases in which copyright, trademarks[14] or privacy[15] have been infringed on as well as cases of defamation. As the same rules apply to both cases (horizontal approach), the rules are a bit cautious regarding blocking transmission of claimed infringing data so as not to harm the freedom of speech.

## III. Internet Auction Operators

*481.* There are no special regulations on internet auctions and the general rules stipulated in the Civil Code are applied to internet auctions. An auction operator bears no liability, in principle, in any disputes between participants, if the auction operator simply provides the brokering sales system for the buyer and seller and is not directly involved in transaction. Nagoya High Court (judgment, 11 November 2008) http://www.courts.go.jp/hanrei/pdf/20081125135128.pdf (*cert. denied*, 21 October 2009) rejected the claimant's damage claim that the defendant operator of an internet auction site should have his own civil liability in case an auctioneer did not perform his delivery obligation.

*482.* However, the auction operator is substantially involved in transactions between users beyond simple provision of the system (virtual market), he/she may be liable to the extent of his/her further involvement. In addition, where the successful bidders had purchased the stolen items, which were claimed by the original owner and this is attributable to the auction operator because the auction operator did not stop the bidding although he/she had been ordered to suspend the bidding by the police commissioner, etc. (A used goods auction broker provides assistance to a person offering goods, which are reasonably suspected as being stolen property,

14. A request for deletion might be made via a credibility affirming agency for the purpose of the TSP's Liability Limitation and Sender Data Disclosure Act Guidelines relating to Copyrights or the TSP's Liability Limitation and Sender Data Disclosure Act Guidelines relating to Trademarks.
15. The Human Rights Organs of the Ministry of Justice may request an ISP to delete some information in accordance with the TSP's Liability Limitation and Sender Data Disclosure Act Guidelines on Defamation and Privacy Issues (Rules concerning the Investigation of Human Rights Infringement Cases, Art. 14, para. 1, Item 1).

the Superintendent-General of the Tokyo Metropolitan Police Department, the chief of the Prefectural police headquarters, or the chief of a police station may request a used goods auction broker to stop the auction involving the applicable used goods. Antique Dealings Act, Article 21*septies*), he/she may be obligated to indemnify the successful bidders.

*483.* The Antique Dealings Act (Law No. 108 of 1949) defines those who engage in auction brokerage businesses (specifically designated as those who use electronic information processing systems specified by relevant ordinances) of used goods as 'used goods auction brokers' (excluding used goods market operators) and applies certain regulations (Article 2, paragraph 2, subparagraph 3). Internet auctions are subject to the regulations stipulated in the Antique Dealings Act (Implementing Order for the Antique Dealings Act, Article 3).

## §4. Limitation of Liability and Disclaimer

### I. Limitation of Liability

*484.* Based on the freedom of contract, the disclaimer or limitation of liability clause is valid to some extent. However, such provisions are void under the Consumer Contracts Act, and the courts have held that a disclaimer or limitation of liability clause is not valid in some cases because such a clause is contrary to public policy under the circumstances. It is the established view that clauses exempting one party from the liability arising from wilful acts are null and void. According to the majority opinion, a limitation of liability clause for misconduct with gross negligence is also considered to be void (Judgment, Supreme Tribunal, 29 January 1916, 22 *Minroku* 200, E. Hoshino, *Minpo Gairon*, Vol. 3, Tokyo: Ryosho Fukyukai, 1976, 61). The limitation of liability is also usually considered to be null and void with respect to personal injury (Judgment, Osaka District Court, 12 June 1967, 18 *Kaminshu* 641, Judgment, Tokyo District Court, 20 September 1978, 911 *Hanrei Jiho* 14, S. Kurusu, *Keiyakuho*, Tokyo: Yuhikaku, 1974, 130).

*485.* Furthermore, it is possible to limit the period within which the parties may bring an action to the court under the Civil Code. Accordingly, a party may provide that any action, whether in contract or tort, arising from or in connection with this contract, may not be brought forward by either party longer than the period specified in the contract after the cause of action has accrued, except that an action of non-payment may be brought forward within the specified period in the contract after the last payment.

*486.* For example, where the network service provider provides an Internet service, the standard contract stipulates, for example, that if the provider fails to deliver the Internet service which otherwise should have been provided, due to reasons attributable to the provider, the damages suffered are deemed to constitute the total amount of the average fee for such an Internet service corresponding to the number of days for which such an Internet service was not available. The provider is liable only to the extent of such damages, except with respect to any subscriber for whom the delivery of the service is suspended. The number of days is counted for every twenty-four hours with respect to the hours the situation continued (only for the hours which are the multiple(s) of twenty-four hours), i.e., that the Internet service was not entirely available for use (including the case in which significant trouble has occurred in all communication through the use of the telecommunication equipment relating to such a contract, resulting in a situation almost equivalent to the entire unavailability of the relevant service), but only after the provider has become aware of such situation. The method to calculate the average use fee is also provided in the general contract, for example:

(1) where the fee for the relevant Internet service is fixed, the daily fee is calculated based on the fee provided in the attached price list; and
(2) where the fee for the relevant Internet service is not fixed, it shall be calculated by using the average daily fee during the six months preceding the billing month during which the Internet service became completely unavailable to the subscriber (in case it is difficult to identify the actual record of the use during those preceding six months, the amount is calculated by the method separately prescribed by the provider).

*487.* At the same time, a widely used standard contract provides that, in case the Internet service is not entirely available for use due to reasons not attributable to the subscriber (including the case in which significant trouble has occurred in all communication through the use of the telecommunication equipment relating to such a contract, resulting in a situation almost equivalent to the entire unavailability of the relevant service), and further in case such a situation were to continue for twenty-four hours or more after the provider has learned of such situation, the fee corresponding to such a number of days (one day shall be counted for every twenty-four hours) will be refunded to the subscriber, provided that the subscriber notified the provider of the situation, in writing, within seven days. The amount is calculated based on the period (only in the integral multiple of twenty-four hours) during which the service was not made available after the provider had learned of the situation.

*488.* Similar provisions can be found in the standard contracts of common carriers, which stipulate that the liability of the common carrier is not limited if the service was not made available due to the carrier's gross negligence or wilful misconduct.

## II. Disclaimer

*489.* Some disclaimer clauses are generally included in network service contracts. The typical provision is as follows: The provider shall not be liable for any damages suffered by any land, building or other structure belonging to the subscriber during the implementation of any work for the installation, removal, repair or recovery of the equipment or other telecommunications equipment relating to the service, to the extent that such damages were caused by an unavoidable situation or by improper instructions from the subscriber.

*490.* In addition, some contracts also provide that, except when expressly provided in the contract, the provider is not liable for any damages arising in connection with the provision of the service by the provider, unavailability of the service, any delay, loss of any information of the subscriber registered, provided or collected through the service of the provider, or another service of the provider.

## III. The Validity of Disclaimer

*491.* Judging by a lower court decision concerning the liability of the former NTT (Judgment, Tokyo High Court, 12 July 1990, 1355 *Hanrei Jiho* 3 (interpretation of Article 109 of the Public Telecommunication Act)), the limitation of liability clause as mentioned above may be judged as valid in cases where the provider was simply at fault. However, a recent Supreme Court decision concerning the liability of the Post Office (Judgment, Supreme Court, 11 September 2003, 1801 *Hanrei Jiho* 28) held that such limitation clauses might be invalid where the loss arose from the provider's gross negligence (*see also above* paragraph 335).

*492.* Moreover, in many cases, network services contracts are made between a business and a consumer, and the Consumer Contracts Act (Law No. 61 of 2000) applies to such contracts. The Consumer Contracts Act provides that clauses that totally exclude a business from the liability, in contract or in tort, to compensate damages to a consumer arising from that business's non-performance are null and void. Clauses which partially exclude a business from liability, in contract or in tort, to compensate damages to a consumer arising from that business's non-performance are void in cases where such non-performance arose through gross negligence or wilful misconduct on the part of the business or the business's representative or employee (Article 8, paragraph 1).

# Part IV. Intellectual Rights

## Chapter 1. Patent Law

### §1. Patent

#### I. Software-Related Inventions and Patentability

*493.* Computer software has, in principle, been eligible for patent protection under the Patent Act (Law No. 121 of 1959). Such protection is available for both computer programs and software-related inventions. Inventions are defined as the highly advanced creation of technical ideas by which a law of nature is utilized (Patent Act, Article 2, paragraph 1). Patents are granted for inventions that are novel, involve an inventive step and are susceptible to industrial applications (Patent Act, Article 29, paragraphs 1 and 2). A patent may not be granted for an invention which could easily have been made, prior to the filing of the patent application, by a person with ordinary skill in the art to which the invention pertains on the basis of an invention or of inventions publicly known, worked or accessible prior to the filing of the patent application either in Japan or in foreign countries (Patent Act, Article 29, paragraph 2).

#### II. Guideline for Software-Related Inventions

*494.* Examination Guidelines for Computer Software-related Inventions (now Examination Guidelines for Patents and Utility Models, Part VII, Chapter 1) of the Japan Patent Office (JPO) have made it clear to grant patents to software in order to adequately protect the software-related inventions as, in addition to a computer-readable medium such as CD-ROMs, the computer network system has been emerging as a tool for distributing a computer program.

*495.* In the Guideline, a 'computer program' that specifies a multiplicity of functions performed by a computer can be defined as 'an invention of a product'. In this respect, 'software' is defined as a program for information processing on a computer while a 'program' is defined as a set of numbered instructions given to a computer to make it perform a particular information process. 'Information processing' is defined as an arithmetic operation or manipulation of information in order to achieve a particular result depending on the purpose of usage. When information processing by software is concretely realized by using hardware resources, the said software is deemed to be 'a statutory invention' prescribed in the Patent Act. Examples for determining the inventive step of the business method-related inventions have increased. Further, it is clear that the claimed invention has no inventive step when the said invention is an exercise of the ordinary creative activity of a person skilled in the art who has knowledge both of the said business field and computer technology.

*496.* Software-related inventions can be protected as an invention of a process or an invention of a product. When a software-related invention is expressed in a sequence of processes or operations connected in a time series (a procedure), the invention can be defined as an invention of a process (including an invention of a process of manufacturing a product) by specifying such a procedure. However, a software-related invention can be defined as an invention of a product by specifying such functions when the invention is expressed as a combination of multiple functions performed by the invention. Accordingly, a 'computer-readable storage medium having a program recorded thereon' can be defined as an invention of a product. A 'computer-readable storage medium having structured data recorded thereon' can also be defined as an invention of a product as long as processing performed by a computer is specified by the data structure recorded thereon. Furthermore, a 'program' that specifies multiple functions performed by a computer can be defined as an invention of a product.

*497.* The claimed invention should be 'a creation of technical ideas utilizing a law of nature' in order to be qualified as a 'statutory invention' under the Patent Law. The Guideline tries to make clear the primary conditions to determine whether a software-related invention constitutes 'a creation of technical ideas utilizing a law of nature':

(1) Where 'information processing by software is concretely realized by using hardware resources', the said software is deemed to be 'a creation of technical ideas utilizing a law of nature'.
(2) The information processing equipment (machine) and operational method thereof that cooperatively work with the said software satisfying condition (1) above, and the computer-readable storage medium having the said software recorded thereon are also deemed to be 'creations of technical ideas utilizing a law of nature'.

*498.* Accordingly, a claimed invention constitutes 'a creation of technical ideas utilizing a law of nature' where information processing by the software is concretely realized by using hardware resources (e.g., an arithmetic unit such as a Central Processing Unit, a storage device such as memory) in the claimed invention. For a 'statutory invention', the information processing equipment (machine) or the operational method particularly suitable for the purpose should be constructed by some concrete means in which software and hardware resources are a cooperatively working and realizing arithmetic operation or manipulation of information depending on the said purpose of usage.

However, a claimed invention does not constitute 'a creation of technical ideas utilizing a law of nature' when information processing by software is not concretely realized by using hardware resources.

## III. 2002 Amendments to the Patent Act

*499.* In 2002, the Patent Act was amended to explicitly include computer programs, etc., as a patentable 'product' (Patent Act, Article 2, paragraph 3) in order to make it clear that the Patent Act also protects patented software in cases when the software is circulated via the Internet, etc. In this context, (computer) 'programs, etc.' are defined as (computer) programs (a set of numbered instructions given to a computer so as to achieve a particular result) and any information used for data processing by a computer and similar to (computer) programs. The latter includes any data structure (e.g., the structure of data compressed). After the 2002 amendments, 'transfer and lending via a telecommunication line' of a (computer) program, etc., is included in the 'exploitation' of a patented product (Article 2, paragraph 3).

## IV. Non-obviousness

*500.* Judgment on an 'inventive step' should be made by precisely comprehending the state of the art in the technical field to which the invention pertains at the time of filing, and then trying to reason whether a person skilled in the art would have easily arrived at the claimed invention on the basis of the cited prior art.

*501.* Attempts are usually made in the field of software to combine methods or means used in different fields or to apply them in another field in order to achieve an intended object. Consequently, combining technologies used in different fields and applying them to another field is usually considered to be within the exercise of an ordinary creative activity of a person skilled in the art, so that when there is no technical difficulty (technical blocking factor) for such combination or application, the inventive step is not affirmatively inferred unless there exist special circumstances (such as remarkably advantageous technical effects).

*502.* A person skilled in the art of software-related inventions is expected to have common general knowledge both of the applied field of the said software-related inventions and of computer technology (e.g., systematization technology):

(1) to use ordinary technical means for research and development;
(2) to exercise ordinary creative activity in changing design; and
(3) to be able to comprehend all the state of the art in the field of technology to which the invention pertains (state of the art in the applied field of the said software and the computer technology) at the time of filing.

*503.* In addition, a person skilled in the art is deemed to be able to comprehend the entire state of the art in the field of technology relevant to the problem to be solved by the invention. There are cases where it is more appropriate to suppose 'a team composed of experts' from plural technical fields will join the project.

*504.* Examples of exercising ordinary creative activity expected of a person having ordinary skills in art are discussed below.

### A. *Application to Other Fields*

*505.* There are a lot of cases in which the procedure or means for realizing the function used in software-related inventions are common in function or operation, regardless of the applied field to which the invention belongs. In such cases, it is within the ordinary creative activity expected of a person skilled in the art to apply such a procedure or means of software-related inventions used in certain applied fields to other fields to realize the same function or operation.

### B. *Addition of a Commonly Known Means or Replacement by Equivalent*

*506.* It is within the ordinary creative activity expected of a person skilled in the art to add a commonly known means for systematization as a constituent element thereof, or to replace part of the constituent elements of the system with a well-known equivalent thereof.

### C. *Implementation by Software of Functions That Are Otherwise Performed by Hardware*

*507.* It is within the ordinary creative activity expected of a person skilled in the art to try to realize such function by means of software that has been so far performed by hardware, such as circuits.

### D. *Systematization of Human Transactions*

*508.* There is a case where the cited prior art describes human transactions but does not describe how to systematize them. Even in such a situation, it is within the ordinary creative activity expected of a person skilled in the art to systematize existing human transactions in an applied field in order to realize this on a computer, if the said systematization can be realized by a routine activity of usual system analysis method and system design methods.

### *E. Reproduction of a Known Event in Computerized Virtual Space*

*509.* It is within the ordinary creative activity of a person skilled in the art to reproduce a known event in a computerized virtual space, provided that the said reproduction would have been made by a routine work using normal system analysis and system design methods.

### *F. Design Modification on the Basis of Known Facts or Customs*

*510.* When different features between the claimed invention and the cited invention are based on known facts or customs, and as a result of considering other publicly known cited inventions and the common general knowledge (including 'evident facts') the said different feature is of the nature to be decided at the discretion of a person skilled in the art, and there is no blocking factor for combination, the difference is no more than a design modification decided depending on the need of a person skilled in the art, it is, therefore, within the ordinary creative activity expected of a person skilled in the art.

## V. Patent Application

### *A. Applicant*

*511.* The Patent Act establishes a right in a patented invention. An inventor or his successor of a patentable invention may apply for a patent to the Commissioner of the Patent Office (Patent Act, Article 36). When two or more persons have the right to obtain a patent jointly, the patent may only be applied for jointly by all the joint owners (Patent Act, Article 38). An employer, a legal entity, or a state or local public entity (hereinafter referred to as the 'employer, etc.') has a non-exclusive licence on the design right concerned when an employee, an executive officer of a legal entity or a national or local public official (hereinafter referred to as the 'employee, etc.') has obtained a patent for an invention which, by reason of its nature, falls within the scope of the business of the employer, etc., and an act or acts resulting in the invention were part of the present or past duties of the employee, etc., performed on behalf of the employer, etc., (hereinafter referred to as an 'employee's invention') or when a successor in title to the right to obtain a patent for an employee's invention has obtained a patent therefore (Patent Act, Article 35, paragraph 1). However, any contractual provision, working regulation or other stipulation providing in advance that the right to obtain a patent or the design right passes to the employer, etc., or that he has an exclusive licence on such an invention, shall be null and void with respect to an invention made by an employee, etc., which is not an employee's invention (Patent Act, Article 35, paragraph 2).

*B. First-to-File Rule*

*512.* When two or more patent applications relating to the same invention are filed on different dates, only the first applicant may obtain a patent for the invention (Patent Act, Article 39, paragraph 1). When two or more patent applications relating to the same invention are filed on the same date, only one such applicant, agreed upon after mutual consultation among all the applicants, may obtain a patent for the invention. If no agreement is reached or no consultation is possible, none of the applicants should obtain a patent for the invention (Patent Act, Article 39, paragraph 2). These rules are applied to the cases where an invention claimed in a patent application is the same as a device claimed in a utility model application (Patent Act, Article 39, paragraphs 3 and 4). When a patent application or a utility model application is withdrawn or dismissed, such application is deemed never to have been made in this respect (Patent Act, Article 39, paragraph 5).

*C. Patentee's Right*

*513.* A patent right comes into force upon registration of its establishment (Patent Act, Article 66, paragraph 1) and endures for twenty years from the filing date of the patent application (Patent Act, Article 67, paragraph 1). However, the term of the design right may be extended, upon application for registration of an extension, by a period not exceeding five years if, because of the necessity of obtaining an approval or other disposition which is governed by provisions in laws intended to ensure safety, etc., in the working of the patented invention, and which is provided for in a Cabinet Order as being such that, in view of the object of the relevant disposition, proceedings, etc., a considerable period of time is required for the proper action for the disposition, it was not possible to work the patented invention for two years or more (Patent Act, Article 67, paragraph 2).

*514.* A patentee has an exclusive right to commercially work the patented invention. However, where the patentee has granted an exclusive licence to another, the patentee does not have the exclusive right to the extent to which the exclusive licensee exclusively possesses the right to work the patented invention (Patent Act, Article 68).

*D. Effect of Registration*

*515.* The following matters do not prevail against a third party unless they are registered:

(1) transfers (except those by inheritance or other general succession), extinguishments by surrender or restrictions on disposal of a patent;

(2) grant, transfer (except those by inheritance or other general succession), modification or extinguishments (except those resulting from a merger or the extinguishments of the patent) of an exclusive licence, or a restriction on the disposal thereof;
(3) grant, transfer (except those by inheritance or other general succession), modification or extinguishments (except those resulting from a merger or the extinguishments of a secured credit) of a pledge on a patent or exclusive licence, or a restriction on the disposal thereof;
(4) transfer, modification, extinguishments of a non-exclusive licence, or a restriction on the disposal thereof, or the grant, transfer (except those by inheritance or other general succession), modification or extinguishments (except those resulting from a merger or the extinguishments of a secured credit) of a pledge on a non-exclusive licence, or a restriction on the disposal thereof (Patent Act, Article 98, paragraph 1, Article 99, paragraph 3).

*516.* Once a non-exclusive licence has been registered, it has effect with respect to anyone who subsequently acquires the patent, the exclusive licence or exclusive licence on such patent (Patent Act, Article 99, paragraph 1).

## *E. Permitted Exploitation*

*517.* The effects of the patent right do not extend to the working of the patent right for the purposes of experiment or research (Patent Act, Article 69, paragraph 1).

*518.* When, at the time of filing a patent application, a person who has made an invention by himself without knowledge of the contents of an invention claimed in the patent application or has learned the invention from a person just referred to, has been commercially working the invention in Japan or has been making preparations, therefore, such a person has a non-exclusive licence on the patent right under the patent application. Such a licence is limited to the invention which is being worked or for which preparations for working are being made and to the purpose of such working or the preparations therefore (Patent Act, Article 79).

## *F. Joint Ownership*

*519.* Each of the joint owners of a patent may neither transfer their share nor establish a pledge upon it without the consent of all the other joint owners (Patent Act, Article 73, paragraph 1). Each of the joint owners may, except as otherwise prescribed by contract, exploit the patent without the consent of the other joint owners, though each of the joint owners may grant neither an exclusive licence nor a non-exclusive licence without the consent of all the other joint owners (Patent Act, Article 73, paragraphs 2 and 3).

### G. Exclusive Licence

*520.* The patentee may grant an exclusive licence on his patent. An exclusive licensee has the exclusive right to commercially work the patent to the extent laid down in the licence contract. An exclusive licence may be transferred only together with the business in which it is exploited, or only with the consent of the patentee or in the case of inheritance or other general succession. An exclusive licensee may establish a pledge or grant a non-exclusive licence on the exclusive licence only with the consent of the rightholder. The provisions regarding joint rightholders (Article 73) apply *mutatis mutandis* to exclusive licences (Patent Act, Article 77).

### H. Non-exclusive Licence

*521.* The patentee may grant a non-exclusive licence on his patent. A non-exclusive licensee has the right to commercially work the patent to the extent prescribed as laid down by the licence contract (Patent Act, Article 78).

### I. Pledge on a Patent

*522.* Where a patent or an exclusive or non-exclusive licence is the subject of a pledge, the pledgee may not work the patent unless otherwise prescribed by contract (Patent Act, Article 95). A pledge on a patent or an exclusive or non-exclusive licence may be exercised against the remuneration received as consideration for the patent or the licence or against money or goods that the rightholder or exclusive licensee would be entitled to receive for the work of the patent. However, an attachment order should be obtained prior to the payment or delivery of the money or property (Patent Act, Article 96).

### J. Infringement

*523.* A patentee or exclusive licensee may require a person who is infringing or is likely to infringe the patent or exclusive licence to discontinue or refrain from such infringement (Patent Act, Article 100, paragraph 1). A patentee or an exclusive licensee who is acting under the preceding subsection may demand the destruction of the articles by which the act of infringement was committed, the disposal of the articles used for the act of infringement, or other measures necessary to prevent the infringement (Patent Act, Article 100, paragraph 2).

*524.* With respect to an invention of a product, commercially manufacturing, assigning, renting, leasing, exhibiting for assignment or leasing, or importing articles exclusively used for manufacturing the patented product are deemed to be infringements of a patent or an exclusive licence (Patent Act, Article 100, No. 1). With respect to an invention of a process, commercially manufacturing, assigning, renting, leasing, exhibiting for assignment or leasing, or importing articles exclusively used for working of such an invention are deemed to be infringements of a patent or an exclusive licence (Patent Act, Article 100, Item 2).

*525.* The Patent Act provides that the plaintiff may seek monetary damages. The amount of the damage can be calculated as follows: the quantity of the articles assigned by the infringing person multiplied by the profits per unit gained from the articles that the patentee or exclusive licensee would have sold if there had not been any infringement as far as they could have worked the utility model right. However, were there to be any circumstances under which the patentee or exclusive licensee could not have sold as much as the infringer had sold, the amount of damages should be decreased accordingly (Patent Act, Article 102, paragraph 1). Where a patentee or exclusive licensee claims, from a person who has intentionally or negligently infringed the patent or exclusive licence, compensation for damage caused to him by the infringement, the profits gained by the infringer through the infringement are presumed to be the amount of damage suffered by the patentee or exclusive licensee (Patent Act, Article 102, paragraph 2). A patentee or exclusive licensee may claim, from a person who has intentionally or negligently infringed the patent or exclusive licence, an amount of money which he would normally be entitled to receive for the working of the patent, as the amount of damage suffered (Patent Act, Article 102, paragraph 3).

*526.* Those provisions do not, however, preclude a claim for damages exceeding the amount referred to therein. In such a case, where there has been neither wilfulness nor gross negligence on the part of the person who has infringed the patent or the exclusive licence, the court may take this into consideration when awarding damages (Patent Act, Article 102, paragraph 4).

*527.* In litigation relating to the infringement of a patent right or exclusive licence, the court may, upon the request of one party, order another party to produce documents necessary for the assessment of the damage caused by the infringement. However, this provision does not apply when the person possessing the documents has a legitimate reason for refusing to produce them (Patent Act, Article 105).

*528.* A person who has infringed a patent right or exclusive licence of another person is presumed to have been negligent as far as the act of infringement is concerned (Patent Act, Article 103). In the case of a patent for an invention of a process of manufacturing a product, where such product was not publicly known in Japan prior to the filing of the patent application concerned, any identical product is presumed to have been manufactured by that process (Patent Act, Article 104).

*529.* Article 101 of the Patent Act provides for the acts deemed as infringing.

*K. Penal Provision*

*530.* Any person who infringes a patent or an exclusive licence may be punished with imprisonment with labour for no longer than ten years and/or a fine not exceeding JPY 10 million (Patent Act, Article 196).

## §2. Utility Model

### I. Utility Model and Invention

*531.* Software or other articles with regard to the ICT sector may be protected under the Utility Model Act (Law No. 123 of 1959), which protects petit inventions or devices regarding the shape, structure or combination of articles (Utility Model Act, Article 1). 'Invention' in this Act can be defined as a creation of technical ideas by utilizing a law of nature. Different from the requirement for patentable invention, the ideas are not required, in relation to the utility model, to be highly advanced, though novelty, industrial applicability and non-obviousness are required (Utility Model Act, Article 3). Inventions regarding the use or methods are not covered, however. In other words, Japan has adopted a two-tier protection system for inventions.

*532.* An inventor may register such an industrially applicable invention as a utility model (*jitsuyo shin'an*) (Utility Model Act, Article 3). Application for registration should be filed with the Patent Office (Utility Model Act, Article 49). Many of the provisions in the Patent Act apply *mutatis mutandis* to utility models (Utility Model Act, Articles 2–5 and 11, Article 18(3), Article 19(3), Articles 26, 30 and 55, etc.).

*533.* There are, however, some significant differences between patents and utility models, other than the difference in the level of invention:

(1) a utility model is registered without examination;
(2) a utility model right endures six years from the day of application (Article 15);
(3) the rightholder or an exclusive licensee may exercise his right against an infringer after giving a warning, presenting the technological evaluation statement on the utility model (Utility Model Act, Article 29*bis*). This is because there is no examination procedure for utility model registration. Anyone may apply for a technological evaluation of a utility model (Utility Model Act, Article 12, paragraph 1). Such an evaluation is carried out by an examiner of the Patent Office (Utility Model Act, Article 12, paragraph 2). The process of technological evaluation is similar to that of examination for patents; and
(4) when the rightholder or an exclusive licensee has exercised his right or given a warning against an infringer and a trial decision that the utility model registration is to be invalidated has subsequently become final and conclusive,

he is liable for the damages suffered by the infringer arising from his exercise or warning unless he has exercised his right or given a warning based on the technological evaluation statement or with due care (Utility Model Act, Article 29*ter*).

## II. Utility Model Right

*534.* A rightholder has an exclusive right to commercially work the registered invention. However, when the utility model right is the subject of an exclusive licence, this provision does not apply to the extent that the exclusive licensee exclusively possesses the right to work the registered invention (Utility Model Act, Article 16). However, if a registered utility model were to utilize another person's patented invention, registered utility model or registered design or design similar thereto under an application filed prior to the filing date of the application concerned for utility model registration, or if the utility model right conflicts with another person's design right or trademark right in an application for registration of a design filed prior to the filing date of the application concerned for utility model registration, the rightholder, exclusive licensee or non-exclusive licensee may not commercially work the registered utility model (Utility Model Act, Article 17).

## III. Exclusive Licences

*535.* A rightholder may grant an exclusive licence on his utility model right. An exclusive licensee has an exclusive right to commercially work the registered invention to the extent laid down in the licence contract. An exclusive licence may be transferred only together with the business in which it is worked, or only with the consent of the rightholder or in the case of inheritance or other general succession (Utility Model Act, Article 18).

## IV. Non-exclusive Licences

*536.* A rightholder may grant a non-exclusive licence on his utility model right. A non-exclusive licensee has the right to commercially work the patented invention to the extent prescribed in this Law or laid down by the licence contract (Utility Model Act, Article 19).

## V. Infringement

### *A. Injunction*

*537.* A rightholder or an exclusive licensee may require a person who is infringing or is likely to infringe the utility model right or the exclusive licence to discontinue or refrain from such infringement. A rightholder or an exclusive licensee may demand the destruction of the articles by which the act of infringement was committed (including the articles manufactured by the act of infringement in the case of a patented invention of a process of manufacture), the removal of the facilities used for the act of infringement, or other measures necessary to prevent the infringement (Utility Model Act, Article 27). However, he may make such a request against an infringer only after giving a warning, presenting the technological evaluation statement on the utility model (Utility Model Act, Article 29*bis*).

*B. Acts Deemed as Infringing*

*538.* Commercial manufacturing, assigning, leasing, importing, or offering for assignment or leasing of articles to be used exclusively for the manufacture of the articles related to the utility are deemed to be an infringement of a utility model right or exclusive licence (Utility Model Act, Article 28).

*C. Calculation of Damages*

*539.* When an infringer has assigned the infringed articles and a rightholder or exclusive licensee claims, from a person who has intentionally or negligently infringed the utility model right or exclusive licence, compensation for damage caused to him by the infringement, the amount of the damage can be calculated as follows: the quantity of the articles assigned by the infringer multiplied by the profits per unit gained from the articles that the rightholder or exclusive licensee would have sold if there had not been any infringement as far as they could have worked the utility model right. However, if there have been any circumstances under which the rightholder or exclusive licensee could not have sold as much as the infringer had sold, the amount of damages should be decreased accordingly (Utility Model Act, Article 29, paragraph 1).

*D. Presumption of Damages*

*540.* In addition, the profits gained by the infringer through the infringement are presumed to be the amount of damage suffered by the patentee or exclusive licensee (Article 29, paragraph 2). A rightholder or exclusive licensee may claim, from a person who has intentionally or negligently infringed the utility model right or exclusive licence, an amount of money that he would normally be entitled to receive for the working of the registered invention, as the amount of damage suffered by him (Article 29, paragraph 3). These provisions, however, do not preclude a claim for damages exceeding the amount referred to therein. In such a case, where there has been neither wilfulness nor gross negligence on the part of the person who has infringed the utility model right or the exclusive licence, the court may take this into consideration when awarding damages (Article 29, paragraph 4).

## Chapter 2. Trademarks and Trade Names

*541.* The Trademark Act protects registered trademarks to maintain the business reputation and standing of those who rely on such trademarks. Trademarks to be protected under the Trademark Act should be registered with the Patent Office (Trademark Act, Article 3, paragraph 1). The term 'trademark' is defined as distinctive written characters, signs, three-dimensional shapes, or a combination of these, which a person uses with a certain class or type of goods (Trademark Act, Article 2, paragraph 1). Service marks can be registered under the Trademark Act (Trademark Act, Article 3). In this respect, a service mark is defined as any type of design or mark used by a service company as its corporate or business symbol, though trade names are not protected under the Trademark Act but under the Commercial Code. A designation of the specific goods with which the trademark will be used as well as the classification of such goods should be included in the registration application, referring to the classification system developed by the METI (Trademark Act, Article 5).

*542.* Where two or more applications relating to the same trademark or service mark are filed on different dates, only the first applicant may obtain a registration for the design (Trademark Act, Article 8, paragraph 1). Where two or more applications relating to the same trademark or service mark are filed on the same date, only one such applicant, agreed upon after mutual consultation among all the applicants, may obtain a registration for the mark. If no agreement is reached or no consultation is possible, none of the applicants may obtain a registration for the mark (Trademark Act, Article 8, paragraph 2).

*543.* Registration of a trademark is valid for a period of ten years from the date of registration, and is renewable (Trademark Act, Article 19). Though the trademark owner has no duty to use the mark, any person may file a request for a hearing regarding the cancellation of the mark if the owner or the exclusive licensee of the mark fails to use the mark for a period of three years or more (Trademark Act, Article 50).

*544.* The owner of a registered trademark or service mark has the exclusive right to use the mark with respect to the designated goods or designated services (Trademark Act, Article 25). However, the use of a domain name similar to any registered trademark or service mark is seldom deemed as the use of the registered mark under the Trademark Act, because the domain name is seldom used with respect to goods or services. Under the Trademark Act, the term 'use' is defined as:

(1) applying the mark on the goods or their packaging;
(2) assigning, delivering, displaying for the purpose of assignment or delivery, or importing, the goods on which or on the packaging of which a mark has been applied;
(3) applying a mark to articles for use by persons to whom the services are provided (including articles assigned or leased, hereinafter the same) when providing services;

(4) providing services by use of articles to which a mark has been applied for use by persons to whom the services are provided when providing services;
(5) displaying, for the purpose of providing services, articles to which a mark has been applied and supplied for use in the provision of services (including articles for use by persons to whom the services are provided when providing services, hereinafter the same);
(6) applying a mark to articles related to the provision of such services belonging to persons to whom the services are provided when providing services; and
(7) displaying or distributing advertisements relating to goods or services, price lists or business papers with respect to the goods or articles on which a mark has been applied (Trademark Act, Article 2, paragraph 3).

*545.* On the other hand, trade names are protected under the Commercial Code, the Companies Act and the Unfair Competition Prevention Act. Merchants, including companies, may, in principle, freely choose their trade name (Commercial Code, Article 11; Companies Act, Article 6). There are, however, some restrictions. First, names identical to the names of other merchants whose principal office is located in the same address, cannot be registered (Commercial Registration Act, Article 27). It should be noted that companies should register their trade name, while unincorporated merchants are not required to register their trade names, although they may register.

*546.* Second, a company should include the word 'company' and the type of the company in its trade name (Companies Act, Article 6, paragraph 2), while non-company entities are prohibited from using any word that suggests the entity is a company in their trade name (Companies Act, Article 6, paragraph 3).

*547.* Third, using a trade name for an improper purpose that is likely to induce persons to believe that the business is that of another person is prohibited (Commercial Code, Article 21, paragraph 1; Companies Act, Article 8). The merchant may demand such a person to stop such a use.

*548.* Finally, if a trade name is well known among consumers or buyers, the trademark will also be protected under the Unfair Competition Prevention Act irrespective of whether it is registered or not. Any person whose interests are likely to be harmed by the use of a name (including the trade name) identical or similar to the well-known name (including the trade name) may demand discontinuance of such a use. There is no purpose requirement for this protection.

*549.* With respect to trade name protection, it is widely accepted that the term 'use of other's trade name' covers the use of a trade name similar to another's. Accordingly, the use of a domain name identical or similar to a trade name may fall within the use of the trade name.

# Chapter 3. Design Protection

## §1. Scope of Protection

*550.* The Design Act (Law No. 125 of 1959) protects a registered 'design' (*isho*). A 'design' is defined as any shape, pattern or colour, or a combination of these in an article, which produces an aesthetic impression on the sense of sight (Design Act, Article 2).

The design to be registered and protected under this Act covers any design that is novel and has an industrial application. Accordingly, the Act does not protect any design that:

(1) was publicly known in Japan or elsewhere prior to the application for the design being filed in Japan;
(2) was described in an application distributed in or outside of Japan prior to the application for the design being filed in Japan;
(3) is similar to any design that would not be protected for the reasons stipulated in (1) and (2) above (Design Act, Article 3, paragraph 1).

*551.* Where a design could easily have been created, prior to the filing of the design application, by a person with ordinary skill in the art to which the design pertains, on the basis of a shape, pattern or colour or any combination of these widely known in Japan, a design registration is not effected for such a design (Design Act, Article 3, paragraph 2).

*552.* Equally, any design that contravenes public order or good morals cannot be registered. Registration may not be effected when a design is similar to articles used in an unrelated person's business and may create confusion (Design Act, Article 5).

## §2. Registration Application

*553.* The registration applications should be submitted to the Commissioner of the Patent Office (Design Act, Article 6). The application should include a specified application form and a drawing of the design. When an ordinance of the METI so prescribes, a photograph, model or sample of the design for which registration is sought may be submitted instead of the drawing. It must describe the scope of the rights that the applicant claims clearly and indicate the article(s) in connection with which the design will be applied, referring to the classification system developed by the METI (Design Act, Article 7).

*554.* Where two or more applications relating to the same design are filed on different dates, only the first applicant may obtain a registration for the design (Design Act, Article 9, paragraph 1). Where two or more applications relating to the same design are filed on the same date, only one such applicant, agreed upon after mutual consultation among all the applicants, may obtain a registration for the design. If no agreement is reached or no consultation is possible, none of the applicants obtains a registration for the design (Design Act, Article 9, paragraph 2).

*555.* An applicant for a patent may convert his application to a design registration application within thirty days from the transmittal of the examiner's first decision that the patent application is to be refused. Equally, an applicant for a utility model registration may convert his application into a design application (Design Act, Article 13).

## §3. Secret Designs

*556.* An applicant for a design registration may demand that the design be kept secret for a period which is designated in the demand and does not exceed three years from the date on which the establishment of the design right was registered (Design Act, Article 14).

## §4. Employees' Design

*557.* The provisions in the Patent Act concerning employee's invention apply *mutatis mutandis* to the creation of a design by an employee, an executive officer of a legal entity or a national or local public entity (Design Act, Article 15, paragraph 3). An employer, a legal entity or a national or local public entity (hereinafter referred to as the 'employer, etc.') has a non-exclusive licence on the design right concerned, when an employee, an executive officer of a legal entity or a national or local public official (hereinafter referred to as the 'employee, etc.') has registered a design which by reason of its nature falls within the scope of the business of the employer, etc., and an act or acts resulting in the design were part of the present or past duties of the employee, etc., performed on behalf of the employer, etc. (hereinafter referred to as an 'employee's design'), or where a successor in title to the right to register an employee's design has registered the design. However, any contractual provision, working regulation or other stipulation providing in advance that the right to register or the design right passes to the employer, etc., or that he has an exclusive licence on such design shall be null and void with respect to a design made by an employee, etc., which is not an employee's design.

## §5. Design Right

*558.* A design right comes into force upon registration of its establishment (Design Act, Article 20, paragraph 1) and endures for fifteen years from the date of the registration of its establishment (Design Act, Article 21). The owner of a design right has an exclusive right to commercially work the registered design and designs similar thereto. However, where the design right is the subject of an exclusive licence, this provision does not apply to the extent that the exclusive licensee has an exclusive right to work with the registered design and designs similar thereto

(Design Act, Article 23). The scope of a registered design should be decided on the basis of the statement in the request and the design represented in the drawing attached to the request or shown in the photograph, model or sample attached to the request (Design Act, Article 24).

The Commissioner of the Patent Office should have applications for design registration examined by an examiner (Design Act, Article 16).

## §6. Permitted Exploitation

*559.* The effects of the design right do not extend to the working of the design right for the purposes of experiment or research (Design Act, Article 36; Patent Act, Article 69, paragraph 1).

*560.* When, at the time of filing of a design application, a person who has created a design or a design similar thereto by himself without knowledge of the contents of a design in a design application or has learned of the design from a person just referred to, has been commercially working the design or a design similar thereto in Japan or has been making preparations, therefore, such a person has a non-exclusive licence on the design right under the design application. Such a licence is limited to the design which is being worked or for which preparations for working are being made and to the purpose of such working or the preparations therefore (Design Act, Article 29).

## §7. Joint Ownership

*561.* Each of the joint owners of a design right may neither transfer his share nor establish a pledge upon it without the consent of all the other joint owners (Design Act, Article 36; Patent Act, Article 73, paragraph 1). Each of the joint owners may, except as otherwise prescribed by contract, exploit the design without the consent of the other joint owners, though each of the joint owners may grant neither an exclusive licence nor a non-exclusive licence without the consent of all the other joint owners (Design Act, Article 36; Patent Act, Article 73, paragraphs 2 and 3).

## §8. Exclusive Licence

*562.* The owner of a design right may grant an exclusive licence on his design (Design Act, Article 27). An exclusive licensee has an exclusive right to commercially work the registered design and designs similar thereto to the extent laid down in the licence contract. An exclusive licence may be transferred only together with the business in which it is exploited, or only with the consent of the owner of a design right or in the case of inheritance or other general succession. An exclusive licensee may establish a pledge or grant a non-exclusive licence on the exclusive licence only with the consent of the rightholder. The provisions regarding joint rightholders (Patent Act, Article 73) apply *mutatis mutandis* to exclusive licences (Design Act, Article 27, paragraph 3).

## §9. Non-exclusive Licence

*563.* The owner of a design right may grant a non-exclusive licence on his design. A non-exclusive licensee has the right to commercially work the registered design and designs similar thereto to the extent prescribed in laid down by the licence contract (Design Act, Article 28).

## §10. Pledge on a Design

*564.* Where a design right or an exclusive or non-exclusive licence is the subject of a pledge, the pledgee may not work the registered design or designs similar thereto unless otherwise prescribed by contract (Design Act, Article 35, paragraph 1). A pledge on a design right or an exclusive or non-exclusive licence may be exercised against the remuneration received as consideration for the design or the licence or against money or goods that the rightholder or exclusive licensee would be entitled to receive for the work of the design. However, an attachment order should be obtained prior to the payment or delivery of the money or property (Design Act, Article 35, paragraph 2; Patent Act, Article 96).

## §11. Effect of Registration

*565.* The following matters do not prevail against third parties unless they are registered:

(1) transfers (except those by inheritance or other general succession), extinguishments by surrender or restrictions on disposal of a design right;
(2) grant, transfer (except those by inheritance or other general succession), modification or extinguishments (except those resulting from a merger or the extinguishments of the design right) of an exclusive licence, or a restriction on the disposal thereof;
(3) grant, transfer (except those by inheritance or other general succession), modification or extinguishments (except those resulting from a merger or the extinguishments of a secured credit) of a pledge on a design right or exclusive licence, or a restriction on the disposal thereof;
(4) transfer, modification, extinguishments of a non-exclusive licence, or a restriction on the disposal thereof, or the grant, transfer (except those by inheritance or other general succession), modification or extinguishments (except those resulting from a merger or the extinguishments of a secured

credit) of a pledge on a non-exclusive licence, or a restriction on the disposal thereof (Design Act, Article 27, paragraph 3, Article 28, paragraph 3, Article 35, paragraphs 3 and 4, Article 36; Patent Act, Article 98, paragraph 1, Article 99, paragraph 3).

*566.* Once a non-exclusive licence has been registered, it has effect with respect to anyone who subsequently acquires the design right, the exclusive licence or exclusive licence on such design right (Design Act, Article 28, paragraph 3; Patent Act, Article 99, paragraph 1).

## §12. Infringement

*567.* The owner of a design right or an exclusive licensee may require a person who is infringing or is likely to infringe the patent or exclusive licence to discontinue or refrain from such infringement (Design Act, Article 37, paragraph 1). The owner of a design right or an exclusive licensee may demand the destruction of the articles by which the act of infringement was committed, the removal of the facilities used for the act of infringement, or other measures necessary to prevent the infringement (Design Act, Article 37, paragraph 2).

*568.* Commercially manufacturing, assigning, leasing, exhibiting for assignment or leasing or importing articles exclusively used for manufacturing the article to which the registered design or a design similar thereto are deemed to be infringements of a design or an exclusive licence (Design Act, Article 38).

*569.* The Design Act provides that the plaintiff may seek monetary damages. When the owner of a design right or exclusive licensee claims, against a person who has intentionally or negligently infringed the design right or exclusive licence, compensation for damage caused to him by the infringement, the profits gained by the infringer through the infringement are presumed to be the amount of damage suffered by the owner of a design right or the exclusive licensee (Design Act, Article 39, paragraph 1). The owner of a design right or the exclusive licensee may claim, from a person who has intentionally or negligently infringed the design right or exclusive licence, an amount of money which he would normally be entitled to receive for the working of the design, as the amount of damage suffered (Design Act, Article 39, paragraph 2).

*570.* Those provisions do not, however, preclude a claim for damages exceeding the amount referred to therein. In such a case, where there has been neither wilfulness nor gross negligence on the part of the person who has infringed the design or the exclusive licence, the court may take this into consideration when awarding damages (Design Act, Article 39, paragraph 3).

*571.* A person who has infringed a design right or the exclusive licence of another person is presumed to have been negligent as far as the act of infringement is concerned (Design Act, Article 40).

*572.* In a litigation relating to the infringement of a design right or exclusive licence, the court may, upon the request of a party, order the other party to produce documents necessary for the assessment of the damage caused by the infringement. However, this provision does not apply when the person possessing the documents has a legitimate reason for refusing to produce them (Design Act, Article 41; Patent Act, Article 105).

## §13. Penal Provision

*573.* Any person who infringes a design right or an exclusive licence may be punished with imprisonment with labour for no longer than three years or a fine not exceeding JPY 3 million (Design Act, Article 69).

# Chapter 4. Copyright Protection in the Digital Context

## §1. 'Work', 'Program' and 'Database'

*574.* The Copyright Act provides for the rights of authors and the rights neighbouring thereon with respect to works as well as performances, phonograms, broadcasts, and wire diffusions (Article 1). In the Act, 'work' is defined as a production in which thoughts or sentiments are expressed in a creative way and which falls within the literary, scientific, artistic, or musical domain (Article 2, paragraph 1, No. 1) and 'program works' (Article 10, paragraph 1, No. 9) and 'databases' (Article 12*bis*, paragraph 1) are included in 'works'.

*575.* In application of the Copyright Act, 'program' is defined as an expression of combined instructions given to a computer so as to make it function and obtain a certain result (Article 2, paragraph 1, No. 10*bis*), and 'databases' is defined as an aggregate of information such as articles, numerical values or diagrams, which is systematically constructed so that such information can be searched for with the aid of a computer (Article 2, paragraph 1, No. 10*ter*).

## §2. Author's Right

*576.* The author of a work is given the exclusive right to do or authorize certain specified restricted acts in relation to the work. The restricted acts are:

(1) to offer to and to make available to the public his work which has not yet been made public (including a work which has been made public without his consent) (Article 18);
(2) to determine whether his true name or pseudonym should be indicated or not, as the name of the author, on the original of his work or when his work is offered to or made available to the public (Article 19);
(3) to preserve the integrity of his work and its title from any distortion, mutilation or other modifications against his will (Article 20);
(4) to reproduce his work (Article 21);
(5) to perform his work for the purpose of making a work seen or heard directly by the public (Article 22);
(6) to present his work publicly (Article 22*bis*);
(7) to make the public transmission of his work (including the making transmittable of his work in the case of the interactive transmission) and to communicate publicly, by means of a receiving apparatus, his work of which the public transmission has been made (Article 23);
(8) to recite publicly his work (in case of an author of a literary work) (Article 24);
(9) to exhibit publicly the original of his work (in case of an author of an artistic work or an unpublished photographic work) (Article 25);
(10) to distribute copies of his work (in case of an author of a cinematographic work or a work reproduced in a cinematographic work) (Article 26);

(11) to offer his work (except for a cinematographic work) to the public by transfer of ownership of the original or copies of the work (excluding copies of a cinematographic work in case of a work reproduced in the cinematographic work) (Article 26*bis*);
(12) to offer his work (except for a cinematographic work) to the public by lending copies of the work (excluding copies of a cinematographic work in the case of a work reproduced in the cinematographic work) (Article 26*ter*); and
(13) to translate, arrange musically or transform, or dramatize, cinematize, or otherwise adapt his work (Article 27).

## §3. Derivative Work

*577.* In addition, the author of the pre-existing work has the same rights as the author of the derivative work in the exploitation of a derivative work (Article 28). The author has the same right as provided for in Articles 18 and 19 with respect to works derived from his work which has not yet been made public (Articles 18 and 19).

## §4. Limitation on Right of Reproduction

*578.* The Copyright Act provides for limitations on the right of reproduction. Apart from reproduction for personal use (Article 30), several cases for limitation are listed. Among them, the examples of limitations that are significant in the context of ICT are as follows:

(1) Reproduction and adaptation by the owner of a copy of a computer program (Article 47*ter*).
(2) Ancillary use of copyrighted work on computers (Article 47*quater*).
(3) Insignificant use of copyrighted work in regard to information processing on computers and the provision of the outcome thereof (Article 47*quinquies*).
(4) Use of copyrighted work where its use is not perceivable (Article 30*quater*).
(5) Creation of thumbnail to upload on the Internet in case of transfer of artistic works (Article 47*bis*).
(6) Transfer of copies made pursuant to limitations on the right of reproduction (Article 47*nonies*).[16]

16. For example, unification of file formats of contents posted by users of bulletin boards, video-sharing websites and social networking services and the reproduction of contents necessary for organizing data are permitted.

§5. Duration of Copyright

*579.* While copyright in a cinematographic work continues to subsist until the end of a period of seventy years following the making public of the work or the creation of the work if it has not been made public within a period of seventy years following its creation Article 54), copyright comes into being upon the creation of the work and in principle continues to exist until the end of a period of fifty years following the death of the author (or following the death of the last surviving co-author in the case of a joint work) (Article 51). However, copyright protection in anonymous and pseudonymous works continues until the end of a period of seventy years[17] after the publication of the work, provided that copyright in such work, the author of which is presumed to have been dead for fifty years, is considered expired as of the time when the author is so presumed to have been dead, unless the pseudonym adopted by the author is generally known to be his own, or the author has registered his true name or has made public his work in which he indicates his true name or generally known pseudonym as the name of the author (Article 52).

*580.* Copyrights in works created or published in the name of a legal person or other corporate body continue until the end of a period of fifty years after the publication of the works or else the creation of the works if they have not been made public within a period of fifty years following their creation (Article 53, paragraph 1). However, where a person who is the author of a work created or published a work in the name of a legal person or other corporate body, and has afterwards made public the work in which he indicates his true name or generally known pseudonym as the name of the author, the provision of Article 51 applies (Article 53, paragraph 2).

*581.* With respect to the copyright in works of which the authorship is attributed to a legal person or other corporate body in accordance with the provision of Article 15 paragraph 2, the provision of paragraph 1 applies to such works, even if not falling within those mentioned in paragraph 1, as if such works were created or published in the name of such a corporate body as the author (Article 53, paragraph 3).

§6. Infringement and Injunction

*582.* The authors as well as the owners of the copyright, the right of publication or tangential rights may make a demand for cessation or prevention of such infringements or against those who infringe or are likely to infringe these rights or moral rights (Article 112, paragraph 1). They may take measures necessary to effect such cessation or prevention of infringement, such as the abandonment of objects

17. In order to adjust relevant laws to the conclusion of the Trans-Pacific Partnership Agreement, the Copyright Act was amended to extend the life of copyright in general to seventy years. Copyright in a cinematographic work continues to subsist until the end of a period of seventy years following the making public of the work or the creation of the work if it has not been made public within a period of seventy years following its creation (Art. 54).

the making of which constituted an infringement, objects made by an infringement or implements and tools used solely for an infringement in making such demand (Article 112, paragraph 2).

*583.* According to paragraph 1 of Article 113, the following acts are considered to constitute infringements on moral rights, copyright, right of publication or neighbouring rights:

(1) importation into Japan, for distribution, of objects made by an act which would constitute an infringement on moral rights, copyright, right of publication or tangential rights if they were made in this country at the time of such importation;
(2) distribution or the possession for distribution, or the making of an offer of distribution, or the exportation by trade or the possession for exportation by trade, of objects made by an act infringing moral rights, copyright, right of publication or neighbouring rights (including those imported as mentioned in the preceding item), by a person who is aware of such infringement.

## §7. Acts Deemed as Infringing

*584.* In addition, the following acts are considered to constitute infringements on moral rights, copyright, or neighbouring rights relating to rights management information concerned (Article 113, paragraph 3):

(1) intentional addition of false information as rights management information;
(2) intentional removal or alteration of rights management information, excluding the case where such act is conditional upon technology involved in the conversion of recording or transmission systems or other cases where it is deemed unavoidable in the light of the purpose and the manner of exploiting works or performances, etc.; or
(3) distribution, importation for distribution or possession for distribution of copies of works or performances, etc., by a person who knows that any act mentioned in the preceding two items has been done concerning such works or performances, etc., or the public transmission or making transmittable of such works or performances, etc., by such person.

*585.* For the purpose of this provision, 'rights management information' is defined as information concerning moral rights or copyright or rights ('copyright, etc.') which falls within any of the following (1), (2) and (3) and which is recorded in a memory or transmitted by electronic or magnetic means or by other means not perceivable by human perception, together with works, performances, phonograms, or sounds or images of broadcasts or wire diffusions, excluding such information as not used for knowing how works, etc., are exploited, for conducting business relating to the authorization to exploit works, etc. and for other management of copyright, etc., by computer:

(1) information that specifies works, performances, phonograms, broadcasts or wire diffusions, owners of copyright, etc., and other matters specified by a Cabinet Order;
(2) information relating to manners and conditions of the exploitation in case where the exploitation of works, performances, phonograms, broadcasts or wire diffusions is authorized;
(3) information which enables to specify matters mentioned in (1) or (2) above in comparison with other information (Article 2, paragraph 1, Item 21).

## §8. Damages

*586.* An author or owner of copyright, publication right or tangential rights may claim damages from a person who has infringed intentionally or negligently any of these rights. In such a case, the profits, if any, obtained by the infringer from that infringement are presumed to be the amount of damages suffered by such owner (Article 114, paragraph 1). The author or owner of such rights may choose to claim the amount equivalent to the amount that would have been received by them through the usual exercise of these rights (Article 114, paragraph 2). However, the provisions of paragraphs 1 and 2 of Article 114 do not prejudice any claim for damages in excess of the amount mentioned therein. In such case, the court may consider the absence of any bad faith and gross negligence on the part of the infringer in fixing the amount of damages (Article 114, paragraph 3).

*587.* However, the Copyright Act permits reproduction of a work for private use (Article 30). Those who intend to use a reproduction of a work for their personal use, family use or other similar uses within a limited circle (private use) may reproduce the work unless such reproduction is made by means of a machine which has reproducing functions and of which all or main parts of the reproducing devices are automatic (automatic reproducing machine) and open for use by the public, and unless such reproduction is made by a person who knows that such reproduction becomes possible by the circumvention of technological protection measures or it ceases to cause obstruction, by such circumvention, to the results of acts deterred by such measures. 'Circumvention' is defined as enabling acts prevented by technological protection measures or to stop causing obstruction to the results of acts deterred by such measures, by removal or alteration of signals used for such measures, though 'removal' or 'alteration' do not include such removal or alteration as is inevitable upon technology involved in the conversion of recording or transmission systems. In this context, 'technological protection measures' are defined as measures to prevent or deter, by causing considerable obstruction to the results of such acts, such acts which constitute infringements on moral rights or copyright or neighbouring rights by electronic or magnetic means or by other means not perceivable by human perception, excluding such measures as used not at the will of the owner of copyright, etc., which adopt systems of recording in a memory or which transmit such signals that have specific effects on machines used for the exploitation of works, performances, phonograms, broadcasts or wire diffusions, together with works, performances, phonograms, or sounds or images of broadcasts or wire diffusions (Article 2, paragraph 1, Item 20).

*588.* In addition, where the ownership of the original or copies of works (excluding copies of cinematographic works, including copies of cinematographic works in cases of works reproduced in cinematographic works), sound or visual recordings of performances or copies of phonograms has been transferred to a person who does not know or has no negligence in not knowing that such original or copies of works, sound or visual recordings of performances or copies of phonograms do not fall within any of the items provided for in paragraph 2 of Article 26*bis*, paragraph 3 of Article 95*bis* or paragraph 2 of Article 97*bis*, respectively, an act by such person to transfer to the public the ownership of such original or copies of works, sound or visual recordings of performances or copies of phonograms are not considered not to constitute infringements on the rights mentioned in paragraph 1 of Article 26*bis*, paragraph 1 of Article 95*bis* or paragraph 1 of Article 97*bis* (Article 113*bis*).

# Chapter 5. Legal Protection of Software

## §1. Copyright

### I. Copyright Protection

*589.* As mentioned above, computer software is protected by copyright. It should be noted, however, that protection by copyright of programs does not extend to any programming language, rule, or algorithm used for the making of such works. In application of this provision, 'programming language' is defined as letters and other symbols as well as their systems for use as a means of expressing a program. A 'Rule' is defined as a special rule on how to use, in a particular program, a programming language mentioned in the preceding item and 'algorithm' is defined as method of combining, in a program, instructions given to a computer (Article 10, paragraph 3).

*590.* It should be noted that the expression of ideas cannot be protected under the Copyright Act where the expression of the idea is limited to ordinary and commonplace forms of expression, because exclusive rights should not be given by the Copyright Law to ideas. For example, the court held in the *System Science* case (Judgment, Tokyo High Court, 20 June 1989, 1322 *Hanrei Jiho* 138) that it could not help having similar combinations of commands where the combinations are constrained by the hardware.

*591.* In addition, there are a few exceptions to copyright infringement in relation to computer programs.

*592.* First, modifications necessary to achieve interoperability are permitted. To this extent, the author's exclusive right to preserve the integrity of his work and its title against any distortion, mutilation, or other modification against his will is limited. Modifications to computer programs are permitted as far as they are necessary to enable the use of a program on a particular computer which would otherwise be unusable on that computer, or to make the use of a program on a computer more effective (Article 20, paragraph 2, No. 3). Other modifications are also allowed when the modifications are deemed unavoidable in the light of the nature of a work as well as the purpose and the manner of exploitation (Article 20, paragraph 2, No. 4).

*593.* Second, an owner of a program work is permitted to copy or adapt (as well as make copies of a derivative work created by means of adaptation) that work provided that it is necessary for the purpose of exploiting that work on a computer by himself and to such extent, unless he is aware of the infringement in making the copy at the time when he has acquired an authority to use the copy (Article 47*ter*). If the owner of copies of a program work ceases to have the ownership of any of the copies (including copies made in accordance with the provision of that paragraph) for reasons other than those of destruction, he may not thereafter preserve other copies in the absence of a declaration of the intention of the copyright owner to the contrary.

*594.* It may be possible for software companies to prohibit the making of copies and adaptations to some extent in the licence agreement. However, terms prohibiting error correction or the making of a backup copy by the licensee are likely to be null and void because the terms are contrary to public policy or good morals (Civil Code, Article 90). In addition, terms prohibiting error correction by anyone other than the licensee could be seen as an unfair restriction on trade or an abuse of a dominant position under the Anti-Monopoly Act.

*595.* Third, it seemed that the reverse engineering of computer programs is permitted to some extent, though some doubt the permissibility of reverse engineering of computer programs under the Copyright Act as there are no explicit provisions allowing reverse engineering (while the Patent Act explicitly allows reverse engineering; Article 69, paragraph 1). It is common understanding that the reason why the Copyright Act has no provisions regarding reverse engineering is that 'works' under the Copyright Act have been so legible or visible that there has been no need for reverse engineering or decompilation.

*596.* Though there is one lower court decision (*Microsoft v. Shuwa*, Judgment, Tokyo District Court, 30 January 1987, 1219 *Hanrei Jiho* 48) that seems to prohibit reverse engineering, it is the dominant opinion that the decision is not authoritative on reverse engineering in general. First, the decision was made before the Copyright Act was amended in relation to the protection of program works. In addition, the courts are cautious in finding infringements in relation to program works (*re* System Science, Decision of Tokyo High Court, 20 June 1989, 1322 *Hanrei Jiho* 138; *ICM v. Mets*, Decision of Tokyo High Court, 31 March 1992, 24 *Chisaishu* 218). Second, the aim of the reverse engineering found in the Microsoft case was different from that of ordinary reverse engineering. This case simply involved what amounted to dead copies because the defendant published in a book the decompiled program of a BASIC interpreter, adding some labels and comments. It should be noted that the court found that the published decompiled program was a reproduction of the plaintiff's object program.

*597.* The 2018 amendments introduced a new exemption in order to cope with the development of IT and the growing use of computers and the internet. First and the most important, Article 30*quater* stipulates that a (copyrighted) work can be used, provided this does not apply where it would unfairly harm the interests of the copyright owner in light of the type and use of the work, where the intention to use the work is not to enjoy the thoughts or emotion expressed in the work, or for another person's enjoyment or the enjoyment of others; for example, in the cases where: (1) testing for the development or practical application of technology relating to recording or other use of the work; (2) information analysis (defined as extracting information, concerned with language, sounds, images, or other elements constituting such information from a large number of works and other large amounts of information and to make a comparison, classification or other analysis of such information); and (3) the use of the work in the course of information processing by computer without the expression of the work being perceived by human beings. According to the explanatory memorandum prepared by the Agency for Cultural Affairs, the expression, 'where the intention to use the work is not to enjoy the thoughts or emotions expressed in the work', excludes use of the work in a form that human beings 'perceive'. 'Information analysis' is included in the explicit examples in order to promote the growth of AI and big data industries, both of whose technologies heavily rely on text and data mining.

*598.* Second, paragraph 1 of Article 47*quater* now stipulates that it is permissible to make use of a (copyrighted) work to be exploited on a computer (including by any methods using information and telecommunication technology) by any methods to the extent deemed necessary, in cases where the work is exploited for making such exploitation on a computer smoothly and efficiently and ancillary to the use of such work on a computer, including the cases where:

(1) a work is exploited on a computer by using copies of such work, or where a work is exploited upon reception of transmission of such work transmitted by means of radio communication or wire-telecommunication in recording such work on a memory of computer in the course of information processing by such computer for such exploitation, to the extent deemed necessary for making such information processing smooth and efficient;
(2) one who engages in the business of providing an interactive transmission server, etc., for the use of the interactive transmission, etc. made by others, makes a transmission for relaying an interactive transmission, etc., of a work of which the transmittable, etc., has been made (excluding a work of which the making transmittable, etc., has been made by means of an interactive transmission server, etc.) in recording such work on a part, to be used for such transmission, of a memory of such interactive transmission server, etc. to the extent deemed as necessary for making an efficient transmission for relaying an interactive transmission, etc., of such work, made after such transmission; and
(3) one offers information using information and telecommunication technology in recording the work on memories or adaptation for the purpose of information processing on a computer necessary for preparation to make such an offer smoothly or efficiently.

*599.* Similarly, paragraph 2 of Article 47*quater* provides that it is permissible to make use of a [copyrighted] work to be exploited on a computer (including by any methods using information and telecommunication technology) by any methods to the extent deemed necessary, in cases where the work is exploited for keeping or making again the use of the work on a computer possible, including the cases where:

(1) in order to conserve or repair a machine in which a memory is built-in, a work recorded in the built-in memory is temporarily recorded in another memory and recorded in the built-in memory again once the maintenance or repairment is finished;
(2) in order to replace a machine in which a memory is built-in with another machine having equivalent functions, a work recorded in the built-in memory of the former is temporarily recorded in another memory and recorded in the built-in memory of the latter; and
(3) one who engages in the business of providing an interactive transmission server, etc., for the use of the interactive transmission, etc. made by others, records a work in a memory for the purpose of restoring a copy, destroyed or damaged, of a work which has been recorded on a public transmission memory, etc. concerned with the making available, etc.

*600.* In both cases, it does not apply where it would unfairly harm the interests of the copyright owner in light of the type and use of the work as well as the form of the use.

*601.* Third, those who create new knowledge or information through information processing on computers and promote the use of works are allowed to use copyrighted works published or made transmittable without any licence as long as the use is deemed as minor to the extent it is necessary and ancillary to searching or analysing information by computers and providing the results thereof as well as any activities designated by a Cabinet Order to meet the needs in the future (Article 47*quinquies*). Typically, under this provision, locating a certain book using specific keywords and displaying a part thereof with the keywords is permitted without the copyright owner's authorization. This enables searchable databases, which are important to carry out data verification of the results and insights obtained through time-division multiplexing as well.

*602.* However, it does not apply where it would unfairly harm the interests of the copyright owner in light of the type and use of the work as well as the form of the use. It neither applies in case where the user knows that the work has been published in infringing the copyright.

## II. Employee's Work

*603.* The authorship of a program work which, on the initiative of a legal person, etc., is made by his employee in the course of his duties, is attributed to that legal person, etc., unless otherwise stipulated in a contract, working regulation or the like in force at the time of the making of the work (Article 15, paragraph 2).

## III. Program Registration

### *A. Registration*

*604.* The author of a program work may have the date of creation of his program work registered, provided that a period of six months has not passed since the creation of that work. Program works, whose dates of creation have been registered are presumed to have been created on the date registered (Article 76*bis*). Registration of a program work is mainly governed by the Act Concerning Exceptions for the Registration of Program Works (Law No. 65 of 1986) (cf. Copyright Act, Article 78*bis*).

### *B. Program Register*

*605.* With regard to the registration of program works, the copyright register may be prepared in whole or in part by means of magnetic tapes (including any similar material object capable of assuring records of given items) (Article 2) in accordance with a Cabinet Ordinance. Any person may demand that the Commissioner of the Agency for Cultural Affairs deliver copies of the entries in the part of the program register prepared by means of magnetic tapes, paying a fee, the amount of which is fixed by Cabinet Order, taking into account actual cost (Article 2).

### *C. Procedure for Program Registration*

*606.* A person who intends to apply for program registration should submit to the Commissioner of the Agency for Cultural Affairs a copy of the program work intended for application as material indicating the content of that program work, unless such program work has already been registered as one of the program registrations other than that for which he applied (Article 3). The Commissioner of the Agency for Cultural Affairs should give public notice thereof as provided by the Ministry of Education and Science Ordinance when a program work is registered (Article 4).

### *D. Designated Registration Body*

*607.* The Commissioner of the Agency for Cultural Affairs may designate and entrust a person with the whole or a part of the program registration service as well as the services carried out upon request and processing public notice. Designation should be made as provided by an ordinance of the Ministry of Education and Science upon application of a person who intends to conduct a registration service. In case the Commissioner of the Agency for Cultural Affairs entrusts the designated registration body to a registration service, he may no longer conduct such registration service as is carried out by that institution (Article 5).

*608.* The Commissioner of the Agency for Cultural Affairs may not make the designation unless he is satisfied that the applicant for such a designation meets the qualifications as follows:

(1) that the person has the knowledge and experience that meet the conditions provided by the Ministry of Education and Science Ordinance to conduct the program registration business, and that the number of such persons is equal to or more than that provided by an ordinance of the Ministry of Education and Science;
(2) that the applicant has a sufficient financial basis and technical capability to conduct the registration service properly and smoothly;
(3) that the applicant is a legal person established and recognized under the relevant statute and that the composition of the officers or staff thereof is not likely to harm the fair conduct of the registration service;
(4) that, in case the applicant conducts business other than the registration service, such business may not lead to an unfair conduct of the registration service;
(5) that the designation does not hinder a proper and smooth conduct of the registration service (Article 7).

*609.* The Software Information Centre is designated as a designated registration body so far.

## IV. Special Provision Regarding Infringement

*610.* In the course of business, using copies made by an act infringing the copyright of a program work on a computer is considered to constitute an infringement on that copyright, so long as the person using such copies was aware of such an infringement at the time he acquired the authority to use these copies (Article 113, paragraph 2).

## V. The Limit to Private Use Exemption

*611.* One may, in principle, reproduce by himself a work forming the subject matter of copyright for the purpose of his personal use, family use or other similar uses within a limited circle (Article 30, paragraph 1). Uploading copyright-infringing contents to the internet and, after 2009 amendments, downloading them are, however, illegal even for personal use, knowing that they are copyright-infringing contents (Article 30, paragraph 1, Item 3). Since 1 October 2012, downloading copyright-infringing contents knowingly has been penalized up to two years in jail or fined JPY 2 million (Article 119, paragraph 3). In addition, reproduction for personal use is no longer exempted in cases where such reproduction is made by a person who knows that such reproduction becomes possible by the circumvention of technological protection measures or it ceases to cause obstruction, by such circumvention, to the results of acts deterred by such measures or by reversion (Article

30, paragraph 1, Item 2). For the purpose of this provision, 'removal' or 'alteration' does not include such removal or alteration as is conditional upon technology involved in the conversion of recording or transmission systems and 'reversion' does not include that made based upon the will of a person who has copyright, etc.

## Chapter 6. Protection of Databases

*612.* Compilation works have been protected under the Copyright Act since 1899. A compilation work is protected under the Copyright Act when such compilations, by reason of the selection or arrangement of their contents, constitute original creations (Copyright Act, Article 12). Databases were considered as compilation works.

*613.* In 1986, however, the Copyright Act was amended to clarify that it also protects databases and it defined 'database'. The Copyright Act provides for the rights of authors and the rights neighbouring thereon with respect to works (Article 1). In the Act, 'database', which is an aggregate of information such as articles, numerical values or diagrams, and which is systematically constructed so that such information can be searched for with the aid of a computer, is included in 'works' (Article 12*bis*, paragraph 1; Article 2, paragraph 1, No. 10*ter*). Information is deemed to be 'systematically constructed' where such information is searchable by a certain index. Such information may be a copyright work or mere data that would not otherwise be protected under the Copyright Act.

*614.* The fundamental requirement for copyright protection for all the categories of works, including database works, is originality. A database is protected under the Copyright Act when the database has originality in its selection or systematic composition. With respect to any work, courts have held that 'originality' is different from creativity in its strict meaning and that it only means the manifestation of the author's personality in the external form of expression (Judgment, Tokyo District Court, 3 March 1986, 1183 *Hanrei Jiho* 148).

*615.* In *Nippon Telephone and Telegram v. Daikei*, the court held that a database comprised of collected telephone numbers classified by occupations is protected under the Copyright Act because the plaintiff's database has creativeness in classifying almost all the occupations for the convenience of users (Judgment, Tokyo District Court, 17 March 2000, 1714 *Hanrei Jiho* 128).

*616.* However, a database does not have originality and is not protected under the Copyright Act when none of the material comprising the database is a 'work'. As databases may have high economic value, the MITI (now the METI) published a preliminary report on the methods of legal protection of databases. The report discussed two possible ways to protect databases: (1) to grant the creator of a database an exclusive right to extract and reutilize the data of the database (sui generis right); or (2) to prohibit extraction and reutilization which causes damages to the database creator. This proposal, however, has not yet resulted in specific legislation, though the creator of a database may be protected under the Unfair Competition Prevention Act.

*617.* Protection of databases under the Copyright Act does not affect the rights of copyright owners with respect to the copyright works comprising a database (Copyright Act, Article 12*bis*). Therefore, the consent of owners of copyright works is necessary where all or a part of the material comprising a database is copyrighted.

# Chapter 7. Chips Protection

## §1. Protection of Topography

*618.* The Act Concerning the Topography of Semiconductor Integrated Circuits (hereinafter referred to as the Semiconductor IC Act) gives a right to the layout of an integrated circuit.

*619.* A creator or his successor (hereinafter referred to as a 'creator, etc.') of a semiconductor topography may register with the Minister of Economics, Trade and Industry a topography right in the topography. If two or more persons have created the topography, they should apply for the registration jointly (Semiconductor IC Act, Article 3, paragraph 1). When the topography was created in the course of a creator's employment, the creator's employer is deemed as the creator unless the contract, the term of employment or other agreement at the time of creation provides the contrary (Semiconductor IC Act, Article 5). Application for registration of a topography right can be made within two years after the first commercial assignment, rental, leasing, exhibition for assignment, rental, leasing, or importation of semiconductor integrated circuits or semiconductor products manufactured by using the topography by the creator, etc., or his licensee (Semiconductor IC Act, Article 6).

*620.* Topography rights require registration (Semiconductor IC Act, Article 10, paragraph 1) and endure for ten years from the date of registration (Semiconductor IC Act, Article 10, paragraph 2). The rightholder may commercially exploit the registered topography right unless he has granted another the exclusive right of exploitation (Semiconductor IC Act, Article 11). Exploitation is defined in paragraph 3 of Article 2 as commercial production of semiconductor integrated circuits using a topography, commercial assignment, rental, leasing, exhibition for assignment, rental, or leasing or importation of semiconductor integrated circuits or semiconductor products manufactured by using a topography.

## §2. Effect of Registration

*621.* The following matter does not prevail against third parties unless they are registered:

(1) transfer (except those by inheritance or other general succession), extinguishments by surrender or restrictions on disposal of a topography right;
(2) grant, transfer (except those by inheritance or other general succession), modification or extinguishments (except those resulting from a merger or the extinguishments of the topography right) of an exclusive licence, or a restriction on the disposal thereof;
(3) grant, transfer (except those by inheritance or other general succession), modification or extinguishments (except those resulting from a merger or the

extinguishments of the topography right or exclusive licence) of a non-exclusive licence, or a restriction on the disposal thereof;

(4) grant, transfer (except those by inheritance or other general succession), modification or extinguishments (except those resulting from a merger or the extinguishments of a secured credit) of a pledge on a topography right, exclusive licence or non-exclusive licence, or a restriction on the disposal thereof (Semiconductor IC Act, Article 21, paragraph 1).

*622.* Once a non-exclusive licence has been registered, it has effect with respect to anyone who subsequently acquires the topography right, the exclusive licence or the exclusive licence on such a topography right (Semiconductor IC Act, Article 21, paragraph 2).

## §3. Permitted Exploitation

*623.* Though Japanese law does not explicitly require that the topography be original, the registration should be rejected if it is obvious that the applicant is not the creator, etc., (Semiconductor IC Act, Article 8, paragraph 1, Item 1). In addition, paragraph 1 of Article 12 provides that the effect of the registered topography right never extends to the exploitation of a topography created by another (Semiconductor IC Act, Article 12, paragraph 1). It is permissible to make a semiconductor using a topography for the purpose of analysing or evaluating that topography (Semiconductor IC Act, Article 12, paragraph 2). It is not an infringement of the topography right to assign, rent, lease, or exhibit for assignment, rental or leasing or import semiconductor integrated circuits or semiconductor products once the topography rightholder, exclusive licensee or non-exclusive licensee has produced the products and assigned them to another (Semiconductor IC Act, Article 12, paragraph 3). The topography rightholder, exclusive licensee or non-exclusive licensee may not commercially exploit the topography if the exploitation falls within the working of another's patent or utility model right (Semiconductor IC Act, Article 13).

## §4. Joint Ownership

*624.* Each of the joint owners of a topography right may neither transfer his share nor establish a pledge upon it without the consent of all the other joint owners (Semiconductor IC Act, Article 14, paragraph 1). Each of the joint owners may, except as otherwise prescribed by contract, exploit the topography right without the consent of the other joint owners, though each of the joint owners may grant neither an exclusive licence nor a non-exclusive licence without the consent of all the other joint owners (Semiconductor IC Act, Article 14, paragraphs 2 and 3).

§5. Exclusive Licence

*625.* The topography rightholder may grant an exclusive licence on his topography right. An exclusive licensee has an exclusive right to commercially exploit the topography to the extent laid down in the licence contract. An exclusive licence may be transferred only together with the business in which it is exploited, or only with the consent of the rightholder or in the case of inheritance or other general succession. An exclusive licensee may establish a pledge or grant a non-exclusive licence on the exclusive licence only with the consent of the rightholder. The provisions regarding joint rightholders (Article 14) apply *mutatis mutandis* to exclusive licences (Semiconductor IC Act, Article 16).

§6. Non-exclusive Licence

*626.* The topography rightholder may grant a non-exclusive licence on his topography right. A non-exclusive licensee has the right to commercially exploit the topography to the extent prescribed as laid down by the licence contract. A non-exclusive licence may be transferred only together with the business in which it is exploited, or only with the consent of the rightholder (in case of non-exclusive licence of the exclusive licence, the topography rightholder and the exclusive licensee) or in the case of inheritance or other general succession. A non-exclusive licensee may establish a pledge on the licence only with the consent of the rightholder (in case of non-exclusive licence of the exclusive licence, the topography rightholder and the exclusive licensee). The provisions regarding joint rightholders (Article 14, paragraphs 1 and 2) apply *mutatis mutandis* to exclusive licences (Semiconductor IC Act, Article 17).

§7. Pledge on a Topography Right

*627.* Where a topography right or an exclusive or non-exclusive licence is the subject of a pledge, the pledgee may not exploit the topography unless otherwise prescribed by contract (Semiconductor IC Act, Article 18). A pledge on a topography right or an exclusive or non-exclusive licence may be exercised against the remuneration received as consideration for the topography right or the licence or against money or goods that the rightholder or exclusive licensee would be entitled to receive for the exploitation of the topography. However, an attachment order must be obtained prior to the payment or delivery of the money or property (Semiconductor IC Act, Article 19).

§8. Infringement

*628.* A rightholder or exclusive licensee may require a person who is infringing or is likely to infringe the topography right or exclusive licence to discontinue or refrain from such infringement (Semiconductor IC Act, Article 22, paragraph 1). A rightholder or an exclusive licensee who is acting under the preceding subsection may demand the destruction of the articles by which the act of infringement was committed, the disposal of the articles used for the act of infringement, or other measures necessary to prevent the infringement (Semiconductor IC Act, Article 22, paragraph 2).

*629.* Manufacturing, assigning, renting, leasing, exhibiting for assignment or leasing, or importing articles exclusively used for imitating a registered topography are deemed to be an infringement of a topography right or an exclusive licence (Semiconductor IC Act, Article 23).

*630.* When a rightholder or exclusive licensee claims, from a person who has intentionally or negligently infringed the topography right or exclusive licence, compensation for damage caused to him by the infringement, the profits gained by the infringer through the infringement are presumed to be the amount of damage suffered by the rightholder or exclusive licensee (Semiconductor IC Act, Article 25, paragraph 1). A rightholder or exclusive licensee may claim, from a person who has intentionally or negligently infringed the topography right or exclusive licence, an amount of money which he would normally be entitled to receive for the exploitation of the topography, as the amount of damage suffered (Semiconductor IC Act, Article 25, paragraph 2).

*631.* Those provisions do not, however, preclude a claim for damages exceeding the amount referred to therein. In such a case, where there has been neither wilfulness nor gross negligence on the part of the person who has infringed the topography right or the exclusive licence, the court may take this into consideration when awarding damages (Semiconductor IC Act, Article 25, paragraph 3).

*632.* In a litigation relating to the infringement of a topography right or exclusive licence, the court may, upon request of a party, order the other party to produce documents necessary for the assessment of the damage caused by the infringement. However, this provision does not apply when the person possessing the documents has a legitimate reason for refusing to produce them (Semiconductor IC Act, Article 26).

*633.* When semiconductor integrated circuits or semiconductor products have been transferred to a person who does not know or has no negligence in not knowing that such semiconductor integrated circuits, etc., were manufactured using a topography which was an imitation of a registered topography on which another has the topography right or an exclusive licence, commercial assignment, rent, leasing, exhibition for assignment or leasing, or importation of such semiconductor integrated circuits, etc., by such a bona fide transferee is considered not to constitute an infringement of the topography right or the exclusive licence (Semiconductor IC Act, Article 24, paragraph 1). The topography rightholder or an exclusive licensee may, however, claim from such person an amount of money which he would normally be entitled to receive for the exploitation of the topography where the bona fide transferee commercially assigns, rents, leases, exhibits for assignment or leasing, or imports the semiconductor integrated circuits, etc., after he has known the fact of the imitation (Semiconductor IC Act, Article 24, paragraph 2). Where the bona fide transferee has paid such an amount, the semiconductor integrated circuits are deemed to be assigned by the topography rightholder or the exclusive licensee (Semiconductor IC Act, Article 24, paragraph 3).

## §9. Compensation

*634.* After the creator or his licensee had commercially assigned, rented, leased, exhibited for assignment, rental, leasing, or imported semiconductor integrated circuits or semiconductor products manufactured by using the topography before the registration, a person who has commercially exploited a topography which is an imitation of the topography, knowing it to be an imitation, is liable to pay the creator, etc., an amount of money which he would normally have to pay for the exploitation of the topography as compensation (Semiconductor IC Act, Article 27, paragraph 1). The creator, etc., cannot, however, request such person to pay compensation until the registration of the topography (Semiconductor IC Act, Article 27, paragraph 2).

## §10. Penal Provision

*635.* Any person who infringes a topography right or an exclusive licence is punishable with imprisonment with labour for no longer than three years or a fine not exceeding JPY 1 million (Semiconductor IC Act, Article 51).

# Chapter 8. Protection of Internet Domain Names

## §1. Internet Domain Name Registration

*636.* The 'jp' domain names and IP addresses are assigned, registered and managed by the Japan Network Information Centre (JPNIC) in accordance with the 'Rules on Registration of JP Domain Names in Accordance with the Nature (Type of Organizations) or Local Type' and 'Rules on the Registration of JP Domain Names for General-purpose' (hereinafter referred to as 'the Registration Rules').

*637.* In 2000, the JPNIC revised the 'JP Domain Name Dispute-Resolution Policy' (hereinafter referred to as 'the JPNIC Policy'), which is incorporated by reference into the Registration Rules. This Policy determines the conditions with respect to a dispute between the domain name registrant and a third party over the domain name arising from the registration and the use of a domain name registered by the registrant. Proceedings on JP Domain Name Dispute Resolution under Article 4 of the Policy are conducted according to the 'Rules for Procedure of JP Domain Name Dispute-Resolution Policy' (hereinafter referred to as 'Rules for Procedure') and the selected administrative dispute-resolution supplemental rules of the dispute-resolution service provider that will be approved by the Centre (hereinafter referred to as 'the dispute-resolution service provider') (the JPNIC Policy, Article 1).

*638.* Article 2 of the Policy requires the applicant, upon application for registration of a domain name, maintenance or renewal of a domain name, to notify the JPNIC that:

(1) the contents of the statements made in the registration application are complete and accurate;
(2) to the best knowledge of the applicant or registrant, the registration of the domain name will not infringe upon or otherwise violate the rights or interests of any third party;
(3) the applicant or registrant is not registering the domain name in bad faith (unfair purposes);[18] and
(4) the applicant or registrant will not knowingly use the domain name in violation of any applicable laws or regulations.

*639.* In case of violation of this duty of notification, the applicant or the registrant deems that he/she agrees that the domain name may be transferred or cancelled pursuant to the JPNIC Policy (the JPNIC Policy, Article 2).

*640.* The JPNIC will transfer or cancel the domain name registration under the following circumstances:

18. An 'unfair purpose' is defined as a purpose of gaining unfair interests, of causing damages to others and other bad faith.

(1) subject to the provisions of Article 8, the receipt by the JPNIC of written instructions from the registrant or its authorized agent to take such action;
(2) the receipt by the JPNIC of the original (a copy of the original may be acceptable, if circumstances require so) of an order from a court or arbitration tribunal, in each case of competent jurisdiction, requiring such action; and/or
(3) the receipt by the JPNIC of a decision of an Administrative Panel requiring such action in JP Domain Name Dispute-Resolution Proceedings to which the registrant was a party and which was conducted under the JPNIC Policy or a later version of the JPNIC Policy adopted by the JPNIC.

*641.* The JPNIC may also cancel or transfer the domain name registration in accordance with the terms of the Registration Rules or other legal requirements. If the transfer has been made, however, the JPNIC will not establish the name server for the domain name unless the qualifications and requirements for registration are satisfied (Article 3).

## §2. JP Domain Name Dispute-Resolution Proceeding

*642.* Article 4 of the JPNIC Policy provides the JP Domain Name Dispute-Resolution Proceeding.[19] The registrant is required to submit to this JP Domain Name Dispute-Resolution Proceeding in the event that a third party (hereinafter referred to as 'Complainant') asserts to the applicable dispute-resolution service provider, in compliance with the Rules of Procedure, that:

(1) the domain name of the registrant is identical or confusingly similar to any mark such as a trademark or service mark in which the Complainant has rights or legitimate interests;
(2) the registrant has no rights or legitimate interests with respect to the domain name registration; and
(3) the domain name of the registrant has been registered or is being used in bad faith (unfair purpose).

In the JP Domain Name Dispute-Resolution Proceeding, the Complainant must maintain that all the three elements are present in the complaint (Article 4, paragraph a).[20]

19. These requirements are quite similar to those provided in the UDRP of the Internet Corporation for Assigned Names and Numbers (ICANN).
20. In case of multiple disputes between the same registrant and the complainant, either the registrant or the complainant may petition to consolidate the disputes before a single panel. This petition should be made to the first panel appointed to hear a pending dispute between the parties. This panel may consolidate before it any or all such disputes at its sole discretion, provided that the consolidated disputes are governed by the JPNIC Policy or later versions of the JPNIC Policy adopted by the JPNIC (Art. 4, para. f).

*643.* The panel of the dispute-resolution service provider should find that the registration or use of a domain name is in bad faith (unfair purpose) if the panel has recognized especially the following circumstances, in particular but not limited to:

(1) circumstances indicating that the registrant has registered or has acquired the domain name primarily for the purpose of selling, renting, or otherwise transferring the domain name to the Complainant or to a competitor of that Complainant, for valuable consideration in excess of the out-of-pocket costs (amount to be confirmed by documentation) directly related to the domain name; or
(2) the registrant has registered the domain name in order to prevent the Complainant from reflecting any trademarks or other indication in a corresponding domain name, provided that the registrant has engaged in multiple occurrences of such interference; or
(3) the registrant has registered the domain name primarily for the purpose of disrupting the business of a competitor; or
(4) by using thc domain name, the registrant has intentionally attempted to attract, for commercial gain, Internet users to the website or other online location of the registrant, by intending to make confusion as to the source, sponsorship, affiliation, or endorsement of the website or location or of a product or service thereon (Article 4, paragraph b).

*644.* The Complainant should select the dispute-resolution service provider from among those approved by the JPNIC by submitting the complaint to that dispute-resolution service provider. The selected dispute-resolution service provider should administer and conduct the JP Domain Name Dispute-Resolution Proceeding, except in cases of consolidation as provided in Article 4, paragraph f (Article 4, paragraph d).

*645.* The remedies available to the Complainant pursuant to any proceeding before a panel are limited to requiring the cancellation of the domain name of the registrant or the transfer of the domain name registration to the Complainant (Article 4, paragraph i).

## §3. Unfair Competition Prevention Act and Domain Names

*646.* In *Jaccs v. Nihonkai Pact* (Judgment, Toyama District Court, 6 December 2000, 1734 *Hanrei Jiho* 3), the court held that the plaintiff was entitled to an injunction against the defendant's commercial use under the Unfair Competition Prevention Act (Law No. 47 of 1993) before the amendments of 2001 (Article 2, paragraph 1, Items 1 and 2). In this case, the plaintiff's trade name was famous at the time of registration of the domain name and the defendant's domain name was identical or confusingly similar to the plaintiff's trade name. At the same time, the court recognized that the defendant had registered and had been using the domain name in bad faith, intent on profiting from that name.

*647.* *Daigyotsusho v. J-Phone Higashi Nihon* (Judgment, Tokyo High Court, 25 October 2001, *unpublished*)[21] affirmed the lower court's decision to issue an injunction against *Daigyotsusho*, stating that for the court to 'prevent unfair competition or the apprehension of unfair competition is only natural. The result of ban on unfair competition, even if speech is restricted to some extent, is not unconstitutional'.

*648.* The Unfair Competition Prevention Act was amended in 2001 and regulates the unfair use of domain names identical or similar to others' trademarks and so on. In order to prevent cybersquatting, the amended Unfair Competition Prevention Act provides that 'unfair competition' covers registration, possessing or using a domain name which is identical or similar to the indication of another's goods, etc. – names, trade names, trademarks, marks and those indicating goods or services in another's commerce – in bad faith and with intent of profiting or harming others (Unfair Competition Prevention Act, Article 2, paragraph 1, Item 13).

*649.* One whose commercial interests have been or are likely to be damaged by unfair competition may require the person who is infringing or is likely to infringe the interests to discontinue or refrain from such infringement (Unfair Competition Prevention Act, Article 3, paragraph 1). Such a claimant may demand the destruction of the articles by which the act of infringement was committed, the disposal of the articles used for the act of infringement, or other measures necessary to prevent the infringement (Unfair Competition Prevention Act, Article 3, paragraph 2).

*650.* The Unfair Competition Prevention Act does not, however, have any explicit provisions with respect to the assignment of domain names. Thus, it would be difficult to obtain a judgment for the assignment of such domain name.

*651.* However, JPNIC and Internet Corporation for Assigned Names and Numbers (ICANN) have formulated dispute-resolution policies for both JP and generic domain names. JPNIC's Regulation Concerning the Registration, etc. of Attribute Type (Organization Class Type) and Regional Type Domain Names (Article 40) and Regulation Concerning the Registration, etc., of General Purpose JP Domain Names (Article 37) provide that whenever there is a dispute between a registrant and a third party over a JP Domain Name registered in the name of the registrant, the registrant shall consent to the dispute settlement agency's authority to resolve the dispute in accordance with the JP Domain Name Dispute Resolution Policy (JP-DRP). The JP-DRP provides that a third-party applicant may seek, as a remedy, the cancellation of the registrant's domain name registration or the assignment of the domain name registration to the applicant (Article 4, Item i). In cases where an award is granted by a dispute settlement agency (presently, Japan Intellectual Property Arbitration Center) recognized by JPNIC, the Japan Registry Service Corporation shall take steps for the assignor cancellation of the domain name registration (JP-DRP, Article 3 and Article 4, item k). In a similar way, with respect to a Generic Domain

21. Available in Japanese at http://www.courts.go.jp/hanrei/pdf/695F1B89FFD8F6D749256B2F00019773.pdf.

Name, a party may seek to cancel or assign its registration by filing an application with a dispute settlement agency recognized by ICANN.

*652.* A person who has intentionally or negligently infringed another's commercial interests should be liable for the damages caused by the unfair competition (Unfair Competition Prevention Act, Article 4). In such a case, the profits, if any, obtained by the infringer from that infringement are presumed to be the amount of damages suffered by the victim (Unfair Competition Prevention Act, Article 5, paragraph 2). The victim may choose to claim the amount equivalent to the amount that would have been received by them through a usual exercise of the right of such a domain name (Unfair Competition Prevention Act, Article 5, paragraph 3, No. 4). However, the provisions of paragraph 3 of Article 5 do not prejudice any claim for damages in excess of the amount mentioned therein. In such a case, the court may consider the absence of any bad faith and gross negligence on the part of the infringer in fixing the amount of damages (Unfair Competition Prevention Act, Article 5, paragraph 4). In litigation involving the infringement of commercial interests by unfair competition, if it is found that damage has been suffered but it is extremely difficult to prove the facts necessary for proving the amount of damage due to the nature of said facts, the court may determine a reasonable amount of damage based on the entire import of oral argument and the results of the examination of evidence (Article 9).

*653.* In addition, the victim may demand that the person who has intentionally or negligently damaged the reputation of the other's business take measures necessary to recover the victim's reputation either instead of compensating damages or together with compensation of damages (Unfair Competition Prevention Act, Article 14).

## Chapter 9. Circumventing Technological Protection Measures

*654.* The Unfair Competition Prevention Act (Law No. 47 of 1993) provides that one whose commercial interests have been or are likely to be damaged by unfair competition may require the person who is infringing or is likely to infringe the interests to suspend or prevent the infringement, destroy the articles that gave rise to the act of infringement, remove the equipment used for the act of infringement, or take any other actions necessary for suspending or preventing the infringement (Article 3). It also stipulates that one who intentionally or negligently infringes on commercial interests of another person through unfair competition is liable for damages resulting therefrom (Article 4).

*655.* For the purpose of these provisions, 'unfair competition' covers:

(1) assigning, delivering, displaying for the purpose of assignment or delivery, exporting, or importing a device (including a machine that incorporates such device and a set of parts for such device that can be easily assembled) with a function that makes it possible to view images, hear sound, run programs or process information, or record images, sound, programs or other information (hereinafter referred to as 'to view images, etc.') which are protected by technological protection measures that are used for commercial purposes (excluding technological protection measures used to restrict all but specific persons from viewing images, hearing sound, running programs or processing information, or recording images, sound, programs or other information), by interfering with the effectiveness of such technological protection measures, or a data storage medium or machine on which a program with such function (including a combination of such a program with other programs) has been recorded; or providing a program or an instruction code (instruction given to a computer to obtain a certain result without any other instructions) with such function over a telecommunications line (if such device or program has a function other than such function, this is limited to an act done in order to provide such a device or program for the purpose of making it possible to view images, etc. by interfering with the effectiveness of such technological protection measures); and providing a service of making it possible to view images, etc. by interfering with the effectiveness of such technological protection measures; and

(2) assigning, delivering, displaying for the purpose of assignment or delivery, exporting or importing, other than to a specific person, a device (including a machine that incorporates such device and a set of parts for such device that can be easily assembled) with a function that makes it possible to view images, etc. which are protected by technological protection measures that are used for commercial purposes to prevent all but a specific person from viewing images, hearing sound, running programs or processing information, or recording images, sound, programs or other information, by interfering with the effectiveness of such technological protection measures or a data storage medium or machine on which a program (including a combination of such a program with other programs) or an instruction code with

such function has been recorded; providing a program or an instruction code with such function over a telecommunications line, other than to a specific person (if such device or program has a combination of functions other than such function, this is limited to an act done in order to provide such device or program for the purpose of making it possible to view images, etc. by interfering with the effectiveness of such technological protection measures); and providing a service of making it possible to view images, etc. by interfering with the effectiveness of such technological protection measures (Article 2, Nos 11 and 12).

655–655 Part IV, Ch. 9, Circumventing Technological Protection Measures

# Part V. Cybersecurity Law

## Chapter 1. Institutional Framework

*656.* The Cybersecurity Strategic Headquarters was established under the Cabinet in 2014 in order to effectively and comprehensively promote cybersecurity policies (FAC, Article 25). It is headed by the Chief Cabinet Secretary, with his deputy – the Minister in charge of Cybersecurity – and composed of the Foreign Minister, the Minister of Defence, the Minister of Trade and Economy, the Minister of Internal Affairs, the Chairman of the National Public Safety Commission, and other knowledgeable experts from academia and business sectors appointed by the Prime Minister (Framework Act for Cybersecurity (Law No.104 of 2014) (FAC), Article 29).

*657.* It can delegate part of its functions by a Cabinet Order to such entities as the Information Technology Promotion Agency. The functions to be delegated include setting standards for cybersecurity measures for national administrative organs; promoting the implementation of evaluative measures, including audits; and coordinating with relevant persons and entities in Japan and abroad where any cybersecurity breaches and threats take place (FAC, Articles 26 and 31).

*658.* The National Center of Incident Readiness and Strategy for Cybersecurity (NISC), which was formerly called the National Information Security Center, has been a secretariat of the Cybersecurity Strategy Headquarters. The NISC coordinates intra-government collaboration and promotes collaborative alliance between the government and industry, academia, public and private sectors. The NISC coordinates cybersecurity policy by formulating: Cybersecurity Strategy; Cybersecurity Policy for Critical Infrastructure Protection; Common Standard on Information Security Measures of Government Entities; Cybersecurity Human Resource Development Plan; and Cybersecurity Research and Development Strategy etc.

*659.* The NISC operates the Government Security Operation Coordination team (GSOC), a real-time government-wide monitoring team. The GSOC not only monitors malicious communications incoming to or outgoing from any government-owned systems but also works as an information-sharing infrastructure among governmental entities. It provides alerts and advice for the governmental entities when they detect suspicious signals or malware.

*660.* The NISC takes a role of a governmental CERT while the Japan Computer Emergency Response Team Coordination Center (JPCERT/CC) works as a CERT for private entities.

*661.* In 2018, the FAC was amended and provides that the government sets up a council that discusses the promotion of cybersecurity measures (FAC, Article 17). The Cybersecurity Council is intended to be the avenue to allow national government agencies, local governments, critical infrastructure operators, cyberspace-related business entities, and educational and research institutions to share information which may facilitate the proposal and implementation of cybersecurity measures. The Cybersecurity Council comprises 265 persons or entities as of 30 June 2021.

## Chapter 2. General Obligations

*662.* The Framework Act for Cybersecurity provides the fundamental framework for the responsibilities and policies of the national and local governments to enhance cybersecurity. It requires the national and local governments to take measures to boost cybersecurity (FAC, Articles 4 and 5). The Act obligates the government to establish uniform cybersecurity standards for government agencies, monitor the government information network system, and detect and analyse unauthorized access or attacks to the system (FAC, Article 13). The government must take necessary measures to enhance cooperation between relevant organizations on cybersecurity and to make those organizations' responsibilities clear, in order to counter cyber-attacks that may affect the nation's security. (FAC, Article 18). It should take measures as well to improve the skills of those who work in the cybersecurity field (FAC, Article 21).

*663.* The current Cybersecurity Strategy (Cabinet Decision of July 27, 2018) shows a basic position on cybersecurity policy, its objectives and its implementation for three years (2018-2020) domestically and internationally.

*664.* The FAC has been implemented to promote the cybersecurity policy by: setting fundamental principles of cybersecurity policy; clarifying the responsibilities of the government, private entities and citizens; setting the framework for cybersecurity policy such as the cybersecurity strategy formulation and the launch of the Cybersecurity Strategic Headquarters.

*665.* The NISC has set the Common Standards on Information Security Measures of Governmental Entities to raise the level of information security for all governmental agencies and related agencies, as the minimum standard (FAC, Article 26, paragraph 1). The standards are a unified framework for improving the level of information security of governmental entities and define the baseline for information security measures to ensure a higher level of information security. The NISC oversees the status of implementation of the Standards across governmental agencies through audits.

## Chapter 3. Sector-Specific Obligations

*666.* The FAC defines 'Critical Infrastructure Operators' as operators of businesses that provide an infrastructure which is fundamental to citizen's lives and economic activities which could be seriously adversely affected by the functional failure or deterioration of that infrastructure (Article 3, paragraph 1). The Critical Infrastructure Operators are required to make efforts to deepen their interest and understanding of the importance of cybersecurity, and to endeavour to take voluntary and proactive measures to ensure cybersecurity in order to provide services in a stable and appropriate manner (FAC, Article 6). The government provides support for cybersecurity measures for such operators (FAC, Article 14).

*667.* The Cybersecurity Strategy Headquarters formulated the Cybersecurity Policy for Critical Infrastructure Protection (the 4th edition was published in 2017 and revised in 2020) as a non-mandatory guideline, which is a common action plan shared by the government which bears a responsibility for protection of critical infrastructure and by critical infrastructure operators and covers designated fourteen critical infrastructure areas: information and communication; financial services; aviation; airport; railway; electric power supply; gas supply, government and administrative supply; medical; water supply; logistics; chemical; credit cards; and petroleum. This document expects stakeholders to: develop and penetrate safety principles; enhance information-sharing system; reinforce capacity to deal with incidents; be thorough in risk management and prepare incident readiness; and build up the basis of critical infrastructure protection.

*668.* The Financial Services Agency (FSA) published the Approach to Strengthen Cybersecurity in the Financial Business Sector in 2015, and updated in 2018. The FSA will: engage in continuous dialogue with financial institutions to grasp their cybersecurity risks; improve information sharing among financial institutions; conduct cybersecurity drills in which financial institutions, the FSA and other public authorities take part in; and foster cybersecurity human resources.

*669.* The FSA's guidelines (e.g., the Comprehensive Guidelines for Supervision of Major Banks, etc.), which are not legally binding but are complied with by banks, encourage banks to, for example: develop surveillance system for cyber-attacks, report and public relations system in the event of a cyber-attack, system for emergency response and early warning such as CSIRT (Computer Security Incident Response Team) in the organization, and information collection and sharing system, etc.; implement defence in depth against cyber-attacks ('entrance' measures that do not allow unauthorized access or malware intrusion such as installation of firewall and anti-virus software, introduction of intrusion detection system/intrusion prevention system; 'internal' measures that minimize damage when intrusion is allowed such as proper management of privileged IDs and passwords, deletion of unnecessary IDs, execution monitoring of specific commands; and 'exit' measures that prevent information from being taken out such as keeping and analysing communication logs, event logs, etc., detection/blocking inappropriate communication); designate a manager in charge of cybersecurity; implement a periodic assessment of cybersecurity, utilizing network intrusion inspections and vulnerability diagnosis; formulate a contingency plan that presupposes cyber-attacks, conduct training and review and participate in cross-industry drills; and formulate and implement a plan for training and fostering human resources for cyber security (III -3-7-1-2(5)).

*670.* Though there is no mandatory requirement to report incidents, the FSA requests banks to report an incident immediately after becoming aware of it. According to the FSA's guidelines, the report should include: the date and time when the incident occurred and the place where the incident took place; a summary description of the incident and which services were affected by the incident; causes of the incident; a summary description of the facilities affected by the incident; a summary description of damages caused by the incident, and how and when the bank recovered or is expected to recover; any harmful effect for other business providers; how the bank responded to enquiries from users and how it notified the incident to users, public authorities and the public; and possible measures to prevent a recurrence of similar incidents.

*671.* Where a serious incident specified in the Telecommunications Business Act and the Implementing Regulation for the Telecommunications Business Act, for example, a temporary suspension of telecommunications services or a violation of the secrecy of communications, arises from a cyber-attack, the telecommunications carrier is required to report the incident to the MIC promptly after the incident took place. Moreover, the carrier should report the details of the incident to the Ministry within thirty days from its occurrence. The report must include: the date and time when the Incident occurred; the date and time when the operator recovered; the place where the incident took place (the location of the facilities); a summary description of the incident and which services were affected by the incident; a summary description of the facilities affected by the incident; the details of the events or indications of the incident, the number of users and the service area affected; measures taken to respond to the incident, including the persons who responded to it, in chronological order; causes which made the incident serious, including how the facilities have been managed and maintained; possible measures to prevent a recurrence of similar incidents; how the operator responded to inquiries from users and how it notified the incident to users; internal rules regarding the incident; a summary description of the past incidents, if the operator experienced similar Incidents in the past; the name of the manager of the telecommunication facilities; and the name and qualifications of the chief engineer of the telecommunication facilities.

## Chapter 4. Liability and Remedies

*672.* In cases where ensuring cybersecurity is deemed as a contractual obligation, the obligor is liable for the failure to perform the obligation in accordance with its purport and meaning (Civil Code, Article 415). In a case involving cyber-attacks (SQL injections) on a computer system which leads to divulging of credit card information of a company's clients, the company sought damages based on breach of contract to the vendor of the system. Though the court decided that the vendor was required to develop a system which is effective to block SQL injections in accordance with the standards when the system was introduced, it found that the incident was also partially attributable to the company that rejected the vendor's proposal to strengthen the system (Judgment, Tokyo District Court, 23 January 2014, 2221 *Hanrei Jiho* 71).

*673.* It is possible for parties to agree on limitation of liability so long as the limitation does not conflict with any mandatory laws and regulations. However, in contracts between a business and a consumer (a natural person, excluding he/she who becomes a party to a contract as any business or for any business (Consumer Contracts Act, Article 2)), any clause that totally exempts a business from its liability to compensate a consumer for damage arising from breach of contract by the business is void. Moreover, any clause that partially exempts a business from its liability to compensate a consumer for damage arising from breach of contract with intention or gross negligence by the business is void. In addition, any clause that allows a business to judge whether he/she is liable or not is void (Consumer Contract Act, Article 8).

*674.* A person who intentionally or negligently violates another's rights shall be liable for the losses caused by the act (torts) (Civil Code, Article 709). Even where an injured suffers mental or psychological harm, he/she can make a claim for compensation (Civil Code, Article 710). Moreover, a person who employs another for a certain business is liable for damages suffered by a third party caused by his/her employee's torts in the course of that business (Civil Code, Article 715). In a similar way to contractual liability, the Consumer Contracts Act provides that some types of clauses that exempt a business from its liability to compensate a consumer for torts are void (Consumer Contracts Act, Article 8).

*675.* The plaintiff is often awarded, however, only a small amount in pecuniary damages for personal data breaches (*See*, e.g., Judgment, Kyoto District Court, 23 February 2001, 265 *Hanrei Chihojichi* 17; Judgment, Osaka High Court, 25 December 2001, 265 *Hanrei Chihojichi* 11 (upheld by Judgment, Supreme Court, 11 July 2002, 265 *Hanrei Chihojichi* 10); Judgment, Tokyo High Court, 23 March 2004, 1855 *Hanre Jiho* 104; Judgment, Osaka District Court, 19 May 2006, 1948 *Hanrei Jiho* 122; Judgment, Osaka High Court, 21 June 2007, unpublished; Judgment, Tokyo District Court, 8 February 2007, 1964 *Hanrei Jiho* 113; Judgment, Tokyo High Court, 28 August 2007, unpublished).

# Part VI. Cybercrime

## Chapter 1. Application of International and Regional Agreements

*676.* Japan joined the Budapest Convention on Cybercrime in 2012. A State Party to the Convention may request mutual legal assistance from Japan in accordance with the requirements of the Convention.

*677.* In addition, when a request comes from a party to another mutual legal assistance treaty (MLAT) or mutual legal assistance agreement (MLAA) with Japan, Japan will provide assistance as required under the treaty or agreement. The current MLAT/MLAA partners are the United States, Korea, China, Hong Kong SAR, EU and Russia. Japan can provide assistance to a state without a mutual legal assistance treaty (MLAT) with Japan based on the principle of reciprocity and domestic law as well.

# Chapter 2. Specific Computer Crimes

## §1. General Legal Development

*678.* The Penal Code (Law No. 45 of 1907)[22] and the Criminal Procedure Code (Law No. 131 of 1948) are the most important sources of criminal law, but there are some special criminal statutes. As there were no specific provisions regarding computer-related crimes in the Penal Code before 1987, the courts interpreted the existing penal provisions so widely that they could penalize some types of computer-related crimes.

*679.* The 1987 amendments to the Penal Code did not introduce comprehensive penal provisions regarding computer-related crimes but introduced provisions regarding electromagnetic records[23] and provisions punishing the manipulation of computer data and computer sabotage. In other words, the aim of the amendments was solely to fill the gap in the application of the penal provisions to electromagnetic records processed by computers. In relation to these new provisions, 'electromagnetic record' was defined as any record that is produced by electronic, magnetic or any other means unrecognizable through natural perception and that is used for data processing by a computer (Article 7*bis*). It should be noted that no provisions were introduced with respect to computer espionage and the illegal use of computers because it did not seem appropriate or practical to introduce such provisions. As there were no penal provisions protecting trade secrets or other secrets then, it was difficult to determine the scope of protection with respect to computer espionage. In addition, the rationale to penalize the illegal use of computers had not been clear and the illegal use of machines had in general not been punishable, except for in the cases of larceny. Accordingly, the courts have until now applied the existing provisions to computer-related crimes by expansive interpretations.

*680.* In 1999, the Unauthorized Computer Access Act (Law No. 128 of 1999) was enacted because the Penal Code did not penalize unauthorized access to computers in general. However, the Criminal Procedure Code had no specific provisions in relation to computer-related crimes, though the Law authorizing wiretapping for crime detection (Law No. 137 of 1999) has a provision regarding encrypted communication (Article 13, paragraph 2).

*681.* In response to the development of IT and the increase of cybercrimes, both the Penal Code and the Criminal Procedure Code were amended by the Act on the Partial Revision of the Penal Code, etc., in order to deal with the Development of Information Processing, etc. (Law No. 74 of 2011).

---

22. The Penal Code was completely restated in modern Japanese in 1995 (Law No. 91 of 1995).
23. It was common understanding that a 'record' should be lasting for some period (Judgment, Supreme Tribunal, 30 Sep. 1910, 16 *Keiroku* 1572) and does not include data in transition or being processed in the CPU of a computer.

§2. Forging Documents

*682.* Articles 154 through 161 of the Penal Code penalize the forgery of official or private documents, though a 'document' is not explicitly defined in the Code. The Supreme Tribunal once ruled that a 'document' with respect to the prohibition of forgery is 'an expression or a statement of a will or intention, fixed on an object by using letters or other signs' (Judgment, 30 September 1910, 16 *Keiroku* 1572). This ruling implies that legibility or visibility of an expression or a statement therein is required for something to be a 'document', which makes it difficult to apply the provisions regarding document forgery to electromagnetic records which are not legible or visible.

*683.* Some lower courts, however, have held that automobile registration files in the form of electromagnetic records fall within 'documents' with respect to paragraph 1 of Article 157 of the Penal Code and the Supreme Court has approved this conclusion without stating any reasons (Judgment, 24 November 1983, 37 *Keishu* 1538). The grounds of the decisions made by a lower court were as follows: An electromagnetic record also expresses ideas or intentions and may easily be converted into a legible and visible document which is inseparably related to the original electromagnetic record. And as the automobile registration files replaced the automobile registration books when the Road Transportation Vehicle Act was amended, they are not essentially different and automobile registration files should be regarded as the 'original of an officially authenticated instrument'.[24] An 'original of an officially authenticated instrument' should be protected more than ordinary documents.

Unfortunately, these justifications were not persuasive for some criminal law scholars, who pointed out that the justification virtually disregarded the requirement of legibility or visibility and that the 'original of an officially authenticated instrument' is nothing but a document. Accordingly, there was a need for legislation to make it clear that the forgery of electromagnetic records constitutes a crime. The 1987 amendments inserted a phrase into Articles 157 and 158 to cover electromagnetic records as the original of an officially authenticated instrument.

*684.* In addition, it is a crime to unlawfully produce an electronic record regarding a right, duty or certification of facts in use for the administration with the intent to make another's administration of affairs improper (Penal Code, Article 161*bis*, paragraph 1). Where such an offence is committed against an electromagnetic record prepared by a public office or a public officer, the offender may be punished with imprisonment with labour for no more than ten years or a fine of no more than JPY 400,000 (Article 161*bis*, paragraph 2). A person who provides an unlawfully produced electronic record regarding a right, duty or certification of facts in use for the administration with an intent to make another's administration of affairs

24. With respect to the record on a magnetic stripe of a bank card, a lower court decision (Judgment, Osaka District Court, 9 Sep. 1982, 1067 *Hanrei Jiho* 159) held that the magnetic record could be regarded as a document because the record can be converted into a visible form and the record and visible document are inseparably connected.

improper is punished with the same penalty as a person who unlawfully produces the electronic record (Article 161*bis*, paragraph 3). Attempts at such a crime are also punished (Article 161*bis*, paragraph 4).

*685.* There are, however, some problems in interpreting the provision of Article 161*bis*. First, does 'unlawful' production of electronic records mean not only an unauthorized production but also the production of untrue electronic records? Some officials of the Ministry of Justice have explained that the production of untrue electromagnetic records is punishable if an unauthorized act is found in the process of producing the record, which may lead to the conclusion that the production of an untrue electromagnetic record constitutes, in principle, the crime provided for in Article 161*bis* because public officers and employees are not authorized to produce untrue records.

*686.* In contrast to this interpretation, it is the prevailing opinion among criminal law scholars that the production of an untrue electromagnetic record is penalized only in exceptional cases because the production of untrue (paper-based) documents is punished only with respect to specific documents.[25] In other words, the Penal Code has made a distinction between the unauthorized production of documents in another's name and the production of untrue documents.

*687.* Second, what does 'an intent to make another's administration of affairs improper' mean? While the provisions regarding the forgery of documents (Penal Code, Articles 154, 155, 156 and 159) require the 'purpose of uttering' in order to protect the evidential value of documents, Article 161*bis* requires 'an intent to make another's administration of affairs improper'. It is said that this intent requirement was adopted in order to exclude computer espionage on the scope of Article 161*bis*. As there is no difference between the original and a copy of an electromagnetic record and as producing a copy of data without authorization falls within 'unlawful production of an electromagnetic record' as provided for in Article 161*bis*, such an act would be penalized without this requirement.

## §3. Forgery or Unauthorized Alteration of Securities

*688.* Though the forgery or unauthorized alteration of securities as well as the untrue entry to securities results in a heavier penalty than the forgery of private documents (Penal Code, Article 162), it is commonly accepted that securities are also documents (Judgment, Supreme Court, 1 May 1969, 23 *Keishu* 907). Accordingly, securities should meet the requirements for documents mentioned above. The provisions regarding securities were not amended in 1987 and it may be natural to interpret that electromagnetic records cannot be regarded as securities.

*689.* However, the lower courts have held that the provisions regarding the forgery of securities should apply to the manipulation of prepaid cards. If the provisions

25. With a few exceptions, producing untrue private documents is not penalized.

regarding the forgery of securities are not applied to the manipulation of prepaid cards, the manipulation of prepaid cards is penalized in accordance with Article 161*bis*. As the dematerialization of some sorts of securities is under discussion, this issue will be more important in the near future.

## §4. Destruction of Electromagnetic Records

*690.* It is obvious that a person is at least penalized in accordance with Article 261 of the Penal Code (intentional destruction of property other than buildings and documents) if he destroys another's computer and memory devices, etc. In addition, it has been the prevailing opinion that the erasure or unauthorized alteration of an electromagnetic record may constitute the destruction of property in general. However, it has been discussed whether such an act constitutes a destruction of documents because the intentional destruction of documents is penalized more heavily (Articles 258 and 259) than the intentional destruction of property other than buildings and documents. The 1987 law reform extended the scope of Articles 258 and 259 of the Penal Code to electromagnetic records.

## §5. Computer Sabotage

*691.* Computer sabotage may obstruct another's business and until the 1987 amendments, it had therefore been a problem whether computer sabotage met the requirements of Articles 233 and 234 of the Penal Code regarding the obstruction of business. With respect to the provisions of Articles 233 and 234, it was not clear whether the spreading of a false rumour, the use of fraudulent means or force could be found in such cases. Some insisted that it is difficult to say whether the manipulation of data constitutes the use of fraudulent means because the offender does not deceive a person conducting business. In addition, it was said that obstructing a computer's functioning could not be regarded as the exercise of force because 'force' should be exerted on a person conducting business and because the courts had interpreted 'force' almost as the exercise of physical power.

*692.* Article 234*bis* was introduced to the Penal Code in 1987 and provides a new type of crime concerning the obstruction of business through the destruction of computers or electromagnetic records and so on. A person who obstructs the business of another by interfering with the operation of a computer used by the latter for his business by damaging the computer or the electromagnetic records used for it, or by providing that computer with false information or instructions, or by any other means, may be punished with imprisonment with labour for no longer than five years or a fine of no more than JPY 400,000. This penalty is heavier than that for the obstruction of business in general (imprisonment with labour for no longer than three years or a fine of no more than JPY 200,000) because the effect of a computer-related obstruction may sometimes be far-reaching. It is the prevailing view that actual obstruction is not required; rather, the danger of obstruction.

## §6. Property Crimes

*693*. Cash withdrawals using a stolen or forged card at an ATM constitute larceny (Penal Code, Article 235) while funds transfers from another's account to the offender's account by using a stolen or forged card at an ATM do not constitute larceny, as the offender does not seize a tangible property but obtains a credit or claim against a financial institution. In the latter case, the offender's act does not constitute fraud (Penal Code, Article 246) as no person is deceived.

*694*. As the legislators believed that such act should be penalized, Article 246*bis* was introduced to the Penal Code in 1987 in order to fill the gap. Article 246*bis* applying only where Article 246 does not apply and the penalty provided for in Article 246*bis* being the same as that in Article 246. Article 246*bi*s provides that it constitutes a crime to acquire an illicit profit or to make others acquire such a profit through the production of a false electromagnetic record regarding the acquisition, forfeiture or alteration of a property right by providing a computer used for the administration of another's business with false information or commands, or through making such a false electromagnetic record for another's use in the administration of a business (*see* Judgment, Supreme Court, 14 February 2006, 60 *Keishu* 165).

## §7. Electronic Certification

### I. Application for Untrue Electronic Certification

*695*. A person who makes a false application before an accredited certification service provider or accredited foreign certification service provider in connection with the accredited certification service and thereby causes an untrue certification will be punished with imprisonment with labour for no longer than three years or a fine of no more than JPY 2 million (Act Concerning Electronic Signatures and Certification Services, Article 41, paragraph 1). Attempts at such crimes are punished (Act Concerning Electronic Signatures and Certification Services, Article 41, paragraph 2). These provisions apply to all persons who commit such crimes both in Japan and abroad (Act Concerning Electronic Signatures and Certification Services, Article 41, paragraph 3; Penal Code, Article 2).

### II. Illegal Use of Mark of an Accredited Certification Service Provider

*696*. A person who places a mark as provided for in paragraph 1 of Article 13 of the Act Concerning Electronic Signatures and Certification Services (marks stating that he has received accreditation on an electronic certificate, etc.) or any mark not clearly distinguishable therefrom on any electronic certificate or like document without receiving any accreditation will be punished with imprisonment with labour for no longer than one year or with a fine of no more than JPY 1 million (Act Concerning Electronic Signatures and Certification Services, Article 42, No. 1).

§8. Unauthorized Computer Access

*697.* The Unauthorized Computer Access Act prohibits unauthorized computer access (Article 3) and stipulates assistance measures to be taken by the Metropolitan or Prefectural Public Safety Commissions in order to prevent the recurrence of such acts, to prevent computer-related crimes that are committed through telecommunication lines and to maintain the telecommunications-related order that is realized by access control functions.

*698.* A person who has committed an unauthorized computer access will be punished with imprisonment with labour for no longer than one year or a fine of not more than JPY 500,000 (Article 8). Under this Act, unauthorized computer access is defined as follows (Article 3, paragraph 2):

(1) making available a specific use which is restricted by an access control function by operating a specific computer which also features that access control function and by entering into it, through a telecommunications line, another person's identification code for that access control function (excluding such acts conducted by the access administrator who has added the access control function concerned, or those which are conducted with the approval of the access administrator concerned or of the authorized user for that identification code);
(2) making available a restricted specific use by operating a specific computer which also features that access control function and by entering into it, through a telecommunications line, any information (other than an identification code) or command that can evade the restrictions placed on that specific use by the access control function (excluding such acts conducted by the access administrator who has added the access control function concerned, or those which are conducted with the approval of the access administrator concerned; the same applies in the following item);
(3) making available a restricted specific use by operating a specific computer, whose specific use is restricted by an access control function installed on another specific computer which is connected, through a telecommunications line, to that specific computer, and by entering into it, through a telecommunications line, any information or command that might evade the restrictions concerned.

*699.* An 'identification code' is defined as a code granted to a person (hereinafter referred to as the 'authorized user') who has been authorized by the access administrator governing a specific use of a specific computer to conduct that specific use, or to that access administrator (hereinafter the authorized user and access administrator are referred to as 'authorized user, etc.') to enable that access administrator to identify that authorized user, etc., in order to distinguish the latter from other authorized users, etc., and that falls under one or more (in case of a combination code) of the following:

(a) a code the content of which the access administrator concerned is required not to make known to a third party want only;
(b) a code which is compiled in such a way as is defined by the access administrator concerned and uses an image of the body, in whole or in part, of the authorized user, etc., concerned, or his or her voice;
(c) a code which is compiled in such a way as is defined by the access administrator concerned and uses a signature of the authorized user, etc., concerned (Article 2, paragraph 2).

*700.* An 'access control function' is defined as a function that is added by the access administrator governing a specific use to a specific computer or to another specific computer which is connected to that specific computer through a telecommunications line, in order to automatically control the specific use concerned of that specific computer, and that removes all or part of the restrictions on that specific use after having confirmed that a code inputted into a specific computer which has that function by a person who is going to conduct that specific use is the identification code (including a code which is a combination of codes, compiled in such a way as is defined by the access administrator concerned) (Article 2, paragraph 3).

*701.* A person who has assisted another's unauthorized access to a computer may be punished with a fine of no more than JPY 300,000 (Unauthorized Computer Access Act, Article 9). It is prohibited to provide another person's identification code which relates to an access control function to a person other than the access administrator for that access control function or to the authorized user for that identification code, while indicating that it is the identification code for which specific computer's specific use, except at the request of a person who has such knowledge, unless such an act is conducted by the access administrator, or with the approval of that access administrator or of an authorized user.

*702.* Where unauthorized computer access is recognized as having been conducted and if, for the purpose of preventing a recurrence of similar acts, assistance is requested by the access administrator of the specific computer involved, attaching to such a request any documents or articles regarding referential matters such as the state of affairs of the operation and management of that specific computer at the time of that act of unauthorized access, the Metropolitan or Prefectural Public Safety Commission should, if it deems such a request reasonable, provide that access administrator with assistance, including the provision of relevant materials, advice and guidance, so that the necessary emergency measures can be properly taken in accordance with the modus operandi of that act of unauthorized access or its cause to protect that specific computer from further acts of unauthorized access (Unauthorized Computer Access Act, Article 6, paragraph 1).

*703.* The Metropolitan or Prefectural Public Safety Commission may entrust a person designated by the National Public Safety Commission Regulation with all or part of the work of implementing a case analysis (which means making a technical study and analysis of the modus operandi of the act of unauthorized computer access relating to that request and the cause of such act) necessary for the provision of the assistance (Unauthorized Computer Access Act, Article 6, paragraph 2).

## §9. 2011 Amendments

*704*. Law No. 74 of 2011 partly amended the Penal Code:

(a) crimes relating to electromagnetic records giving unauthorized commands (so-called computer viruses) were provided (Article 168*bis* and 168*ter*);
(b) the constituent elements of the crimes of distribution of obscene objects were improved and expanded (Article 175);
(c) attempt to obstruct business by damaging a computer became punishable (Article 234*bis*, paragraph 2).

*705*. It is punishable to create or provide electromagnetic records of a computer virus (electromagnetic records of an unauthorized command preventing computers from acting corresponding to the user's intention or making computers act against the user's intention) or electromagnetic records and other records describing the computer virus (records of source codes that may not function as a virus by itself but which is executable as a virus after translation into machine code), in order to put them into for use on a computer of another person (Article 168*bis*, paragraph 1), to put or attempt to put electromagnetic records of a computer virus into for use on a computer of another person (Article 168*bis*, paragraphs 2 and 3), or to obtain or store records of a computer virus or records describing the computer virus (Article 168*ter*) without justifiable grounds. For the purpose of these provisions, 'to put' them 'into for use on a computer of another person' means making it possible that another person would (unknowingly) execute them on a computer. Intentional (including *dolus eventualis*) conducts are punishable and program errors which inevitably occur during the process of program development (bugs) are not subject to these provisions. Moreover, it is considered that creating or storing computer viruses for the purpose of the development and research of anti-virus measures has justifiable grounds.

*706*. Even before the amendments, distributing, selling or displaying obscene documents, drawings or other objects were punishable. However, in order to make it clear that the provision covers such actions as sending obscene pictures by e-mail, recording media with electromagnetic records to the objects, and distributing obscene electromagnetic records or other records by sending them via telecommunications are explicitly provided (Article 175).

# Chapter 3. Traditional Crimes in a Digital Context (Offences Against Decency, Hate Speech, Defamation, Etc.)

## §1. Defamation

*707.* A person who defames another by alleging facts in public, regardless of whether such facts are true or false, is punished in principle, while a person who defames a dead person shall not be punished unless such defamation is based on a falsehood (Penal Code, Article 230).

*708.* Punishment shall not, however, be imposed if the alleging facts are proven to be true when alleging facts in public that defame another is found to relate to matters of public interest and to have been conducted solely for the benefit of the public (Penal Code, Article 230*bis*, paragraph 1). Matters concerning the criminal act of a person who has not been prosecuted are deemed to be matters of public interest (Penal Code, Article 230*bis*, paragraph 2).

*709.* In addition, in cases where alleging facts in public that defame another is made with regard to matters concerning a public officer or a candidate for election, punishment shall not be imposed if an inquiry into the truth or falsity of the alleged facts is made and they are proven to be true (Penal Code, Article 230*bis*, paragraph 3).

## §2. Offences Against Decency

*710.* A person who distributes or displays in public obscene objects such as documents, drawings or recording media contained in electronic or magnetic records is punished. The same applies to a person who distributes obscene records including electronic or magnetic records through the transmission of telecommunications. The same applies to a person who possesses obscene objects or stores electronic or magnetic records for the purpose of distributing them for consideration (Penal Code, Article 175).

*711.* Before the 2011 amendments, Article 175 of the Penal Code provided that a person who distributes, sells, displays in public, or possesses for the purpose of sale obscene documents, drawings or other objects shall be punished. The Supreme Court, however, held that a hard disk that stores obscene electromagnetic records is an obscene object for the purpose of Article 175 (at that time) (Decision, 16 July 2001, *Keishu*, Vol. 55, No. 5, p. 317). It was decided that the defendant displayed in public since reproduction of obscene image data was possible by a simple procedure.

§3. CHILD PORNOGRAPHY

*712.* The Act on Punishment of Activities Relating to Child Prostitution and Child Pornography, and the Protection of Children (Law No. 52 of 1999) provides that the term 'child pornography' shall mean photographs, recording medium containing electronic or magnetic records (i.e., a record used in computerized information processing which is created in electronic form, magnetic form, or any other form that cannot be perceived by the human senses) or any object which depicts, in a form recognizable by the sense of sight: any image of sexual intercourse or any conduct similar to sexual intercourse with a child or between children; any image of a child having the genital organs, etc. touched by another person or of a child touching another person's genital organs, etc. which arouses or stimulates sex drive; or any image of a child wholly or partially naked, in which sexual parts of the body of the child (genital organs or the parts around them, buttocks or chest) are exhibited or emphasized and arouses or stimulates sex drive (Article 2, paragraph 3).

# Chapter 4. Criminal Procedural Aspects

*713.* Roughly speaking, there are three types of problems in relation to a criminal procedure:

(1) problems in investigating computer-related crimes;
(2) problems in investigating other crimes; and
(3) problems in court, especially the evidential value of electromagnetic records.

## §1. Search and Seizure

### I. Before 2011

*714.* As electromagnetic records in data carriers are not invisible, just unrecognizable through natural perceptive functions, problems arise with respect to the search for and the seizure of electromagnetic records in the course of an investigation of computer-related crimes. As the Criminal Procedure Code has, however, no specific provisions regarding electromagnetic records, the courts have interpreted the provisions in the Criminal Procedure Code in order to apply these to electromagnetic records and computer facilities.

*715.* Search and seizure is, in principle, not allowed unless a judge issues a warrant (Criminal Procedure Code, Article 106; Constitution, Article 35). However, investigators or judges do not always have sufficient knowledge concerning the computer system. Accordingly, it is rather exceptional for the data carrier, the object of seizure, to be specified in a warrant as the investigator cannot judge which of the data carriers should be seized in order to obtain the necessary data for the investigation of a crime. It may happen that the investigators seize excessively. For example, when computer users have a lot of records or data on a hard disk, problems arise as to whether it is allowed to seize that hard disk as a whole, disregarding the fact that almost all of the records or data on the hard disk are not related to the crime for which the warrant has been granted.

*716.* However, there are cases where knowledge of the computer system in question is necessary for the appropriate execution of a search and seizure warrant. Though the investigators may execute a warrant with the help of some general experts on computer systems (Criminal Procedure Code, Article 111, paragraph 1), this may not necessarily be sufficient for a search and seizure and there are cases where the cooperation of the experts working on the system in question is indispensable. Where such cooperation cannot be obtained on a voluntary basis, the prosecutor may request a judge to grant permission for the interrogation of a person who has the necessary information as a witness, insofar as the person is not a suspect (Criminal Procedure Code, Article 226).

*717.* Furthermore, there is still discussion as to whether it is allowed for the investigators to print out or make visible or legible the seized electromagnetic information, using the computer system in question, because there may be cases where the electromagnetic information cannot be made visible or legible without using such a computer system. Though some insist that this is lawful because this is a necessary measure as permitted in paragraph 1 of Article 111 or a similar disposition allowed in paragraph 2 of the same article regarding the seized articles, it is doubtful whether such acts are indeed allowed under Article 111 and as a result, others think it only lawful as an inspection, for which another separate warrant is required (Criminal Procedure Code, Article 129). The court may order the production of legible or visible evidence in accordance with paragraph 2 of Article 99, which provides the court's authority to decide which articles are to be seized and orders the owner or possessor of such articles to submit them.

## II. 2011 Amendments

*718.* Law No. 74 of 2011 partly amended the Criminal Procedure Code and copying electromagnetic records from the recording medium connected by way of telecommunication lines to a computer which is the object of seizure into another computer is explicitly allowed (Criminal Procedure Code, Article 99, paragraph 2, and Article 218, paragraph 2).

*719.* A court may order a person authorized to access electromagnetic records, such as the one who maintains them, to record or print necessary ones on a recording medium, and then seize them (Criminal Procedure Code, Article 99*bis*). A public prosecutor, a public prosecutor's assistant officer or a judicial police official may, if necessary for the investigation of a crime, do so upon a warrant issued by a judge (Criminal Procedure Code, Article 218, paragraph 1).

*720.* The methods for executing the seizure of the recording medium containing electromagnetic records were provided in detail (Criminal Procedure Code, Article 110*bis*, Article 222, paragraph 1). In addition, a public prosecutor, a public prosecutor's assistant officer or a judicial police official may request to preserve the electromagnetic records of telecommunications history (Criminal Procedure Code, Article 197, paragraphs 3 through 5).

## III. Criminal Justice Access to Evidence Stored on Servers in the Cloud and in Foreign Jurisdictions

*721.* The Supreme Court held that (Judgment, 1 February 2021) in cases where the recording medium containing the electromagnetic records is located in a contracting party to the Convention on Cybercrime and there exists the legitimate and voluntary consent of a person who has the legitimate authority to disclose the records, remote access to recording media and copying the records is permitted without mutual legal assistance.

*722.* According to the judgment, a police officer may remotely access the recording medium from a computer at the search location specified in the search and seizure warrant that permits the disposal of copies of electromagnetic records by remote access and copy electromagnetic records such as e-mails, etc. relating to the e-mail address of the user of the computer. He/she may copy electromagnetic records by remote access from a computer outside the same place, such as by using an account of a computer user located in the same place since it is a procedure based on the permit issued after a judicial examination.

*723.* The judgment held as well that it is permissible to dispose of the copy of each electromagnetic record without checking the contents individually so long as there is a possibility that information related to the alleged fact is recorded in the electromagnetic record subject to the disposal of the copy by remote access with the search and seizure permit and it is difficult to confirm the contents of the electromagnetic record at the site of seizure or information may be damaged during the confirmation.

## §2. Wiretapping

### I. Before 1999

*724.* Because the use of computers and means of telecommunication has become widespread, some serious and organized crime makes it necessary to find a more effective means of investigating crimes than the traditional compulsory means of investigation. Among them, the permissibility of wiretapping of communications has been under discussion.

Since Article 21 of the Constitution prohibits censorship and protects the secrecy of communications[26] and as the Criminal Procedure Code has no provisions allowing wiretapping,[27] the prevailing view before 1999 was that wiretapping was unlawful and as a result, it was only authorized a few times.[28]

### II. The Act on Communications Interception in the Course of Criminal Investigations

*725.* Under strong pressure from the US government, the Bill on Communications Interception in the Course of Criminal Investigations was approved by the Diet

26. Article 104 of the Telecommunications Business Act and Art. 14 of the Wire Telecommunications Act prohibit wiretapping as well.
27. Article 197 of the Criminal Procedure Code provides that no compulsory means are permitted without special provisions in the Act or other statutes.
28. Wiretapping was once authorized with a warrant to seizure (Judgment, Tokyo High Court, 15 Oct. 1992, 45 *Kokeishu* 85). However, it seems that the police had wiretapped without any authorization in some cases. For example, the court found that Kanagawa Prefectural Police had unlawfully wiretapped the telephone at the residence of a senior member of the Japanese Communist Party (Judgment, Tokyo High Court, 26 Jun. 1997, 1617 *Hanrei Jiho* 35).

in 1999. The Act on Communications Interception in the Course of Criminal Investigations (Law No. 137 of 1999) authorizes wiretapping for cases involving narcotics, large-scale smuggling of foreigners, weapons, guns and gang-related murders (Annexed Table I to the Act). Wiretapping is permitted with a communications interception warrant valid for no longer than ten days (twice renewable) issued by a judge of a district court upon application by a public prosecutor or judicial policeman designated by the Chief Prosecutor, by the National Public Safety Commission or by a prefectural public safety commission (hereinafter referred to as 'investigator') (Article 4, paragraph 1; Articles 5 and 7). A wiretapping warrant may be granted, provided that the above-mentioned crimes have been or are likely to have been committed in conspiracy and it looks as if it would be very difficult to specify the offender or the crime through other means of investigation (Article 3). The communications interception is subject to review by a judge (Article 27, paragraph 3). The investigator who conducts the interception should notify the party of the wiretap in writing, after the interception has taken place (Article 30). The 2016 amendment (Law No. 54 of 2016) expands the scope of crimes in which investigators may wiretap in the course of investigation. The use of explosives, arson, murder, bodily harm, the confinement of people, kidnapping of a minor, human trafficking, robbery, fraud (including computer fraud), and violations of the law against child prostitution and child pornography have been added to the crimes in which suspects' communications may be intercepted (Annexed Table II to the Act). In regard to the newly qualified crimes, a communications interception is permitted, provided that investigators must suspect that these crimes are being committed by a group consisting of persons who act in accordance with assigned roles (Article 3, paragraph 1, Item 1. This applies *mutatis mutandis* for Items 2 and 3).

The amendment further provides two new methods of wiretapping in which the presence of a person on behalf of the telecommunications company that manages the communications facility (if impossible, an official of the local authority) is not necessary. Article 9 stipulates methods using the encryption and temporary storage of communications by a telecommunications company in which the court provides encryption and decryption keys to the telecommunications company and the investigator.

The investigator orders the telecommunications company to encrypt the communications during the period specified by the investigators in accordance with the communications interception warrant and store the information (Article 20, paragraph 1). Once the interception is completed, he/she orders the telecommunications company to decrypt the encrypted communications by using the key provided by the court and reproduce the relevant part of communications at the site of interception in the presence of him/her (Article 21, paragraph 1).

In accordance with the communications interception warrant, the investigator orders the telecommunications company to encrypt and transfer the intercepted and encrypted communications to a specified computer (Article 23, paragraph 2) at the site of the interception. The investigator then sends the intercepted communications from the specified computer at the site of interception to a second location. The intercepted and encrypted communications are examined in real-time or stored temporarily until they are examined. The investigator decrypts the communication by using the key that was provided by the court (Article 23, paragraph 1).

## §3. Electromagnetic Record and Evidence

*726.* It is well accepted that a copy is admissible as evidence if the original is admissible as evidence, if the process of making the copy is deemed appropriate and if there is justification for not producing the original. As a printout of an electromagnetic record can be regarded as something similar to a copy of the record, a printout can be admissible as evidence as long as the requirements similar to those for a copy of a (paper-based) document are met.

*727.* Hearsay evidence is not admissible as evidence (Criminal Procedure Code, Article 320) except in the cases provided for in Articles 321 through 328. This rule also applies to electromagnetic records and to printouts thereof, with the important exception that electromagnetic records and printouts thereof are considered as trading books, logbooks or other documents prepared in the ordinary course of business (Criminal Procedure Code, Article 323, Item 2).

# Conclusions

*728.* Some important characteristics can be emphasized with respect to cyber law in Japan. First, legislators are trying to cope with the rapid evolution in ICT technology and internationalization. Moreover, the national ministries and agencies are quite active in this field and online application and communication with the administrative governments are becoming widely available to the citizens of Japan. The efforts there towards an e-government seem successful so far.

Second, there are remarkable differences between private law and public law with respect to the developments in IT. In order to make the administration process as transparent as possible, many statutes and ordinances, as well as written guidelines, have come into being. So-called unwritten administrative guidance (*gyosei shido*) has become extremely rare. The same holds true for the utilization of information and telecommunication technology. Deregulation has taken place, especially in the telecommunications market. On the other hand, there are few provisions in codes and statutes with respect to private law, except for those relating to consumer protection and company law. Most of the problems are open for interpretation (with finality by the courts). For example, the liability of an ISP or certification service provider to the victim is governed by the general principles stipulated in the Civil Code. It is not clear whether and how a certification service provider can limit his liability against the victim. The cases where an ISP is liable for damages suffered by a non-contracting party victim are still unclear. Neither the Civil Code nor the Civil Procedure Code provides for the treatment of electronic signatures, certified by an accredited certification service provider or not.

Third, while the protection of intellectual property rights has been strengthened, the activity of the Fair Trade Commission or of the other authorities in competition policy seems less active.

Fourth, privacy protection and the regulation of commercial communications are developed in Japan. Regulation over advertisement or unsolicited commercial communication via the Internet was introduced. However, sufficient and effective remedies and an enforcing mechanism against infringement are not necessarily available.

# Selected Bibliography


**Books (in English)**

Bälz, M. *Business Law in Japan – Cases and Comments*. Frederick: Kluwer Law International, 2012.

Matsushita, M. *International Trade and Competition Law in Japan*. Oxford: Oxford University Press, 1993.

**Books (in Japanese)**

Hoshino, E. *Introduction to the Civil Code* (Minpo Gairon). Vol. 3. Tokyo: Ryosho Fukyukai, 1976.

Kurusu, S. *Contract Law* (Keiyaku-ho). Tokyo: Yuhikaku, 1974.

Matsui, S., H. Suzuki & I. Yamaguchi. *Internet Law* (Internet-ho). Tokyo: Yuhikaku, 2015.

Matsumoto, T., M. Saito & Y. Machimura. *Electronic Commerce Law* (Denshi-shotorihiki-ho). Tokyo: Keiso Shobo, 2013.

Nakayama, N. (ed.). *Interpretative Guidelines on Electronic Commerce and Information Property Trading and the Explanation* (Denshi Shotorihiki oyobi Johozai Torihiki tou ni kansuru Junsoku to Kaisetsu). Vol. 2016. Tokyo: Shoji Homu, 2016.

Nakayama, N. *Legal Protection of Software* (Software no Hoteki Hogo). 2nd edn. Tokyo: Yuhikaku, 1988.

Nakayama, N. *Copyright Law* (Chosakuken-ho), 2nd edn. Tokyo: Yuhikaku, 2014.

Nakayama, N. *Patent Law* (Tokkyoho). 3rd edn. Tokyo: Kobundo, 2016.

Natui, T., H. Okamura & M. Kakegawa (eds). *Q&A Law and Tax of Internet* (Q&A Internet no Homu to Zeimu). Tokyo: Shin Nihon Hoki, 2000.

Nishimura Sogo Horitsu Jimusho. *Net Media Practice Team, Compendium of IT Law* (IT-ho Taizen). Tokyo: Nikkei BP, 2002.

Saito, H. *Introduction to Copyright Law* (Chosakuken-ho). Tokyo: Keiso Shobo, 2014.

Sakka, F. *Commentary on the Copyright Act* (Shokai Chosakuken-ho). 5th edn. Tokyo: Gyosei, 2018.

Sonobe, S. & E. Uemura. *Traffic and Telecommunication Law* (Kotsu Tsushin-ho). 2nd edn. Tokyo: Yuhikaku, 1984.

Tagaya, K. et al. (eds). *Commentary on the Telecommunications Business Act* (Chikujo kaisetsu denki- tsushin-jijyo-ho). Tokyo: Denki Tsushin Shinkokai, 2008.

## Selected Bibliography

Takahashi, K., S. Matsui & H. Suzuki (eds). *Internet and Law* (Internet to Ho). 4th edn. Tokyo: Yuhikaku, 2010.

Takashima, M. *Practical Telecommunications Business Act* (Denki- tsushin-jijyo-ho). Tokyo: NTT Shuppan, 2015.

Uchida, H. & T. Yokoyama (eds). *Internet Law* (Internet-ho). 4th edn. Tokyo: Shoji Homu Kenkyukai, 2003.

Umetani, M. *Legal Protection of Database* (Database no Hoteki Hogo). Tokyo: Shinzansha, 1999.

### Edited Collections (in English)

Bank of Japan, 'Payment Systems in Japan'. In *Payment Systems in EMEAP Economies*, East Asia-Pacific Central Banks and Monetary Authorities, EMEAP Working Group on Payment and Settlement Systems, 2002.

Iwahara, S. 'The Practical Execution and Legal Framework of International Funds Transfers in Japan'. In *Legal Issues in International Credit Transfers*, edited by W. Hadding & U.H. Schneider. Berlin: Dunker & Humblot, 1993.

### Articles (in English)

Ando, N. 'Activities of Designated Certification Services under the E-Signature Law'. *ECOM Journal* 3 (2002): 68–70.

Yanaga, M. 'A Bill Regarding the Electronic Declaration of Intention in Japan'. *Zeitschrift für Japanisches Recht* Heft 11 (2001): 255–258.

Yanaga, M. 'New Regulations for E-Commerce in Japan'. *Zeitschrift für Japanisches Recht* Heft 12 (2001): 145–158.

Yanaga, M. 'Recent Developments in Computer Law in Japan'. *Zeitschrift für Japanisches Recht* Heft 13 (2002): 185–193.

### Articles (in Japanese)

Ikeda, K. 'Creating Procedures for Collecting and Conserving Evidences Including Electromagnetic Records (*Denjiteki kiroku wo fukumu shouko no shushu hozen ni muketa tetsuzuki no seibi*)'. *Jurisuto*, No. 1431 (2011).

Imai, T. 'From the Viewpoint of Substantive Law: Revision of the Penal Code etc. to Respond to an Advancement of Information Processing (*Jittaiho no shiten kara: Johoshori no Koudoka tou ni Taiou suru tame no Keiho tou no Kaisei*)'. *Jurisuto*, No. 1431 (2011).

Iwahara, S. 'Electronic Funds Transfers (*Denshiteki Shikin Ido*)'. *NBL*, No. 385 (1987).

Kaneko, N. 'Introduction of Electronic Certification Services (*Denshi Ninsho Seido no Donyu*)'. *Jurisuto*, No. 1183 (2000).

Matsumoto, T. 'Liability of ISP for Illegal Information (*Iho Joho ni tsuite no Provider no Minji Sekinin*)'. *Jurisuto*, No. 1215 (2002).

Ogawa, H. 'Launching the Electronic Notary System (*Denshi Kosho Seido no Sosetsu*)'. *Jurisuto*, No. 1183 (2000).

Sakai, H. 'The Law Concerning Electronic Signatures and Electronic Certification Service (*Denshi Shomei oyobi Ninsho Gyomu ni kansuru Horitsu*)'. *Jurisuto*, No. 1183 (2000).

Sakuma, O. 'Protection of Digital Information under the Criminal Law (*Denshi Joho no Keihoteki Hogo*)'. *Jurisuto*, No. 1215 (2002).
Shiraishi, T. 'Database Protection and Competition Policy (*Database Hogo to Kyoso Seisaku*)'. *Kosei Torihiki*, No. 562 (1997).
Sugiyama, N. & M. Yoshida. 'Comments on the Act for Partial Revision of the Penal Code, etc to Respond to an Advancement of Information Processing (*Joho Shori no koudoka tou ni taishosuru tameno keihou tou no ichibu wo kaisei suru horitsu' ni tsuite*)'. *Hoso Jiho*, Vol. 64, Nos 4 and 5 (2012).
Uchida, T. 'Electronic Commerce and Law (*Denshi Shotorihiki to Ho*) (1)–(4)'. *NBL*, Nos 600, 601, 602 and 603 (1996).
Uchida, T. 'Transactions in the IT Era and the Civil Law System (*IT Jidai no Torihiki to Minji Hosei*)'. *Hogaku Kyokai Zasshi*, Vol. 118, No. 4 (2001).
Uga, K. 'Administration in the IT Era and Law (*Denshika Jidai no Gyosei to Ho*)'. *Jurisuto*, No. 1215 (2002).
Yamaguchi, A. 'Electronic Commerce and Criminal Law (*Denshi Torihiki to Keiho*)'. *Jurisuto*, No. 1183 (2000).
Yamamoto, Y. 'Legal Problems in Electronic Contracts (*Denshi Keiyaku no Hoteki Shomondai*),' *Jurisuto*, No. 1215 (2002).
Yoshida, M. 'History and Outline of the Amendments: Revision of the Penal Code etc. to Respond to an Advancement of Information Processing (*Ho Kaisei no Keii to Gaiyo: Johoshori no Koudoka tou ni Taiou suru tame no Keiho tou no Kaisei*)'. *Jurisuto*, No. 1431 (2011).

**Useful Websites to Find Relevant Japanese Law in English**

Framework Act on the Formation of an Advanced Information and Telecommunications Network Society (http://www.japaneselawtranslation.go.jp/law/detail/?printID=&id=111&re=02&vm=02).[29]
Copyright Act (http://www.japaneselawtranslation.go.jp/law/detail/?printID=&re=01&id=2506&vm=02).
Law on Exceptional Provisions for the Registration of Program Works (http://www.cric.or.jp/english/clj/cloj4.html).
Patent Act (http://www.japaneselawtranslation.go.jp/law/detail_main?vm=&id=42).
Utility Model Act (http://www.japaneselawtranslation.go.jp/law/detail/?id=43&vm=04&re=02).
Design Act (http://www.japaneselawtranslation.go.jp/law/detail/?id=44&vm=04&re=02).
Trademark Act (http://www.japaneselawtranslation.go.jp/law/detail_main?vm=&id=45).
Anti-Monopoly Act (http://www.jftc.go.jp/en/legislation_gls/amended_ama09/index.html).
Law Concerning Electronic Signatures and Certification Services (http://www.japaneselawtranslation.go.jp/law/detail/?printID=&id=109&re=01&vm=02).

29. It should be noted that the translations are not necessarily updated and that the websites are sometimes under construction for updating.

## Selected Bibliography


Unauthorized Computer Access Law (http://www.japaneselawtranslation.go.jp/law/detail/?printID=&re=01&id=2250&vm=0).

Law concerning Limitation of Damages to Specific Telecommunications Service Provider and disclosure of Sender Information (http://www.soumu.go.jp/main_sosiki/joho_tsusin/eng/Resources/laws/pdf/H13HO137.pdf).

Implementing Regulation for the Telecommunications Business Act (http://www.soumu.go.jp/main_sosiki/joho_tsusin/eng/Resources/laws/ministerial/Telecom_Law/).

Law Concerning Nippon Telegraph and Telephone Corporation, etc. (NTT Act) (http://www.soumu.go.jp/main_sosiki/joho_tsusin/eng/Resources/laws/NTTLaw.htm).

Radio Act (http://www.soumu.go.jp/main_sosiki/joho_tsusin/eng/Resources/laws/090204_3.pdf).

Broadcast Act (http://www.soumu.go.jp/main_sosiki/joho_tsusin/eng/Resources/laws/pdf/090204_5.pdf).

Implementing Regulation for the Broadcast Act (http://www.soumu.go.jp/main_sosiki/joho_tsusin/eng/Resources/laws/ministerial/020624_1.pdf).

Manual for Market Entry into Cable TV Business (http://www.soumu.go.jp/main_sosiki/joho_tsusin/policyrcports/cnglish/misc/CATV-Manual/contcnts.html).

# Index

*The numbers here refer to paragraph numbers.*

## Index

www.ingramcontent.com/pod-product-compliance
Ingram Content Group UK Ltd.
Pitfield, Milton Keynes, MK11 3LW, UK
UKHW020140290926
15471UKWH00003B/598

9 789403 549651